UPON
FURTHER
REVIEW

UPON FURTHER REVIEW

THE GREATEST WHAT-IFS IN SPORTS HISTORY

MIKE PESCA

TWELVE

NEW YORK   BOSTON

Twelve
Hachette Book Group
1290 Avenue of the Americas, New York, NY 10104
twelvebooks.com
twitter.com/twelvebooks

First Edition: May 2018

Twelve is an imprint of Grand Central Publishing. The Twelve name and logo are trademarks of Hachette Book Group, Inc.

The publisher is not responsible for websites (or their content) that are not owned by the publisher.

The Hachette Speakers Bureau provides a wide range of authors for speaking events. To find out more, go to www.hachettespeakersbureau.com or call (866) 376-6591.

Names: Pesca, Mike, author.
Title: Upon further review : the greatest what-ifs in sports history / Mike Pesca.
Description: First edition. | New York : Twelve, 2018.
Identifiers: LCCN 2017041897| ISBN 9781455540365 (hardback) | ISBN 9781478911845 (audio download) | ISBN 9781455596997 (ebook)
Subjects: LCSH: Sports—Anecdotes. | Sports—Miscellanea. | BISAC: SPORTS & RECREATION / Sociology of Sports. | SPORTS & RECREATION / Essays. | SPORTS & RECREATION / History. | HUMOR / Topic / Sports.
Classification: LCC GV707 .P47 2018 | DDC 796—dc23
LC record available at https://lccn.loc.gov/2017041897

ISBNs: 978-1-4555-4036-5 (hardcover), 978-1-4555-9699-7 (ebook)

Printed in the United States of America

LSC-C

10 9 8 7 6 5 4 3 2 1

To Milo, maestro of the hypothetical, Michelle, lovingly guiding us toward the realistic, and Emmett, commenting from the side, "Really Dad? Really?"

Contents

Foreword

—

Malcolm Gladwell

1.

In the fourth round of the 2009 British Open at Turnberry, Tom Watson had a clear lead at the start of the eighteenth hole. He was fifty-nine years old. He needed only a par to win. He hit an approach shot right at the pin. It looked for all the world like it would settle happily near the hole. The gallery gasped in anticipation. Watson must have felt the first thrill of victory. But suddenly and unexpectedly the ball took a strange little bounce and trickled down off the edge of the green. Now Watson needed to get up and down for his par. But his putt was too strong. He bogeyed the eighteenth, leaving himself tied with Stewart Cink, who went on to win the four-hole playoff.

I watched Watson on that final day. That approach shot on the eighteenth hole broke my heart. Watson had birdied 17. He was flying home. He hit a beautiful shot. But it took a strange bounce. Did it hit a stray pebble? An imperfection in the green? We'll never know. All that matters is that at the worst possible moment he was unlucky and Stewart Cink was given the gift of his first—and only—major.

So what happens if that little pebble isn't there? Watson would have been the oldest player ever to claim a major championship. Jack Nicklaus was forty-six when he won the Masters in 1986. Julius Boros was forty-eight when he won the PGA in 1968. In 2009, Watson was more than a decade older than both of them.

And by the way, let's not limit this conversation to golf. Watson would have been the oldest athlete to win an international competition in any major sport, ever. I've heard people say that it is unfair to compare golf to other sports, because golf is unusually forgiving to athletes as they age. That is not true: Professional golfers peak in their early thirties, and the odds of winning a major decline precipitously past the age of thirty-five. The age profile of successful golfers is only a shade different from the age profile of successful distance runners or baseball players. Had Watson won at Turnberry, his achievement would have fallen outside the optimal performance range for his profession by a quarter century. I will go further: Had Watson parred the eighteenth, it would have stood as one of the most extraordinary athletic performances of the modern age. But he didn't. He hit a pebble. A few months later, *Sports Illustrated* picked its Sportsman of the Year. Guess who? Derek Jeter. In case you're wondering, Jeter hit .334 in 2009, and played with his typical wooden immobility in the field.

2.

Upon Further Review is a book about what-ifs. What if the U.S. had boycotted Hitler's Olympics? What if Bobby Fischer had received proper psychiatric help? What if the 1993 Phoenix Suns had answered a bit of fan mail? What if the National League had adopted the designated hitter? What if football had been invented in the twenty-first century instead of in the nineteenth?

At first blush, some of those subjects seem trivial, or at least the kind of thing that you would need to be a hardcore sports fan to appreciate. (I mean: the Phoenix Suns and fan mail?) Do not fall into that trap. Counterfactual history is, in a way that real history is not, a true test of the imagination. But it has a second level as well. The what-if forces us to think. The intuitive paradigm we use in evaluating the march of progress is all too often the evolutionary model: natural selection. We accept the course taken as the fittest option, the one optimized for success. The National League didn't adopt the DH because baseball is better that way, right? But if you tease out the full alternative trajectory, where Bartolo Colón never gets his chance at one glorious dinger, you realize that maybe the way we went wasn't better. It was just an accident.

It happened that way, for whatever random reason, and if the random reason had gone the other way there is an entirely plausible scenario where all of baseball plays by a single rule. Just like Tom Watson. What if the pebble hadn't been there? Then we talk about Watson in 2009 the way we talk about Bob Beamon in 1968, or Michael Jordan against Utah in 1998, or Joe DiMaggio's magical streak in 1941. Come to think of it, why don't we rank Watson up there with Beamon, DiMaggio, and Jordan? Why does the presence of an imperfection on the eighteenth green at Turnberry—which Watson had nothing whatsoever to do with—somehow make him unworthy of being ranked with the all-time greats? When Jeter won *Sports Illustrated*'s Sportsman of the Year in 2009, Watson got robbed: A fifty-nine-year-old coming within one unbelievably bad break of a major is a bigger accomplishment than a thirty-five-year-old waving haplessly at routine ground balls. The counterfactual, in that case, ought to make us angry—not just for Tom Watson but for everyone else who is denied a place in history by the width of a pebble.

3.

Let me run a counterfactual by you. It's a little bit complicated—but it is precisely that complication that makes it interesting. It's about the slave trade. Most slaves who came to North America came—for obvious logistical and geographical reasons—from countries such as Nigeria on the Atlantic coast of West Africa. But let's leave those logistical and geographical reasons aside. What would have happened if the slave trade had been centered on East African countries such as Kenya and Ethiopia?

In the main, that fact would make no difference at all. The point of slavery, as an institution, was that it was supremely indifferent to the particulars of the people it enslaved. The plantation owners of Jamaica and South Carolina and Mississippi cared not one whit what language their slaves spoke, or what traditions they carried with them, or what heritage they represented. You just had to have dark skin.

But this is a book about sports, and I'm posing a sports-specific question: What happens if you replace, in the Americas, Nigerians for Kenyans? If you look at the top one thousand performances in the track and field events that involve speed and power—the sprints and the jumps—you will see that the overwhelming majority of the athletes on that list are of West African heritage. If you look at the top one thousand performances in long-distance events, you will see that the overwhelming majority of the athletes on that list are of East African heritage. The numbers, if you care to look them up, are astonishing. Among the top eighty times in the marathon, there is just one non–East African: American Ryan Hall.

All kinds of people have all kinds of debates about why this is so. (For the best treatment of this question and others, I recommend David Epstein's *The Sports Gene*.) But there is no denying the fact of this division: One side of Africa gives us endurance athletes, the other side power and speed. I'm part Jamaican. I had my DNA tested a few years ago and discovered—to no one's surprise—that my African heritage is Igbo, one of the dominant ethnic groups of Nigeria. Jamaica, a country of several million people, produces more great sprinters on both a per capita and an absolute basis than any other country on earth. The tribe in Kenya that has produced more long-distance runners than any other group in the history of organized running is the Kalenjin. The slave trade brought the Igbo to the Americas. It did not bring the Kalenjins. So what if it had?

I suspect that this line of inquiry makes some of you a little uncomfortable. Good. That's my intention. Because the point of this counterfactual is to raise the uncomfortable question of whether the long, dark shadow of the slave trade extends even to the world of professional sports. The United States as a country is obsessed with power and speed sports: basketball, football, baseball, games involving sprinting and jumping.

At endurance sports, by contrast, the United States is puzzlingly weak. In long-distance cycling, there is Lance Armstrong and there is Greg LeMond and then there is, as they say in baseball, praying for rain. In distance running, there is Joan Benoit Samuelson and Mary Decker on the women's side and Frank Shorter, Galen Rupp, Ryan Hall, and a handful of other names on the men's side. But for goodness' sake, there is a case to be made that New Zealand has a better historical record of distance running than the United States. Is this an accidental fact?

I am writing this on a Sunday afternoon, with an NFL game playing in the background, and if the market choices of a bunch of slave traders three hundred years ago had been different, maybe I'd be watching a marathon. Sports fans sometimes retreat into a fantasy where they imagine that their world is somehow immune from the complexity and ugliness of the world outside the arena. Counterfactual history reminds us that this is nonsense.

4.

One more thing. The what-if should not just open our eyes or rob us of our illusions. It should also instruct us. There is an essay in this volume by Nate Jackson that asks what football would look like if it had been invented in 2018, instead of in the nineteenth century. I'm not going to spoil Nate's argument for you. But it is worth pointing out that in this case the what-if is not a hypothetical. Football actually needs to start over: It is a sport that was created in a moment of fundamental physiological ignorance and that subsequently evolved in defiance of known physical laws. We now understand, to cite just one of a million new facts, that hits to the head sustained during football games are altering the brain tissues of high school players. The response of the sport thus far has been to take measures at the margin. When a concussion happens, make sure it is diagnosed. Penalize hits to the head. Teach better tackling techniques. These are the sorts of reforms dreamed up by people who believe that the world as we see it evolved for a reason— that the institutions and practices we live with are the product of some form of natural selection. That is not true, of course. The world in general—and sports in particular—are the way they are because of random events and arbitrary choices and a pebble on the green where it isn't supposed to be. The challenge facing football's governors is not to take the sport as it is and tweak it at the margins to make it better. Somebody get the NFL a copy of *Upon Further Review*. They need to go back to the beginning and ask: "What if?"

Introduction

Mike Pesca

America exists because the sky was foggy.

To be fair, it was particularly and peculiarly foggy on the side of the East River where it needed to be foggy. It was August 29, 1776, and George Washington and the colonists had been badly beaten in the Battle of Long Island. They had not even covered the spread. If the British troops under Admiral Richard Howe had finished the rebels, historians agree, they probably would have snuffed out the American Revolution right there. But then, in the small hours of morning, the fog rolled in and the colonists rowed out. In historian David McCullough's telling, in his book *1776*:

> Incredibly, yet again circumstances—fate, luck, Providence, the hand of God, as would be said so often—intervened. Just at daybreak a heavy fog settled in over the whole of Brooklyn, concealing everything no less than had the night. It was a fog so thick, remembered a soldier, that one "could scarcely discern a man at six yards distance." Even with the sun up, the fog remained as dense as ever, while over on the New York side of the river there was no fog at all.

This is one of the great what-ifs in our country's history. But for a low-lying cloud—paired with the rough currents of the river and some guerrilla tactics acquired by Washington while fighting in the French and Indian War—a great nation might never have been.

This is how the best what-ifs work. Find the bend in history's path and straighten it out, perhaps along the way convincing ourselves that the imagined did become real, with the fog of memory as sufficient cover.

In sports we accept the turning point, as such, more readily than we do in the real world. We much prefer to think of our history as a march of inevitabilities rather than as a series of contingencies. The alternatives can be too big to contemplate.

After all, if Washington hadn't escaped the British, perhaps I wouldn't even be sitting here, protected by a First Amendment, blithely turning our sports heroes to goats all in the name of a thought exercise. Can we really say that there wouldn't have been an America? The United States of America does seem like a pretty compelling idea—stronger, certainly, than the thickest of fog. But to watch and to be invested in sports is to know how much our world is shaped by happenstance—how all would be different but for one errant pass, one blown coverage, one fumbled exchange, one bungled coaching decision.

Sports are a celebration of turning points. In recent years this has been made explicit with the advent of real-time win probability charts, graphs that pinpoint a team's odds of victory even as play is underway. You can actually follow along as your team's chances for victory plummet in real time when, for instance, your offense decides to take a twelve-yard sack and commit a holding penalty with an eight-point lead in the fourth quarter of the Super Bowl. For the record I did not commission a "What if the Falcons had not done sixteen things wrong in Super Bowl LI?" essay, just as I decided not to commission "How much damage would an Olympic rifle team do to a school of fish, provided said fish were neatly stacked in an oak barrel?"

We readily acknowledge that games, seasons, careers, and legacies can turn on single plays. And when the play does not break right, the eternal cry of "Wait 'til next year" is invoked. Close on the heels of that lament comes the question "What if?"

What-if is a fundamental part of sports. Without what-if there'd be no draft, no spring training, no trades, no free agent acquisition. Every roster rebuild in pro sports has been a multi-million-dollar exercise in what-if. Every tweak of the replay rules, every announcement of innovation via the "competition committee," is an official endorsement of what-if. Every excuse of "I thought it was good leaving my hands" or "I could have sworn I was on the base when he tagged me" is the athlete engaging in his or her own version of what-if.

But when we fans propose a what-if scenario, we most often are proposing an if-only. If you hear a voice on sports talk radio, or sports talk podcast, make reference to "one of the great what-ifs," they usually do not mean, "What a fascinating cascade of unforeseen occurrences might have transpired." They usually mean, "Had we taken the road not traveled, we'd have been much better off." Run instead of passed, drafted the forward instead of the center, traded for prospects instead of veterans. These, the usual what-ifs, are rueful reactions to scenes of trophies hoisted by rivals, parades down someone else's Main Street, your own mayor paying off a stupid bet concerning regional foodstuffs.

In this book I wanted to avoid the diehard's what-if—the one where the answer is, "Some other team or player would have won." That may be true, but it doesn't excite the imagination. Neither am I interested in the other common what-if, the one where the fan rewrites the script for a key play. Sports fans love this sort of thing. We want to what-if our favorite teams or athletes over the obstacles that felled them in real life. I get it. It's human. I can't tell you how I yearned to what-if St. John's over Patrick Ewing in the 1985 Final Four, but simply turning a loser into a victor, or redoing a draft pick, or correcting a blown call did not seem like the best use of this magical institution of the what-if. Rather, I chose to propose hypotheticals that sparked the imagination, that opened the door to a hidden history or set off a plausible chain reaction we might not even have considered.

As I went about soliciting contributions and debating what would make good topics, some trends emerged.

Baseball proved to be the sport that provided the most fertile ground. There are a few reasons for that. One, it has been around the longest, and has been well chronicled along the way. Two, writers usually like baseball. Three, baseball is the sport that most embraces the sort of whimsy at the heart of any what-if. To ask "What if?" also has the whiff of nostalgia about it, and nostalgia drives baseball as surely as ethanol drives Indy cars or oats drive horse racing.

Football, though the most popular game in America, and a favorite of mine, did not inspire granular what-ifs. Our contributors were more compelled to address football as a phenomenon rather than football as fodder for rewriting on the play-by-play level. Former Denver Broncos player Nate Jackson attempts a rewrite of the rules of football, and Jason Gay attempts a rewrite of the American weekend without football. I was eager to see if anyone would attempt to rewrite entire dynasties, and to that end Steve Kornacki does a nice job of thwarting the Belichick-Brady dynasty. But there were a couple of what-ifs left unpursued. In 1960 Tom Landry was offered head coaching jobs for both the Dallas Cowboys and the Houston Oilers, but it was hard to imagine a scenario where he would cast his lot with the upstart AFL. I also thought there might be interesting bookend what-ifs to the Pittsburgh Steelers' dynastic run in the 1970s. What if the Immaculate Reception in 1972 had been ruled an incompletion? No definitive angle of that play exists, after all. Similarly, what if Oilers receiver Mike Renfro's catch in the corner of the end zone against the Steelers in the 1979 AFC title game had been ruled inbounds? There, a definitive angle did exist, and it showed that the referees had incorrectly ruled it an incompletion.

The problem with these questions is that the answers do not reverberate beyond the narrow context of the games themselves. Broader history is not implicated. In 1972 the Pittsburgh Steelers did beat the Oakland Raiders, but no matter how much help Franco Harris got from the Father, Son, and Myron Cope, neither they nor any other team were going to get past the undefeated Dolphins that season. As for the 1979 play, yes, that one catch would have tied the AFC Championship Game in the third quarter. And then what? Who's to say the Oilers ever would have taken the lead or prevented the Steelers from doing so? The Steel Curtain held Earl Campbell to seventeen yards on fifteen carries that day. And even if the Chuck Noll Steelers had faltered, they go down as having won three Super Bowls. Still dynastic, if somewhat less fantastic.

So if those particular potential what-ifs do not make the cut, what does? I believe a good what-if has to fall into one of a few categories. It has to:

a) posit a plausible counterfactual and tease out the implications of said counterfactual. Ideally, along the way, other ruptures occur, which in themselves rewrite reality as we currently know it;

b) provide an opportunity to delve into a history that we perhaps didn't know about, but should. This history should have a compelling connection to the present. Claude Johnson's essay, "What If Nat 'Sweetwater' Clifton's Pass Hadn't Gone Awry?"—the longest essay in the book—does this expertly;

c) examine a sporting event that had a great impact on society and explore ways the event might have been rewritten, and in doing so reshaped society;

d) answer a what-if question that has long been posed, and come up with an interesting or authoritative answer. Or both, as is the case with Neil Paine's look at the worst NBA injuries and Ben Lindbergh's examination of drug testing in baseball;

e) be funny.

A what-if, done well, need not provide a definitive answer to the question. The fun is in the asking. Questions are fundamental to the fan experience: "How do you not foul there?" "What was he thinking?" "Why would you make that trade?" "Did you even *know* how many timeouts you had?"

As I write these words I sit a few blocks from Brooklyn's Old Stone House, where brave troops from Maryland fought the British so that by dawn General Washington could deftly use the fog as a blanket. I never think about that. A few blocks in the other direction is the Barclays Center, where one can see the Washington Wizards puncture a foggy Nets defense with three-pointers. I constantly think about the Nets' ineptitude and begrudge the trade that sent a series of top picks to the Boston Celtics for an aged Paul Pierce and Kevin Garnett. Why? Why the obsession with one counterfactual but the neglect of the other? Why do I take my basic freedoms for granted while engaging in hypotheticals about adults in matching outfits who play games?

I think the answer lies in the very nature of sports, and how they give us a space to indulge in mental rewrites and the opportunity to wish away the bad things without paying the psychological costs of clinically being in denial. It's fundamental to the escapism of sports. Under cover of the conditional mood, we flee the confines of history, like Washington's troops into the early morning mists.

1

___

What If Muhammad Ali Had Gotten His Draft Deferment?

Leigh Montville

The hearing took place away from the spotlight that usually followed Muhammad Ali wherever he went. The site was a courtroom in the United States Post Office, Court House and Custom House, a five-story limestone building that covered a city block at Broadway and Sixth Street in Louisville, Kentucky. The date was August 23, 1966. The mood was reserved.

No reporters or spectators were allowed. Ali was accompanied by his mother, his father, two character witnesses, and his new lawyer. They appeared in front of retired judge Lawrence Grauman as requested. The histrionics of the previous six months—begun when the twenty-four-year-old heavyweight champion of the world said, "I don't have no personal quarrel with those Viet Congs"—were replaced by quiet explanation.

This was business. Serious business.

"I never understood why the so-called Negroes had to turn their cheeks and have to take all the punishment while everyone else defends themselves and fought back," Ali told the judge first, describing the seeds of his conversion to the Nation of Islam. "I never understood why our people were the first fired and the last hired. I never understood why when I went to the Olympics in Rome, Italy, and won the gold medal for great America and I couldn't go in a downtown restaurant in Louisville."

The hearing was to consider his application as a conscientious objector to military service for the Vietnam War. Every CO applicant had the right to plead his case before a specially appointed judge. Grauman, retired, a sixty-six-year-old legal scholar in Louisville, white, a member of local society, known more in his judicial career as a strong disciplinarian than for any civil rights decisions, was appointed to hear Ali's case.

The background was that members of the Nation of Islam historically had refused to fight in "white man's wars." The Honorable Elijah Muhammad, the leader of the religion, had served four years in jail for refusing to fight in World War II. Now there was this war. Ali, a member of the NOI, did not want to be drafted.

The issue originally had been moot because he flunked the written test twice when he was eighteen years old. This resulted in a 4-F classification as unfit for service. In the following six years, however, the war had escalated, which brought a larger need for young American bodies. The Army recently had lowered the passing grade for the written test. Ali's score now was acceptable.

Notified on February 17, 1966, that he was reclassified to 1-A, he stood on a lawn in Miami, Florida, and told America how unfairly he thought he was being treated, how his position as heavyweight champion was more important than any position he might occupy in any war effort. He sounded self-centered and cocky. Religion was not mentioned. A day later he said the words about the Viet Cong. America was not happy with any of this.

His fight in Chicago against Ernie Terrell quickly was canceled. Politicians denounced him. Promoters across the country refused to schedule a bout domestically. He was forced to fight once in Toronto, twice in England. His next scheduled title defense was against Karl Mildenberger in Frankfurt, Germany. The message was clear: If a fighter would not fight for America, he could not fight *in* America. The irony seemed obvious to the general public. Ali said this was nothing new.

"I have, I would say, caught more hell for being a Muslim, even before the Army talk came up," he said, religion now the major part of his argument. "With my wife [whom he divorced] and boxing, and the movie rights that I turned down...and I have done all this before the Army came up and it's just not saying that I would not participate in war, but we actually believe it and feel it."

The hearing lasted three and a half hours. The government case was contained in a lengthy report from the FBI. There were no government witnesses. Ali's testimony, restrained but forceful, dominated the proceedings. He was guided by his lawyer, Hayden Covington. Hired only a week before the hearing, Covington was a specialist in these kinds of cases and had defended countless Jehovah's Witnesses in conscientious objector situations. Judge Grauman asked questions at the end.

"It would be disrespect for the American government to say what happened," Ali told reporters as he left the building. He added that the hearing "was run just like I was in a courtroom."

Ali went to Germany a week later to fight Mildenberger, a bout that ended with a technical knockout in the twelfth round after the challenger was dropped to the canvas three times and cut badly around the eyes. Judge Grauman went home to 3939 Napanee Road in Louisville with a 129-page transcript of the hearing to make his decision, which he did in two weeks, sending his recommendation to the U.S. Justice Department in Washington.

The results were not made public until two months later, on November 25, 1966. They were contained in a letter the Justice Department sent to Local Board No. 47, Ali's draft board in Louisville.

Grauman had ruled in favor of the champ. The white disciplinarian southern judge recommended that a Conscientious Objector classification should be granted. This was the upset of upsets. Ali's quiet words had worked. Covington's questions had worked. The hearing was a grand success.

Except the hearing didn't matter.

Grauman's decision didn't matter.

The Justice Department rejected the judge's recommendation. Its letter to Local Board 47 recommended that Muhammad Ali, heavyweight champion of the world, should—indeed—be classified 1-A and subject to the draft. The draft board's decision was pro forma, following the Justice Department's direction. Ali was not only eligible for the service but was at the top of the list.

The course was now set. The unpopular draft resister was on the way to becoming the most famous athlete who ever lived. The Greatest of All Time.

And so, we begin...

What if the decision by Judge Grauman was stamped and approved by the Justice Department? How easy would that have been? Approval was the norm in most CO cases, the judge's decision routinely ratified. What if the Justice Department followed procedure instead of a political animus against the outspoken famous black man and Muslim? What if Muhammad Ali were allowed to simply go ahead with his business? What if?

One minor change, a bit of clerical work, was all that was needed. How different would his story have been? That was the important question. Would there even have been a story? That's an even bigger question.

The stretch of time between Grauman's decision and Ali's eventual acquittal by the United States Supreme Court on June 28, 1971, covered more than four and a half years. Ali was inactive for more than three and a half of those years, his titles stripped, his passport revoked when he refused to step forward to take the oath to join the Army on April 28, 1967.

In most appraisals of his career, great laments are heard about how he was forced to miss all that time in the middle of his prime. What if he had been allowed to keep fighting when he was young and seemingly invincible, a heavyweight with speed that no one had ever seen in a ring? How many more victories might he have accumulated? How much more history could he have made?

A better argument can be made in the other direction. What if he hadn't lost that time? Those missing years were what defined his career, what made his life so different from all the other boxers who came along before or have come along since. How could he have been the

Greatest of All Time, the icon of icons, an important figure in politics and art and everyday life if he had plugged along on a normal athletic arc? How could he have been Muhammad Ali if he simply...boxed?

Blessed with speed, strength, and charisma, Ali worked to achieve great mastery of the skills of his sport. But it was this ordeal, these troubles, that made him everything he became.

1.

If he had not been banned from boxing, his voice would have been silenced. Oh, maybe not silenced, because he surely was a vocal man, but his words would not have meant nearly as much. He would not have been the rebel, the aggrieved party, the perpetual squeaky wheel.

When he could not fight, he found that a way to make a living was to visit college campuses, where he gave speeches to students. This was his major source of income. He became probably the most accessible athlete of the twentieth century. If you were a student at the time, you had a chance to see Ali in person somewhere near your school and you probably did.

Armed with boilerplate speeches that preached the doctrine of the Nation of Islam, hardened by question-and-answer sessions at each stop, he was a one-man evangelical tour. He was funny sometimes, but serious most of the time. He said things that athletes never had said, certainly not black athletes. He riled emotions, stirred the national pot.

"Man, I go places where only the professors went before," he told Dave Kindred of the *Louisville Courier-Journal*. "Harvard. UCLA. California State. Tennessee State. Me, a boxer. I'm doing this.

"I give them hour and a half lectures. Like 'The Negro Must Clean Himself Up Before Anyone Will Respect Us.' And on how we should treat our women. Women are the fields that grow nations."

He also talked about the separation of races, the NOI dream of a black society away from the white devils. (He said he didn't vote, but would vote for George Wallace for president if he did.) He talked against interracial couples. He talked against the white man's war. He talked about black pride, talked about how black people should live in black neighborhoods and spend their money with black merchants and go to black colleges.

This was heavy stuff. There was no real affinity for the civil rights struggles that were taking place led by Dr. Martin Luther King. There was no real affinity with the anti-draft movement that grew daily as kids burned their draft cards and took over the offices of college presidents. The debates started by his points of view were noisy in the moment—he was booed at more than one stop, challenged pretty much everywhere—but the impression he left was more important than the words.

He was Ali! He was the Champ! He was a famous black man, young, strong, challenging authority. That was what counted. That was the bedrock of his future image. He stood up. He fought for his rights. These were the sixties. He fought for himself. That was the image that remained.

It would not have existed if he had not been banned from boxing.

2.

His career would have chugged along the usual set of tracks if allowed to continue uninterrupted. At the time when Grauman's decision became public, Ali already had returned to the U.S. market, defeating Cleveland "Big Cat" Williams in the Houston Astrodome. He was preparing to fight Ernie Terrell, the opponent from that canceled bout in Chicago, also at the Astrodome. The European fights, shown on American television, broadcaster Howard Cosell providing friendly commentary, had softened American resistance. People might buy tickets to boo Ali now, but they would buy tickets.

That situation would have stayed the same if he were a conscientious objector. He could have fought and fought and fought. The problem was that there really wasn't anyone left for him to fight. He already had cruised through the major heavyweight contenders, knocking them off in a rush as he worried about his future. If he had continued to fight, he would have had to cruise through the field again and yet again.

His big fight at the end of his enforced layoff, the first fight against

Joe Frazier at Madison Square Garden, was set up by Ali's absence. Frazier had arrived on the scene, climbed through the same contenders Ali had beaten, and established himself as the alternative heavyweight champion. The attraction of two heavyweight champions in the ring at the same time, both unbeaten, was irresistible. This was the biggest sports event anyone could remember.

Ali fought two warm-up bouts and, bam, came head-to-head with Frazier. Frank Sinatra took pictures for *Life* magazine. Woody Allen, Marcello Mastroianni, Ted Kennedy, Diana Ross, and Miles Davis were there. Hugh Hefner and Col. Harlan Sanders were there. Everybody was there.

If Ali had not missed so much time, none of this would have existed. Frazier would not have been the heavyweight champion. The curiosity would not have existed. Maybe Frazier would have waited this long to fight Ali, but probably not. The match would have happened earlier, simply due to popular demand. Would Frazier have won that fight against a younger, faster Ali, as he did at the Garden, establishing the basis for the next two fights in the famous trilogy? Would Ali have been as easy to hit?

Possibly not. Probably not.

3.

The rest of Ali's career would have been perfunctory, simply about boxing. He would have made noise, no doubt, showman that he was, but it wouldn't have been the same important noise. The bite, the edge, would have been gone.

The Ali who America largely grew to respect as time passed in his suspension and as resistance to the war grew larger and larger wouldn't exist. He would have been another name on the 1970s scorecard, another name on the sports page. The Ali who became beloved after his career ended, the valiant figure struck early by Parkinson's, the soft-talking, slow-moving symbol of fire and resistance, wouldn't exist. He would have been another used-up athlete, his condition a shame but far from unique.

He wouldn't have captivated Zaire, wouldn't have captivated the world with his rope-a-dope, comeback win over George Foreman. The Thrilla in Manila would not have been nearly so thrilling. The other fights—the trilogy with Ken Norton, the collisions with no-names like Chuck Wepner, Joe Bugner, and Ron Lyle, even the loss and then win against Leon Spinks—would not have contained the same drama, the idea that you should see this man now, today, because he was part of history.

Would he have been the choice to light the torch at the 1996 Olympics in Atlanta if he hadn't been banned from his sport? Would he have been so memorable, standing on that platform, familiar and vulnerable, above the crowd?

It was the U.S. Justice Department—strange as it seemed—that handed him his chance for immortality. Not that they deserved more credit than did the heavy bag, or barbell, or some other millstone that a fighter could turn into a sharpening stone. And it was Ali who took the opportunity. He grew far bigger than the squared-off section of life that he was supposed to occupy. If the idea was to punish him for his beliefs, it failed badly. The time away from boxing was the most important time of all. He flourished because of it. He grew his legend, expanded his influence. He became different, so different from any other athlete in American history.

An irony arrived as his fight with the draft board neared its conclusion. When his case finally reached the Supreme Court in the spring of 1971, the first vote did not go well for him. With only eight members of the court voting because Justice Thurgood Marshall had recused himself, the decision was 5–3 to uphold Ali's conviction. He was going to be sent to prison for five years and fined $10,000. The majority and minority opinions had to be typed and the public had to be notified, and he would be gone.

Justice John Harlan was assigned to write the majority opinion and he passed the job on to his law clerks. The clerks, younger, more aligned with Ali's thought about the war, found passages in Nation of Islam literature that bolstered his request for a CO exemption. What to do? They presented these passages to Harlan and argued for acquittal, and to the surprise of everyone, the justice changed his mind.

This made the vote 4–4. Ali still would be sentenced to jail with this decision, but the justices felt that a tie would not satisfy the American public's need for a true verdict. They looked for a procedural hook to set Ali free. They found it in the wording of the Justice Department's letter that—voila!—had overruled Judge Lawrence Grauman's decision long ago. This led the justices to vote 8–0. Ali's conviction was over-turned, and he was free to finish out his career.

What if the hook never had been found? What if the wording from the Justice Department had been bulletproof? What if the icon of American sports icons, the Greatest of All Time, had been sent to jail? What if?

Ah, that would be another story.

2

What If Football Had Been Deemed Too Boring in 1899?

Jason Gay

Many of us are familiar with the origin story of North American football—its rugby roots, twenty-man sides, two-way players, the early domination by the Ivy League, cracked skulls, Walter Camp, forward passing...all the way to its modern zenith: Marshawn Lynch riding atop a Super Bowl duck boat, throwing fistfuls of Skittles at Seattleites.

Today, North American football—oh, let's just call it football, what is this, Belgium?—is America's undisputed national pastime, far ahead of baseball, basketball, and writing horrible things in Internet comment sections. It is a TV ratings juggernaut, a sponsor magnet, the last non-Marvel-comic entertainment property in this country that can claim true mass appeal. Football has revolutionized the country's leisure habits, transforming us from an adventurous society of curious, self-determined explorers to weekend shut-ins who open the door only for the pizza guy or wing guy.

Yes: It is perfect.

And yet it is so perfect, so thoroughly rooted in the culture, that it is difficult to present the unimaginable: What if football had never taken off? What if the evolution of football's rules and equipment had never happened, had not created the more dynamic, modern game and led us down a glorious path to the nirvana of *Sunday Night Football*? What if nobody had bothered to "invent" the forward pass? What if Walter Camp had said, "Eh, screw it, let's just run the ball again."

In 1876 Princeton protested Camp's landmark pass to teammate Oliver Thompson; their appeal was overturned by a coin flip. What if the coin had gone Princeton's way, and a frustrated Camp had not gone on to transform the football rulebook as a coach and writer, but returned, melancholically, to installing wheels and levers in the Camp family clock business?

What if football had simply stayed grinding, violent, and, worst of all, dull, and eventually died off, like the woolly mammoth, or dinnertime conversation (other than "When will the wing guy get here already?")?

What if football had never escaped the nineteenth century?

What would America look like then?

The casualty of a football-less America would first be felt in the wallet. Without football, there would be a complete undermining of the American leisure economy. Here are just a handful of industries that would not exist if football had gone extinct: the canned beer industry, the outdoor grill industry, the crappy leather sofa industry, the coozie industry, the buffalo wing industry, the buffalo-wing-pizza industry, the buffalo-wing-pizza-with-cheesy-crust industry, the chip industry (Big Chip), almost all dips (I think guacamole would still be here), the microwave industry, whatever industry makes that plastic hat thing with the two beer containers on the sides and the giant straws, the Breathalyzer industry, the plastic football phone manufacturing industry, and therefore mid-1980s *Sports Illustrated* subscriptions, the sweatpants industry, divorce mediation services, the handmade JOHN 3:16 sign industry, the clever *D*-with-an-actual-picket-fence combo sign, and therefore perhaps the entire American picket fence industry, and of course, the NO. 1 foam finger industry.

Now I know what you're thinking: "Wouldn't NO. 1 foam fingers have simply caught on in another sport?" And I'll admit that could have happened, that folks may have simply taken NO. 1 foam fingers to horse races, or Wimbledon, or the Masters, but who is kidding whom here? Football is the only authentic, gloating NO. 1 foam finger experience. Without football, I don't think the NO. 1 foam finger industry gets off the ground, which is kind of like imagining America without the Rocky Mountains, or NASA.

The lack of football would radicalize the American weekend, creating a giant pocket of freshly available time. Consider the modern football calendar: There are somewhere between a zillion and a zillion and a half college football games, beginning Wednesday (Wednesday!) and running late into Saturday; on Sunday, the NFL kicks off with a garbage export game from London, followed by an afternoon-to-evening slate that swallows up the entire day until midnight EST. If you're desperate, or gambling, which I guess is the same thing, there's *Monday Night Football*, and if you're lonely, or questioning your existence, or perhaps a Jacksonville Jaguars fan, which I guess is the same thing, there's *Thursday Night Football*.

Deprived of these events, the American calendar dramatically loosens up. The hopeful assumption is that American productivity or at least active time would surge—no longer couch-bound, the country would be free to rake leaves, prune hedges, fix plumbing, go on hikes, learn second languages, perhaps third languages, build a working rocket ship in the backyard out of popsicle sticks, go to church, or even read books. But a thought: Is it possible that football has been the only thing that activated our brains on weekends, and without it we'd be even more slothful, more prone to day-drinking and couch-napping?

It's something to consider.

Other cherished cultural rituals would have died had football faded: I don't think marching bands would still be here. That would be a shame. Marching bands are synonymous with the football experience, especially school football, where Americans love to watch talented student musicians march and play wretched Billy Joel songs. It's one of the things that really makes college football great. At least I assume it's one of the things that makes college football great, because they don't show college marching bands on television anymore, they just cut to a lifeless studio where, instead of pimply sophomores cheerily playing slide trombone to "Uptown Girl," they show dead-eyed, middle-aged analysts talking about the first half.

And forget about marching bands—what would have happened to university life as a whole? We're constantly told that football is booster catnip and a critical economic engine for colleges, a steady and lucrative source of income that is immediately funneled into . . . well, it's mostly funneled back into football, and even then, most athletic departments lose money. But just try sending the math team to the Beef O'Brady's Bowl, you ingrates.

Without football, we'd have lost a soundtrack of most mellifluous and/or aggravating American voices: Keith Jackson, Howard Cosell, Al Michaels, Verne Lundquist, Brent Musburger, Jim Nantz, Joe Buck. Yes, I know all those guys did or do other sports, too, but football is really where their voices became godlike and/or drove us crazy. At the same time, we'd probably have far fewer pregame sports shows in which ex-players in crisp suits laughed at each other's jokes. We might not even have ESPN, or ESPN might revert to its earliest programming with full coverage of Aussie rules. Without football, we'd have a lot less to argue about on sports radio, which would possibly mean a lot less sports radio. I admit that does make the demise of football sound like the polio vaccine.

Similarly, without football we wouldn't have any fantasy football, which would be great, because nobody cares about fantasy football except for the people who play it. Have you ever tried to talk to someone about their fantasy football team? I'd rather have a stranger remove my gall bladder on the floor of a subway car. It would mean the end of all those fantasy football apps, and the ubiquitous commercials with the thirty-seven-year-old virgin winners holding humungous checks for guessing right on the Jaguars. To be honest, not having fantasy football is probably the best thing about football never becoming popular.

I don't know what would have happened to the Guy Who Invented the Yellow Line. He's my favorite football beneficiary. I love that there's a guy out there who, at the moment, is sitting atop the deck of a Mediterranean yacht called the *Yellow Line*, or, perhaps, *Third and Six*, and whenever someone asks him where he got the coin to afford a mega-yacht, he begins with: "Do you remember how hard it once was, watching football on TV, to figure out how many yards the offense needed to get a first down?" (Though we are in the Mediterranean, so there's a better than average chance the questioner isn't going to know what he's talking about, so he's going to really have to start from scratch.)

I don't know what the Guy Who Invented the Yellow Line would have done without football. Maybe he invents the on-screen strike zone before the On-Screen Strike Zone Guy does. Or the glowing hockey puck. Maybe he works at Lady Foot Locker.

If there had been no football, I think Roger Goodell is running an award-winning string of Applebee's in southeast Maryland.

I think Bill Belichick is the grumpy ranger in the national park who tells you not to touch the prehistoric tree.

I think Marshawn Lynch is secretary of state.

I think, somehow, Dick Butkus can still be seen in reruns of *My Two Dads*.

I think Peyton Manning is my kids' orthodontist.

It's also true that without football, a lot of very talented football players would have found their way into other professional sports. Jim Brown would have stuck with lacrosse, but baseball would have gotten a windfall. Mike Ditka may have been a star outfielder in baseball, and the Chicago Cubs could have knocked out another World Series much earlier. John Elway would have been a Yankee. Deion Sanders would have stayed a Brave. Bo Jackson would have been merely Vincent Jackson. And maybe still playing. Barry Sanders would have eight hundred Olympic medals.

Not to be fancy, but we should consider the impact the early death of football would have had upon language, because American discourse, especially corporate lingo, is littered with football terms and allusions. "Who is going to quarterback this project?" . . . "Make sure to protect our blind side"..."He really spiked the ball in the meeting"..."I'm sorry I had to punt on Thursday lunch."

Think about it: A "Hail Mary" will no longer mean an improbable effort, a la an Aaron Rodgers heave into the end zone, but will simply mean...a Hail Mary. I haven't even gotten to the biggest loss to the language, which would be the inability to lazily call something "the Super Bowl of." No more Super Bowl of spelling bees, Super Bowl of flower shows, Super Bowl of awkward weddings. I suppose we could just shift everything over to World Series, but do you want to go to the World Series of awkward weddings? Me neither.

Finally, I know there's a lingering question here about the "other" football, aka soccer, and whether or not the demise of North American football would have created a kind of sports butterfly effect in which gridirons were replaced by pitches, and American soccer stars were as idolized as Odell Beckham Jr. It's an intriguing question, but I have to tell you: It's already happening.

Every week, it seems, there's a new story about a retired NFL player suffering from dementia, or some other type of postconcussive trauma. In reaction, youth football enrollments are trending down, and if you ask a current coach, they'll tell you head injuries are the number one worry they hear about from parents. It's possible that soccer won't need to do anything, since football might die from its roots. As for sports idols, have you been inside an elementary school lately? Increasingly, the corridors are amok not with Colts or Steelers paraphernalia, but kits from F.C. Barcelona, Manchester City, or the U.S. Women's National Team. Not long ago, I spoke to a class of American fifth graders, and when I asked them to name their favorite athletes, they ticked off not Tom Brady or J. J. Watt, but Cristiano Ronaldo, Diego Costa, Lionel Messi, Alex Morgan. Granted, this fifth grade was in Brooklyn, New York, which is basically France, but it felt like a harbinger of what's coming. Football may have overcome its early, ugly history, but its survival is not assured. I'm not saying it's imminent, or that we should panic, but just to be careful, let's begin rationing the buffalo wings and stash a few NO. 1 foam fingers.

3

What If the United States Had Boycotted Hitler's Olympics?

Shira Springer

Judge Jeremiah T. Mahoney saw the future, saw it in a way that wouldn't let him rest. It made him a crusader, an evangelist, an activist, whatever you call a man compelled to share what he knows and take a defiant stand. It made him frustrated, sometimes infuriated, with the blindness of other powerful men. How could they not see that Nazi Germany was playing a shell game with the truth? How could they not see what was coming? He saw it with unshakable clarity. It made him rail against Adolf Hitler's Olympics in letters, on college campuses, at rallies, and at the Amateur Athletic Union's general convention on December 7, 1935.

Bristling with conviction, Mahoney took the floor and argued for the United States boycotting the upcoming Berlin Games. "The Nazi government wants more than American participation in a sporting contest," he warned the AAU delegates gathered at the Hotel Commodore in New York City. "It wants to bring the American dollar into the very weakened Nazi treasury. And it wants to picture Hitler with Uncle Sam standing behind him and saying, 'We are with you, Adolf!'" Mahoney probably thought if some delegates momentarily imagined goose-stepping on the Hotel Commodore's marble floors, all the better. The former New York State Supreme Court jurist wasn't above rhetorical scare tactics, not now, not when he saw how Hitler's racist, anti-Semitic regime was gathering momentum.

Some in the audience shared Mahoney's alarming vision of the future and nodded in agreement. They saw the symbolic potential of the Nazi Games, the stage dangerously set for political propaganda, the world's athletes enlisted as props and pawns. No doubt the United States would send the largest foreign team to Germany, a roster led by Jesse Owens and filled with medal favorites who would be living, breathing, sprinting rebuttals to all the Third Reich's repulsive ideologies. But U.S. athletes would still be in Berlin, marching in the opening ceremony as the German people and the world watched. That image alone would give Hitler the legitimacy he craved. It would be perfect, raw material for manufacturing his version of reality.

Others in the Hotel Commodore audience shifted uneasily in their seats with rising anger of their own. They preferred that sports remain separate from politics. More than that, they worried that Mahoney, not only a skillful speaker but also president of the AAU, would persuade enough delegates to trigger a boycott. A vote on the issue loomed, a vote that was about more than the Olympics. Whether U.S. athletes stayed home or sailed for Germany, they would be ensnared in the international politics of the day. The time for separating sports and politics was long past, if it ever existed.

But where Mahoney saw a moral imperative to boycott, Avery Brundage saw a Jewish-Communist plot behind pro-boycott efforts. Brundage was a stubborn, blinders-on construction magnate from Chicago and president of the American Olympic Committee. In late summer 1934, amid growing concerns about Nazi policies, Brundage toured Germany and talked with sports officials there. It was a fact-finding mission in name only. Brundage saw what he wanted and believed German assurances that Jewish athletes would be treated equally. Brundage operated with a willful blindness that International Olympic Committee members would perfect in future decades.

The boycott vote took place in this atmosphere, with these egos and agendas in play. And the vote was close, 58¼ to 55¾, so close it could easily have gone the other way. What if it had? What if two delegates had changed their minds? What if the United States had boycotted Hitler's Olympics?

Headlines around the country and overseas spread the news: "U.S. Says 'Nein' to Nazis, A.A.U. Backs Olympic Boycott," "Mahoney Calls on Other Nations to Follow," "President Roosevelt on Way to Middle West, Silent on Sports Leaders' Decision," "No Olympic Glory for World Record Holder 'Buckeye Bullet' Owens." The AAU vote shocked Olympic-caliber athletes around the United States. While they heard the boycott talk led by Mahoney and countered by Brundage, many never imagined they would stay home. They were too good, too much of a main attraction, too integral to any sports competition organized for the world's best. And so the U.S. boycott struck a crippling blow to the Nazi Games.

But that was not how American athletes wanted to use their talents. Leading up to the vote, they spoke strongly against a boycott. Black sprinter Ben Johnson even confronted Mahoney during a Columbia University symposium, telling the AAU president he should "put his own house in order before criticizing others" and citing discrimination against black athletes in the United States. Owens, Ben Johnson, Ralph Metcalfe, Cornelius Johnson, and Eulace Peacock, all African-American track stars, wrote to Brundage in favor of participating in Berlin. For Owens, it marked a reversal of earlier radio comments, but more accurately reflected his eagerness to compete on the world stage. Now, with the boycott news, U.S. athletes were reeling with disappointment, frustration, and anger. They saw a missed opportunity to show up Hitler, especially for African-American and Jewish team members.

It was easy to envision African-American athletes, especially Owens, as counterarguments to Hitler's Aryan ideal. Owens was barely six months removed from the greatest track and field performance ever. At the Big Ten championship meet, in the span of forty-five minutes, he broke world records in the 220-yard dash, 220-yard low hurdles, and long jump, and he tied the world mark in the 100-yard dash. And he had competed that day with a back so badly injured he had almost withdrawn from the meet.

Some might call that record-setting Big Ten performance miraculous, but Owens had nothing on Betty Robinson. After winning gold in the 100-meter dash at the 1928 Amsterdam Olympics, she came back from the dead. In June 1931, she was involved in a biplane crash and found unconscious beneath the wreckage; she was placed in the trunk of a car and driven to an undertaker, then was discovered to be alive. Robinson had a deep cut across her forehead, a left leg fractured in several places, and a broken left arm. No one thought she would race again. As the 1936 Berlin Olympics neared, she couldn't bend down into a proper starting crouch, but she would earn a spot on the 4×100 relay. Or, she would have. More than three hundred other American athletes would have joined Owens and Robinson in Berlin, all with compelling personal stories and impressive athletic résumés. And almost all would be lost to history because of the boycott.

Great Britain and France quickly followed with Olympic boycotts of their own, adding to the number of athletes left with disappointment, frustration, and anger instead of medals. Both European countries had long worried about Hitler as Olympic host and long debated what to do. Like U.S. sports officials, members of the British Olympic Association and French leaders doubted Nazi assurances that Jewish athletes would be welcomed onto the German team. They also feared the reach of Hitler's propagandistic ambitions. The absence of Great Britain and France, two of the biggest teams after the German and U.S. delegations, would turn the Berlin Olympics into little more than a sports exhibition. That would tempt other countries to boycott, too.

The International Olympic Committee was collectively slack-jawed and apoplectic about the rapid disintegration of the 1936 Summer Games, having spent years guarding against exactly that outcome. Hitler was beyond infuriated. But the Games would go on.

Ironically, Hitler wasn't always the fast-clapping, enthusiastic Olympic fan captured in documentary footage. Nazi ideals ran counter to Olympic ideals. On principle, the Führer and his followers objected to sports competitions that mixed black, Jewish, and what they considered racially pure athletes. But once convinced that the Berlin Games held immense propaganda value, Hitler endorsed the event and Propaganda Minister Joseph Goebbels went to work.

In the wake of boycott announcements by the United States, Great Britain, and France, Nazi Germany doubled down on the propaganda, more determined than ever to create its own reality and go forward with its sports celebration of Aryan supremacy. The Third Reich portrayed the boycotters as cowardly, afraid to compete against the New Germany, unwilling to expose their citizens to a model nation that would make them question their own governments. The propagandists aggressively targeted the United States, taking anti-boycotters' arguments and throwing them back in the faces of sports and political leaders. They seized on racism in America. Black athletes would be welcomed in Germany, while the southern United States banned interracial competition and black college stars such as Owens couldn't live on campus. Owens also wasn't given a scholarship to Ohio State University. Playing off remarks by Ben Johnson, "Put your house in order" became a recurrent taunt. *"Bringen Sie Ihr Haus in Ordnung,"* proclaimed German newspapers, and the *Volk* echoed that message, all eagerly forming a gleeful, gloating Nazi chorus.

It wasn't long before Mahoney and Brundage had heard enough from the Nazi propaganda machine and from U.S., British, and French athletes who wanted an opportunity to compete. Despite hard feelings over how the boycott vote went down, they would join forces and organize a series of athletic competitions across the United States for athletes from all boycotting countries and for Jewish athletes kept off the German team. In Barcelona, another effort to protest the Nazi Games and provide an alternative competition had taken the name the "People's Olympiad." But when the outbreak of the Spanish Civil War forced organizers to cancel the event, Mahoney and Brundage used the same name for their competition and invited some of the athletes originally headed to Spain.

Let Hitler have his German sports exhibition and call it the Olympic Games, they thought. Let him show off Berlin's Olympiastadion and its seating for more than a hundred thousand spectators. Let him introduce a torch relay and bask in whatever Olympic theater the propagandists dreamed up and Leni Riefenstahl filmed. The United States would supply counterprogramming: a series of track and swimming meets, as well as road cycling races, fencing bouts, and soccer matches to satisfy the British and French. And what the hastily organized international competitions, the newly named People's Olympiad, lacked in pageantry, they would make up in athletic drama and world records.

Owens would set new marks in the 100, 200, 4×100 relay, and long jump as President Franklin D. Roosevelt watched and American crowds chanted, "Jess-e, Jess-e." Robinson and her miracle comeback from the dead would captivate her home country and international reporters. Adolph Kiefer, the eighteen-year-old world record holder in the 100-meter backstroke, would set new world records every time he entered a pool. Mack Robinson, older brother of Jackie Robinson, would gain fame as the man who came astonishingly close to beating Owens in the 200.

Even Germans, the top German-Jewish athletes, would compete in the People's Olympiad and savor the warm embrace of U.S. sports fans. Helene Mayer easily won the women's foil competition with the form and technique that would later earn her recognition as the greatest fencer of the twentieth century. High jumper Gretel Bergmann, another Jewish athlete denied a place on the German team, triumphed in her event.

From the stands of various contests, Mahoney delighted in the success of the People's Olympiad as a sports event and rebuke of Nazi Germany. He knew some Americans, athletes included, still objected to the boycott and wondered what might have been. But summoning the same conviction and rhetorical flourishes he displayed at the AAU convention and in letters, Mahoney told critics, "Participation in the Games under the swastika would have implied the tacit approval of all the swastika symbolizes. What glory would have come from laurels won in Hitler's house? The boycott is a victory for all that Americans hold dearest, a victory more precious than any Olympic medal."

If this is where a U.S. boycott led, would it matter that all the records set at the People's Olympiad, all the historic moments, happened far away from the actual Games? Would the athletic feats of blacks and Jews carry the same message, the same weight, outside Nazi Germany? Would Jesse Owens still be *Jesse Owens*?

Sports immortality requires three basic elements: talent, dramatic historical context, and storytellers. You don't go from superstar to hero to enduring, iconic symbol without some combination of all three. The talent must be overwhelming, almost unbelievably so. It must be the kind of talent that lends itself to media mythmaking. Owens had that kind of talent. Take his record setting at the 1935 Big Ten championships. He didn't merely run faster and jump farther. He did it while injured and while making it look effortless. He was described as floating above the track that day, as having wings. Even without four gold medals at the 1936 Nazi Games, Owens wouldn't have faded into history. He wouldn't have been some largely forgotten champion rediscovered decades later like Betty Robinson. His talent was too great to let that happen.

But without Hitler watching from the stands, without Nazism and racism coloring the Games, without politics on both sides of the Atlantic Ocean amplifying the significance of black medalists, Owens wouldn't have been a transcendent sports figure. He was a legend born as much from four gold medals as from Hitler's long-mythologized snub after the 100-meter final. He was a legend born as much from soaring past eight meters in the long jump and setting an Olympic record on his final attempt as from German silver medalist Luz Long, an embodiment of the Aryan ideal, offering him friendship, congratulations, and a handshake immediately after the event. And not only did Owens win the 100, 200, 4×100 relay, and long jump and set two world records in the process, he won over the largely German crowd at the packed Olympiastadion. There was a magic, can't-be-replicated quality to what Owens did and how people responded in the moment.

As surely as American boxer Joe Louis knocked out German Max Schmeling in the first round of their rematch, Jesse Owens felled the Aryan ideal, and he did it by being the man in the arena, not by achieving success against stopwatches and friendly rivals.

With a U.S. boycott, there is no real or perceived snub by Hitler, no Long handshake, no in-your-face symbolism. Any records Owens sets elsewhere wouldn't have echoed through history in the same way. They can't, not if the hero and the villain of the Nazi Games act upon different stages in different places. The United States holding its own international competitions while the greatly diminished Berlin Games go on would have been the sports equivalent of two people shouting past each other.

But the United States would definitely be shouting, trying to draw attention to its best athletes and its athletic rebuttals of Nazi ideology. To counter Hitler's fawning over German champions, Mahoney would encourage Roosevelt to personally congratulate American winners at the People's Olympiad. It was an easy way to confront Germany, which many Americans in the mid-1930s were still reluctant to do. Owens would get the presidential recognition he wanted but would have never received after Berlin. When Owens returned home with his four gold medals, it stung him that Roosevelt never called and never extended an invitation to the White House.

Still, after 1936, boycott or no boycott, presidential congratulations or no presidential congratulations, racism in the United States limited how Owens could live and make money.

It would be entertaining to imagine his future dramatically changed by a U.S. boycott. But it would gloss over the realities of the day. Even as an Olympic hero, he worked as a playground janitor. It was the best job he could find after he returned from Berlin. He was stripped of his amateur status by Brundage and the AAU because he didn't participate in a post-Olympics meet in Stockholm. This freed Owens to pursue any payday that was available, and he did. He raced horses, dogs, and all manner of motor vehicles. Owens even raced Joe Louis, tripping and falling to let the world heavyweight champion win.

As the years passed, the myth of Jesse Owens grew and gave the man behind it more financial opportunities. Speaking of his gold medals, he once said, "Time has stood still for me. That golden moment dies hard." Without that golden moment and all the meaning invested in it, his fame would have been its greatest during his record-setting days, then receded, reversing what actually happened. And Owens would have found far fewer opportunities to cash in on his fame.

Meanwhile, the Olympics would have emerged better for the boycott. In the absence of the United States, Great Britain, France, and other countries, the extravagant pageantry and naked nationalism of the Nazi Games would have been viewed as more of a threat to the Olympic movement. The IOC would have seen more clearly how the Olympic Games could be co-opted by dictators and corrupted. And maybe, just maybe, decades before Russia and China followed the propaganda model of Nazi Germany, host countries would have been prevented from sinking extraordinary amounts of time, money, and other resources into what they envisioned as international advertising for whatever ideologies they held superior.

If Mahoney and his proboycott crowd had succeeded, then Brundage would never have been IOC president for twenty controversy-filled years. The Olympics would have emerged better for that, too. The sports world would have been spared Brundage's blind-eyed, iron-fisted leadership, a reign marked by such strict enforcement of the amateur athlete ideal that he earned the nickname "Slavery Avery." Brundage was racist, anti-Semitic, and sexist—slow to condemn the apartheid state of South Africa in the 1960s, quick to declare the Games must go on after the Munich Olympic massacre in 1972, and ever eager to limit women's participation.

Instead of Brundage, the IOC would have turned to Mahoney. During an IOC presidency half as long as Brundage's, Mahoney would have recognized the increasing influence of politics on sports and vice versa, and adapted. The boycotts of the 1980 Moscow Olympics and 1984 Los Angeles Olympics would have been avoided. Not because the IOC kept world leaders from mapping Cold War ideologies onto the Olympics and its athletes, but because Mahoney would have prepared the committee for exactly that inevitability. It's largely forgotten that the Soviet Union, along with Spain, boycotted the Berlin Games in reality and planned to participate in the People's Olympiad instead. Mahoney would have remembered both countries' political objections and factored their motivations into his thinking. The IOC molded by

Mahoney would have listened for the earliest rumblings of a Moscow boycott, then worked to neutralize the idea before it reached the highest levels of government and resulted in the 1980 and 1984 tit-for-tat boycotts.

In the wake of World War II, the judge would have set the Olympic movement on a more progressive and more proactive course, one that also addressed professionalism, commercialism, and the Games' gigantism with intelligence, relying on a prescience and moral compass honed during the Berlin boycott battle. That same prescience and moral compass would have put in place checks and balances to guard against the IOC's natural elitist and power-hungry leanings. Today, maybe, just maybe, IOC members would be less "Lords of the Rings" and more responsible stewards of the Olympic movement.

The U.S.-led boycott could have been the wakeup call the Olympic movement desperately needed, leaving a legacy of smaller Games that focused more on sports and less on the symbolic fanfare and architectural excess inspired by Hitler's Olympics. And it could have left the Olympic movement with leadership equal to that vision. Instead, allowing the Nazi Games to take place became the Olympic movement's gravest sin.

4

What If the 2017 Golden State Warriors Traveled Through Time to Play the Greatest Teams in NBA History?

Ethan Sherwood Strauss

Oracle Arena, Oakland, CA, January 1, 2018

"We're gonna beat everyone who's ever been!" Warriors owner Joe Lacob screams to his coterie in the Bridge Club, Oracle Arena's VIP room that's become a salon of sorts for tech movers and shakers. Blood is dripping from Joe's trembling lips. Not blood in the technical sense, as he's just taken a chomp of the Impossible Burger, the ground-breaking meat imitation that threatens to eventually make vegetarianism a societal norm.

Another droplet of heme-blood falls onto the dining table as Joe motions toward the device in an enthusiastic gesture that would dislocate most shoulder blades. The timing couldn't be better. Steph Curry *just* sprinted past the Bridge Club, as per his pregame ritual, *precisely* as the machine whirrs into wakefulness. The device is of a modest size, all black, no bigger than an iPad. The display flashes "Light Years" in alternating blue and gold text.

"Right now, it can only take us backward and return us to the present day," Joe says with chagrin. "Our ability for future travel is imminent."

Valley bigwigs Elon Musk, Mark Zuckerberg, Eddy Cue, Ron Conway, Marc Benioff, and Bob Kagle are all present. The tech tycoons are trying but mostly failing to look happy. How did Joe stumble upon the world's greatest invention, all because he commissioned some Stanford grad students to study whether artificial intelligence could replace Klay Thompson? That lucky asshole.

There's some nervous laughter as Joe shuffles over to a marked spot on the floor. Lacob belts, "Search Cleveland, June eleventh, 2015!" A flash of light and he's gone. Seconds later, Lacob reappears, but this time with an extra championship ring on his finger. His oversized Warriors 2016 champions shirt is soaked in champagne. "Convincing Draymond not to hit LeBron in the balls was harder than sneaking past the time-space continuum! Amazing!"

A polite golf clap greets the feat. The Valley peanut gallery starts asking questions all at once. "Is Trump still president?" "Could this result in a disaster beyond our comprehension?" "Is this ethical?" "Does this mean we can somehow live forever?"

Joe gives a dismissive wave. "Light Years isn't about your doubts. As John Galt said, 'Do not let the hero in your soul perish in lonely frustration for the life you deserved but have never been able to reach! The world you desire...can be won!'"

Joe's fists are shaking now as he tilts his head back and puffs his chest. Somehow even more plant-based blood is oozing from his lips. Zuckerberg passes out. Musk slowly shakes his head. Joe presses on.

"You want to know why I did this?! Why I gave you Light Years?! It's not about some piddling quest to change politics or the nature of being! It's about being the greatest team of all time! In *any* time!"

The room is silent. Lacob's arms loosen. He smirks, then softly says, "You're welcome."

After some tedious negotiations with the league office, it is decided that Golden State will face two opponents during All-Star weekend: the 1997 Chicago Bulls and the 2000 Los Angeles Lakers. The other owners begged Lacob not to travel too far back in the past, for fear he might butterfly-effect away their lucrative national television deal.

Eventually all time-traveling parties agree to certain terms. The main edict: no forewarnings. To limit butterfly effects, there will be no answers to questions about the present, no matter how tempting it may be. Adam Silver is clear on this. Also, no technology—iPhones and the like are not permitted. This rankles most of the roster but pleases Andre Iguodala, who always has a book handy.

Many time travelers secretly plan to violate these rules. Steve Kerr wishes to warn his younger self about a future botched back surgery. Curry needs to warn his younger self about the Chef Curry dad shoes that got him roundly mocked on social media in 2016. Experienced Draymond Green has some sage advice to young Draymond regarding showing his penis to the world. Nick Young can't remember what he'll tell younger Nick Young, but he's sure he'll come up with it once the journey begins.

The Warriors have a week to prepare for a different style of play, and that's no small thing. The modern Golden State Warriors are products of their time, just as much as they are on its vanguard. There's a misunderstanding when arguing over the historic, and it's the assumption that conditions are static, that mastery of "basketball" means the same thing in every era.

This is because we don't want to believe that conditions matter, that there's a Darwinian element at play beyond talent and grit. The rules of the game alter the game, shaping its incentives, helping different kinds of talent prevail. Environment matters. Different islands produce different finches.

Take the 1990s, a halcyon age for hoopheads. Many bemoan the death of the big man, how today's bigs are soft, and worse. And there's certainly some data to back up the lack of the modern bigs' prowess. Rik Smits, for example, had a higher usage rate than any current center. Gone are the days of Hakeem Olajuwon, Shaquille O'Neal, Patrick Ewing, and Alonzo Mourning.

So what happened? It's the rules, dummy. In 2002, the NBA ended illegal defense restrictions, against the loud protestations of Pat Riley. Few casual NBA observers knew what the hell those were, beyond annoying, occasional game interruptions that led to technical free throws, but it represented a meaningful shift. Illegal defense dictated that a team could not play zone; that is, if you were to send a double team in the post, you could not shift your defense to fill in necessary gaps. In short, this legislated space for post-up behemoths. It meant that were a Lilliputian to fly at a big man, the larger fellow would always know exactly where to pass the ball.

So 1990s possessions often meant tossing the ball down low and waiting for your center to work his magic in an unhurried manner. But after 2002, when you tossed the ball down low, defensive pressure could come from anywhere, terrorizing the big man into inefficient shots and choices.

There are still those who yearn for post play. Ironically, Steve Kerr himself famously begged Mike D'Antoni of the "7 Seconds or Less" Suns to run more post offense. But now that the rules have shifted, it makes increasingly less sense to throw it to the big man with his back to the basket. Looking back, it's odd such a form of offense was ever considered intuitive. Think of it this way: Why would it be sensible to not face one's goal in a task at hand? There's a fairly obvious reason why defensive linemen don't begin their rush with backs facing their offensive line foes. (Though I wouldn't be surprised if Rob Ryan tried this prior to his last firing.)

Anyway, the 2002 rule changes gently nudged teams away from inside-out offense and led to the spread-floor carnival Golden State thrills its fans with. The 2018 Warriors players are briefed on this matter, as nobody on the current squad ever played under the old rules. Defensive guru Ron Adams conducts drills according to the constraints. Kevin Durant practices post-up play in scrimmages, and remarks on how much easier it is with all this space.

72-Win Bulls vs. the 2017–18 Warriors

After the time hop, it really wasn't that hard to set this battle up. Sure, it was a bit jarring to the 1997 public when the Warriors magically appeared at the fifty-yard line of the Packers-Patriots Super Bowl, but Steve Kerr's presence granted some credibility. It helped that he hadn't aged much, despite the painful effects of the aforementioned botched back surgery.

The public really bought that the Warriors were from the future and there to organize a basketball game. After Dolly the Sheep was cloned in 1996, the world was ready for any kind of scientific advancement. What the public did have a hard time buying was that anybody could beat the Bulls.

Whatever metaphysical questions time travel might prompt were mostly obviated by Michael Jordan's status as God incarnate. He eagerly agreed to the challenge, and thus it was scheduled right after the All-Star break.

This exhibition game becomes the singular focus of American pop culture for a moment. President Bill Clinton announces he'll attend the game, as does the Dalai Lama. The Warriors find themselves followed by crowds and media scrums that rival Jordan's Bulls. Durant does a cameo on *Friends*, per his agent's suggestion. He plays a snooty food reviewer who'll make or break Monica's restaurant. He wears a Nike beret.

Chicago, March 4, 1997

On game night, the United Center is packed. The first low, warbling noise in the Bulls' theme song evokes the boom that plays in Christopher Nolan's *Inception*, only don't tell anybody that, because *Inception* is thirteen years away and nobody knows who the hell Christopher Nolan is. When the PA announcer yells "Your Chicago Bulls!" you can see a smile spread across Draymond Green's face. He's always loved the "Jordan song" intro, and he has said as much in the past—er, future.

After some first-quarter jitters from the Dubs, the game isn't close. The problem for the Bulls is that 1997 rules were more incidental to their success than essential. Perhaps that makes their seventy-two-win run even more impressive. They've no skilled bigs to punish the Warriors with illegal defense rules. Sure, Jordan torches an awestruck Klay Thompson for forty-five points, but Chicago just can't keep pace in the other direction. Young Steve Kerr can't get a shot off because

Draymond keeps breaking from the defensive game plan and blitzing him, between taunts. "This guy is impossible!" young Steve tells old Steve during a timeout. "Ya," old Steve snorts. "Try coaching him."

Golden State evolved far beyond what was the vanguard of versatility and skill in 1997. Illustrative to the difference is Dennis Rodman, a Hall of Famer and to be sure a great player for his era. But not a small forward in the modern sense, for a reason. The Warriors have a legendary shooter at the three in Kevin Durant, and frequently play small-ball lineups where everyone can hoist from distance. The Bulls have no more than three three-point shooters at any given time, and often, when the Worm is in the game, are reduced to two. Chicago would be even more bereft of shooting if not for the shortened three-point line of this time period. Unfortunately, the shortened three-point line helps KD, Klay, and Steph combine for sixteen treys.

Hand checking, the rule that sports talk show hosts insisted would give the Bulls a defensive edge, does little to stem the tide. The issue is that hand checking is useful for preventing a drive to the rim and less useful for containing Curry's step-back thirty-footers. Jordan contains Klay off the ball, holding him to fourteen points. All-world defender Scottie Pippen does well to hound Durant on his post-ups, but he can do little about Golden State's spread-floor fast breaks. Green delights in racing past the likes of Luc Longley and Bill Wennington for twenty-five points, mostly off fast breaks.

The Bulls probably would have fared better if they'd been more adept at switching on defense. This strategy is popular in 2017, but it arose in response to modern offensive strategy. Chicago has good defensive tools (smart wing-sized players who can play multiple positions), but never had reason to apply tools in this manner. Back when offense meant lobbing the ball down low, stopping a perimeter pick-and-roll attack didn't take precedence. The effectiveness of Chicago's individual defensive talent is compromised as they try to fight over screen after screen. Phil Jackson coyly smiles as he watches his defense disintegrate. Bruised egos make for better practices. This will help them prepare for the playoffs.

Jay Mariotti starts writing his scathing takedown titled "Lack to the Future" before the final buzzer sounds: 130–99 Warriors.

Kerr breathes a sigh of relief. Younger Kerr gives the old man a high five. Jordan storms out of the arena, livid to be so helpless against a foe he'll only face once.

Joe smiles as he waves to a crowd of fans after the game, as he directs the team toward the Light Years blast zone. He can't wait to talk about this with his Kleiner Perkins buddies.

Coming back to 2017 is a bit of a letdown for Joe. Nobody's surprised that the 2018 Warriors beat the '97 Bulls. Everyone knows. Everyone remembers. There was even a 2012 film based on the game, titled *Winning Time*, starring Paul Giamatti as Lacob, Owen Wilson as Steve Kerr, and Golden State's players as their future selves. It wasn't exactly a box office hit. This subject has been extensively studied, extensively documented. What was once novel is now old hat. On the upside, Kerr enjoys being 100 percent healthy.

The process of coming home dulls Golden State's enthusiasm for the next battle. All the glory to be gained lives in the past, back in 1997. It's a high that cannot be recaptured. When the Charlotte Hornets come to Oracle, now Hornets owner Michael Jordan keeps saying the same thing to Warriors staff members: "So now you know what it's fucking like, huh?"

The 1999–2000 Lakers vs. the 2017–18 Warriors

The Warriors come to Los Angeles with too much pride and not enough motivation. The practices are light. While Draymond is excited for the chance to guard Shaquille O'Neal and Klay Thompson is enthusiastic about playing childhood idol Kobe Bryant, all share the collective memory of how little the glory lasted from winning in 1997. Moreover, the people of 2000 are far less enthusiastic about Golden State's sudden appearance. Lacob had already mentioned they'd return at this time in a 1997 press conference, so it's not a surprise. The Warriors' appearance from the future is just another news item. Plus there's some bitterness, some questions about why the time travelers made this their priority. There was some expectation, after the 1997 appearance, that more time travelers would visit and offer suggestions on how to quell disease and famine. Society even had to tackle the Y2K bug on its own.

The first press conference is mostly reporters shouting at Kerr, demanding forewarnings. Kerr starts to say something about Donald Trump but is ushered off the stage by Golden State PR man Raymond Ridder. Scheduling the game is difficult, as Shaq demands a significant pay bump for his efforts. In a secret meeting, Joe offers a stock market forewarning as compensation. Shaq is told to buy Apple and to short-sell the mid-2000s housing bubble. Shaq likes the idea of "shorting" for the novelty/irony factor alone, and, in the future, will frequently, randomly scream the phrase on *Inside the NBA*. He will be the wealthiest man in America by 2013.

Los Angeles, February 4, 2000

Phil Jackson learned a few things about the Warriors in the last go-around, and he actually switches pick-and-rolls, shocking a Golden State organization that had become accustomed to Phil's persona as a doddering fool in his Knicks days.

Zaza Pachulia gets in foul trouble immediately, leaving Draymond to deal with Shaq. The illegal defense rules prevent Golden State from effectively swarming the big man, and Draymond soon also gets in foul trouble. The Lakers are more difficult to contain, due to better three-point shooting. Shaq's early success scatters Golden State's defense, leaving Glen Rice, Derek Fisher, and Rick Fox wide open behind the arc. Los Angeles leads at halftime by four, having drained eleven triples early.

It doesn't help Golden State that Kobe's silky moves are giving Klay the kind of headache usually visited upon him by Kyrie Irving. Klay is a dedicated defender, but a bit balky, and not necessarily intuitive with his movements. Kobe's grace overwhelms his efforts. With the Warriors bereft of bigs, Bryant repeatedly gets to the basket. The Warriors' offense is productive enough (110 points), but it has one of those days where the three just won't fall. Steph goes 2-of-10 from deep, shanking a few wide-open ones. Durant has the best game of anyone, earning forty points against a Laker roster that's a bit light on rim protection. Klay manages a frustrating eleven.

The reffing isn't helping matters, something many Laker foes of this era might sympathize with. While it's not lopsided enough to prompt a concerned letter from Ralph Nader, the calls are going the way of LA. The Warriors, who often struggle to earn free throws, end the game at a 33–10 disadvantage on freebies. The jeers and boos start in the fourth quarter, when Golden State falls down by ten.

Golden State goes small and pushes the pace, hoping to exhaust Shaq. But this is the year Shaq's in shape, and he's ready for the challenge. After flushing an alley-oop from Kobe, he stares down Draymond and sprints back down the floor. The Warriors lose by seven. The LA crowd chants "OVER-RATED," as Golden State's players trudge off the floor.

Many of the postgame press conference questions are sneering in nature. "Tell us about the future" has been replaced by "Tell us why you're overhyped." Shaq takes the mic during one of Kerr's questions and booms, "SHAQ TO THE FUTURE! Thank you everybody!" and waves. The attending media laughs uproariously. In the *LA Times*, Bill Plaschke writes, "Tales of Golden State's dominance were, apparently, science fiction."

The Warriors largely shrug. If winning in 1997 didn't matter, what difference does losing in 2000 make? They are quite naïve.

When the Warriors transport themselves back to their practice facility floor, a large media crowd greets them. Everybody remembers having seen this game, but they're eager to relive it. Resentful fans around the league have been waiting for this. Golden State's been winning too much, and people have taken solace in sharing miscues and associated memes from this disaster of a performance. There's a non-HD GIF of Klay slipping and falling in front of Bryant, another one of Shaq dunking at Draymond and pointing.

Shaq goes on *Inside the NBA* and brags nearly weekly about owning the Warriors. He's been doing this for years, but has really ratcheted it up for Golden State's return from 2000. He calls JaVale McGee a "bum." Barkley affirms that the Warriors only got lucky against Jordan's Bulls, that this Laker game exposed them. Trump mocks the modern Warriors on Twitter, says he'll make the NBA great again, like it once was.

Skip Bayless froths over how soft the NBA's gotten. Various think pieces are out about basketball's decline over the past two decades. There's already talk of production on a massive documentary, set to commemorate the upset's twentieth anniversary in 2020. The most commonly worn piece of Laker-affiliated apparel, aside from Kobe Bryant's jersey, is a purple-and-gold Nike shirt that reads BEAT THE FUTURE, with silhouettes of Shaq and Kobe high-fiving over text that reads "2/4/2000." That one Laker victory kicked off a popular ad campaign in the early aughts, a convenient bridge from the "Just Do It" slogan of the '90s. Other Warriors shoot Durant dirty looks when he shows up to practice wearing the shirt. He shrugs. "To be honest, I was a Kobe fan as a kid. I was rooting against us."

The Warriors have a team meeting dedicated to whether they should go back in time to correct this humiliation. Adam Silver has requested it, on account of how it has lessened faith in modern basketball. He's sick of Barkley's tirades. Most of the players hate the mockery but are tired of time travel. Nobody wants to guard Shaq again.

Lacob is ambivalent. He feels a measure of shame but also is, for the first time, wary of his own powers. It was nice to expunge the failure of 2016, and fun to defeat the vaunted Bulls, but he misses a less complicated life. He's a little shaken by the dissonance of two histories in his head, the one where he'd discovered his future life path when an older Lacob visited in 1997 and the one where he had no knowledge. He resents the part of himself that never had to worry about the future ever since 1997. He resents the part of himself that made life boring by removing its mystery. He's lonely like this. And when will his future self visit? Why hasn't this happened already?

Lacob paces around Golden State's rooftop practice facility. "Silver really owes us an easier schedule next season," he mutters to GM Bob Myers, who abstained from the trips due to a busy college scouting season schedule. Joe strolls out the facility doors, out to the parking lot that hangs over downtown Oakland. He reaches into his pocket and pulls out Light Years. It's cool to the touch. It hasn't been used in a month or eighteen years, depending on how Schrödinger's cat meows. Joe sighs, collects himself, and stares at the greatest invention he's ever known. "They'll never invite me back to Davos if I do this," he says. And with that, he throws Light Years, screaming "WAIT!" just after it leaves his fingertips. It's already too late. Light Years can't withstand a five-story fall. Horrified, Lacob watches the device hurtle toward asphalt, when suddenly, out of nowhere, a gray-haired Lacob appears, with a baseball glove that safely snags the machine. The Joes give each other a thumbs-up.

Future Joe gently places the time machine atop a rectangular parking meter before evaporating behind an artisanal cheese stand. Present Joe races downstairs and snatches the device back, feeling a wave of relief as his fingers absorb that polycarbonate cold. Order is restored; he was thinking crazy just five minutes ago. Light Years has the potential to do so much more. How was he so foolish as to focus on something as prosaic as the Lakers? It's time to do what's right, to think bigger than the NBA for once.

He mutters a line from *Atlas Shrugged*: "Ask yourself whether the dream of heaven and greatness should be left waiting for us in our graves—or whether it should be ours here and now and on this earth."

Heaven and greatness will be his, because this isn't just a reverie. This is a reality where a beloved dream can't just be attained. It can be conquered, pummeled into submission. Joe smiles as he looks across the Bay, in the general direction of his yet-to-be-built San Francisco stadium. Then he texts his assistant to fetch a water bottle and also book the team a hotel in Barcelona, near the Olympic Village, in the summer of 1992. Playing Jordan isn't enough. Real fulfillment means demolishing his entire vaunted Dream Team. They might have popularized basketball the world over, acting as something between ambassadors and rock stars. They might have done all that, that is, unless Joe's Warriors steal their thunder and their place in history. To be the best, you have to replace the best. To be Light Years ahead, you must first be decades behind.

5

What If Horse Racing Was Still the Most Popular Sport in America?

Peter Thomas Fornatale

September 21, 2012, was a truly great day in sports history. It saw the return of big-time professional sports to Brooklyn after an absence of more than fifty years. The old railyards at the intersection of Atlantic and Flatbush Avenues had long been discussed as a possible site for a sports stadium. As far back as the fifties, the Dodgers wanted to move there to play in a geodesic dome designed by Buckminster Fuller. After many decades of stops and starts, and a dubious use of eminent domain, the place was finally ready for business.

Politicians, city planners, and celebrities were on hand to christen the new venture, none more prominent than Jay-Z and Beyoncé, who were also investors and among the driving forces behind the project.

I'm talking, of course, about the opening of Blue Ivy Downs, the United States' first luxury racetrack, complete with three racecourses, a nightclub, and a performance venue that doubled as a hockey arena with perfect sight lines. The Sport of Kings had conquered the County of Kings, and horse racing had cemented its standing as America's most popular sport.

What alternative universe is this? It's one where horse racing is as popular in 2018 as it was in 1938.

I'm not one of these doom-and-gloom guys when it comes to the current state of horse racing. As my friend Nick Tammaro is fond of saying, "Racing is as Hyman Roth is described in *Godfather II*: dying of the same heart attack for the past twenty years." Only in racing's case it's more like seventy years. But that said, it's clear that in that time frame racing has gone from the top of the sports pyramid to scuttling along somewhere in the desert sand.

What led to racing's decline? Racing, which had been the most popular spectator sport for most of the second half of the nineteenth century and the first half of the twentieth, is said to have been killed off by television. But the fact is, racing *did* embrace television in the 1950s. Racing was broadcast nationally throughout the decade. In fact, the "Grey Ghost," Native Dancer, was named the number three television star of 1953 by *TV Guide*, behind only Ed Sullivan and Arthur Godfrey. The problem wasn't that racing failed to jump on the television bandwagon, the problem was that it didn't make for very *good* television.

At the start of the 1950s, there were just over five million TV sets in America. By the decade's end, that number rose to more than forty-two million. Almost overnight, television changed the way Americans consumed their news and sports. Boxing and pro wrestling were the biggest winners in the early days of TV. Both were great fits for the limitations of the new medium, confined to well-lit squares and easy to shoot.

Racing, a high-speed sport requiring panoramic angles, was difficult to broadcast effectively with fifties technology. But that's not a great excuse, as it wasn't exactly a picnic to capture the NFL's spread-out game flow back then, either, and football was still able to ride the new medium to unprecedented levels of popularity. Come to think of it, it's not a coincidence that Native Dancer was gray: While the many bay and chestnut horses blended in with the background on the black-and-white TV sets of the day, his striking pale color made him stand out.

Then there was the matter of length. It's never been easy to fill a sixty-minute block of programming with the few minutes of action that two or even three horse races can provide. Viewers of the new medium wanted lots of spectacle—and racing's excitement was compressed into too short a window.

Another problem with racing and TV is that the broadcasts—then and sometimes now—hid a key aspect of racing's appeal: gambling. TV networks found it unsavory to promote this element of the sport. After all, we are a country founded by Puritans. But without the thrill of cash changing hands and the chance to make a score, a big part of what makes the sport so appealing in person was gone. TV viewers were not getting what made the mare go, as it were.

But TV is just part of the picture of racing's slide. The other part is that the sport never recognized a central authority, preferring to stay a collection of independent fiefdoms in the form of different state racing organizations and track operators. Competing racing interests have continually struggled and fought for slices of an ever-diminishing pie. Imagine if the AAFC, AFL, WFL, USFL, and NFL all still existed. Maybe they would work together occasionally, but more likely they'd spend most of their time in direct competition, diluting the talent pool and the fan base. Or, if you prefer, don't imagine. Look at boxing. The alphabet soup of WBC, IBF, WBF, and WBO creates a byzantine morass of licensing bodies, state commissions, and stakeholders. That's the same type of fractured structure that holds racing back outside of its biggest events (the Triple Crown races and the Breeders' Cup).

Racing's lack of centralized power left it vulnerable to competing gaming interests. One key moment came in the early 1960s: New York lawmakers proposed a constitutional amendment to legalize lotteries for the stated purpose of raising money for education. On November 8, 1966, 60 percent of New Yorkers voted yes on the measure. A lot of the money that once flowed racing's way was then diverted to scratch-offs and jackpot chasers. All it takes is a dollar and a dream, no equines necessary. Casinos provided another easy way for racing's former fans to rid themselves of cash.

Where racing was once the only game in town, now people could spend their gambling dollars on pursuits that have been better promoted and regulated than racing has ever been. Americans spent $70 billion on lotteries in 2014. In 2015, casinos' gross gaming revenues were also approximately $70 billion. In 2016, horse racing handled just under $11 billion—not nothing, but a comparatively small slice.

It should be noted that while gambling adds to racing's appeal, it is one part of the mosaic. No sane person would lecture you on the history, pageantry, strategy, or majesty of pulling the arm of a slot machine. Racing is built on all of those things. But the lottery, table games, and slot machines do offer a steady dopamine gambling rush that racing can't hope to compete with. Consider racing a sip of single-vineyard Barolo from a hand-blown crystal glass, whereas a scratch-off ticket is like taking a deep pull off a bottle of Mad Dog.

Oddly enough, racing also faces competition from itself. You can't comprehend racing's problems without a short economics lesson. I wish I could give you Margot Robbie in a bathtub (or even Angel Cordero) but I'm afraid you're stuck with me. First of all, racetracks don't care who wins. In racing, you're not playing against the house, you're playing against other bettors with the house taking a cut, known as the takeout. This is why racing is such a great gambling game—the individual gambler can win because he or she can tilt the odds in his or her favor by being smarter than the competition.

In the old days, you had to be present at the track where a race was taking place to make a bet. This changed because of something that became known as simulcast wagering, where you could eventually make bets from a variety of venues (other racetracks, OTB parlors, online). Over time, racing's action shifted heavily away from being bet on track toward being bet offtrack—the problem is that racing's cut of the money bet offtrack is a fraction of what it is when one bets on the live racing at Saratoga, Santa Anita, or Keeneland. This led to all manner of in-fighting and economic problems too numerous to list.

Think about this for a second. In real life, a team like the New York football Giants makes $75 million or so from their stadium and they make $180 million from TV. In total, the NFL generated $7.3 billion from its TV contracts in 2014. But if the NFL operated under the revenue structure of racing, the Giants would receive their full share of revenue only if a patron attended the game in person. TV viewers would amount only to a tiny cut, with a middleman raking in most of the money.

Let's see what might have been for racing. Let's have our fictional universe split off from reality in the mid-1950s and have racing emerge as America's game. The first thing that happens in our fantasy is that racing finds a better way to work with television. A young hotshot television producer named Roone Arledge comes up with the idea to combine racing broadcasts with those of college football—a far more popular sport than pro football in the fifties. College halftimes offer the perfect opportunity to cut away for short "Raceday in America" segments, hosted by a young theater actor named Ed Sabol.

These segments and others like them firmly plant racing in the national consciousness fifty-two weeks a year. Sabol goes on to found a production company, Equine Films, where he and his son Steve win more than a hundred Emmy Awards creating a mythology around a sport that readily lends itself to morality tales of underdogs and champions.

In the world of Blue Ivy Downs, our Brooklyn racetrack of tomorrow, an alliance is struck between various regional racing interests in the early 1960s, culminating in the hire of Pete Rozelle away from the Los Angeles Rams. In this fantasy world, Rozelle doesn't become NFL commissioner after Bert Bell dies. Instead Rozelle takes many of his—and Bell's—best ideas and implements them in racing, centralizing power into the NRO (National Racing Organization) and creating formidable national TV deals with revenue-sharing components that allow smaller tracks to stay vibrant as the big-boy tracks not only survive but thrive. (Just as, in reality, the NFL allowed small market teams like the Green Bay Packers and Baltimore Colts to compete on equal footing with teams in major cities like the New York Giants and Chicago Bears.)

A former public relations executive, Rozelle understands the issues racing faces, and he fights to fix them. For one thing, there's the whole gambling issue. The NFL's Rozelle took a fierce anti-gambling stance. In 1969, he threatened his league's biggest star, Joe Namath, with suspension if he didn't sell his interest in a nightclub known to be frequented by gamblers. But our Rozelle understands how essential gambling is to racing.

He comes up with a game-changing idea that will eventually improve the way the sport is covered on television. Seeing an opportunity for the sport to grow, he seeks to tie racing to the state lotteries that are springing up around the country. He cuts a deal with New York State where the lottery numbers are generated not by random Ping-Pong balls in a glorified popcorn machine but by the results of actual horse races. There is a cultural precedent for this: Neighborhood numbers rackets, which were ultimately put out of business by the lottery, used the last three digits of the day's handle at the track to generate the winning combination of numbers. But in our case, the numbers are determined by the first six past the post.

The resulting lottery is expanded to other states (just as eventually happened with Powerball and Mega Millions). The jackpots become enormous, especially when the number goes unhit for several weeks at a time, creating millions of ticket-clutching viewers at TV sets nationwide as the crowd at Churchill Downs sings "My Old Kentucky Home" on the first Saturday in May, all hoping to become the $100 million Power-Derby winner.

The sport flourishes: All the casual lottery-style money fuels pools, and since smart horse players have an opportunity to win, racing-related hedge funds become an important part of the country's economics, especially as they offer an investment vehicle not correlated to other asset classes. In related news, in 1978 revolutionary racing writer for the *Washington Post* Andrew Beyer wins the first-ever EGOP—Eclipse, Grammy, Oscar, People's Choice Award—the latter for his three-episode arc alongside Adrienne Barbeau on *Maude*.

The existence of the national office prevents racing's simulcast problem from ever coming into being—potentially competing interests have a strong leader who prevents them from cutting each other's throats. Because they're already working so much in partnership, racing's various jurisdictions are able to broker mutually beneficial deals that evolve as time moves on. Racing isn't wasting time fighting itself—there's simply too much money to be made by cooperating.

This symbiosis between racing, TV, the lottery, and eventually simulcasting pushes racing to a place in the sports landscape that the NFL and NBA could only dream about. When Secretariat wins the Triple Crown, he is not only on the covers of *Time* and *Newsweek* on the same day, he also receives more votes for president in 1976 than Gerald Ford. Secretariat, in fact, carries not only Ron Turcotte but Rhode Island.

Rivalries continue to be an important part of the sport's promotion, with Affirmed and Alydar (and later Easy Goer and Sunday Silence) persuaded to stay in training to contest multi-million-dollar match races that are promoted with more zeal than any heavyweight fight ever was. This brings another revenue stream, pay-per-view, into play. With so much additional money in purses, racing's top stars can be persuaded to stay in training longer than would ever make economic sense in real life, where they are whisked off to stand at stud for up to hundreds of thousands of dollars per live foal before they even reach their peak. When there's more money to be made racing than breeding, racing has more stars and the sport perpetuates itself.

Racing and popular culture become further entwined. After his romp in the 1984 Florida Derby, Claiborne Farm's color-bearer, Swale, records a novelty record with Seattle Slew and Affirmed called the "Triple Crown Shuffle." His Triple Crown bid falls short in the Preakness, but the single peaks at #41.

Celebrities, of course, have long been a part of actual racing history, from kings and queens to Bing Crosby and his cronies founding Del Mar racecourse in 1937, to M.C. Hammer taking off his gold-sequined shirt in the Belmont owners' boxes and swinging it around over his head when his filly Lite Light won the 1991 Mother Goose Stakes. Well, in our fictional world, celeb involvement is immense, with major figures from finance, technology, Hollywood, and, of course, music all becoming major players in racing.

This leads to some memorable moments for racing in the 1990s. The whole East Coast–West Coast hip-hop rivalry plays out on the track instead of the street, with Biggie Smalls's Bad Boy Stables locking horns with Tupac Shakur's Death Row Racing on multiple occasions.

On September 7, 1996, Tupac isn't in Vegas for the Mike Tyson fight; he is back in New York because he has one in at Belmont the next day.

And of course, there are scandals along the way, even in our fantasy world. Computer programmer Chris Harn finds an exploitable flaw in the betting technology and uses it to hijack the pick-six pool on Breeders' Cup Day in 2002. This happened in our reality, but the difference is that in our fantasy world the pot is worth $300 million instead of $3 million.

Have I taken this too far? Forgive me. I love the sport. In our reality, despite all its problems, horse racing is still the greatest gambling game in the world. And it's more than that. Racing itself may not be exactly pure, but its equine protagonists are. As the racing writer William Murray once wrote, horses are "incorruptible in their innocence and beauty," and they lend the game a primal appeal no other game can match.

And that's why it's so fun to imagine horse racing as a sport where the nation watches it more than a few days a year. Where the hundred-thousand-attendance capacity at Belmont Park is tested more than once a year. Where the words *Saratoga, Santa Anita,* and *Ascot* evoke the same awe and envy as the words *Hamptons, Malibu,* or *Ibiza.* Where Beyoncé, vibrant in her Givenchy gown, stands on the steps of the Gravesend Pavilion at Blue Ivy Downs, a giant set of novelty scissors in hand to cut the red ribbon. At her snip on this promise-festooned day, the crowd of racing fans cheers wildly, their sport's past glorious, its present vibrant, and its future secure.

6

What If I Hadn't Written That Fan Letter to Dan Majerle in April 1993?

Jesse Eisenberg

The 1992–93 NBA season was a tour de force for the Phoenix Suns. They won a franchise record sixty-two games, clinched first place in the competitive Western Conference, and boasted the league's MVP: the Round Mound of Rebound, "Sir Charles" Barkley. If there were ever a team designed to stun Michael Jordan's charging Chicago Bulls, it was the 1993 Phoenix Suns.

The world was shocked, then, when Chicago upended this dream team in the final seconds of Game 6 of the 1993 NBA Finals. Suns fans around the world watched the final fourteen seconds of this game like it was the Zapruder film, parsing each moment, wondering what went wrong. The Bulls, down by two, ran a play called the Blind Pig, where every player touched the ball, and with three seconds left, it wound up in the hands of John Paxson, a largely unheralded marksman whose life was about to change.

The Suns looked comparatively amateur, flummoxed as the ball changed hands: Barkley frantically chased B. J. Armstrong. Suns point guard Kevin Johnson collapsed on the floor. And my favorite player, Thunder Dan Majerle, a two-time all-defensive player, raised his hands helplessly under the basket, twenty feet from the man with the ball, as if to signal surrender.

It was a shocking decade of seconds. What happened? How were the scorching Suns stubbed out so quickly? Where did John Paxson's surge of confidence come from? And how did Dan Majerle, a defensive master, so helplessly lose focus?

It was June 11, 1993. I was nine years old, living in the middle of New Jersey. And yet, I am responsible.

Yes, I am the reason the Phoenix Suns lost the NBA Finals that year. Majerle was just my fall guy—the Oswald to my Hoover; the Bush to my Cheney; the Gulf of Tonkin to my Need to Irrationally Spread Capitalist Hegemony Throughout Southeast Asia.

Here is how it happened:

In 1993, I was in fourth grade and had the same number of friends as I had enemies: one. And both my friend and my enemy were not such good versions of either one; that is, my friend, Teddy, was not such a good friend and my enemy, Stephen, was not such a vicious rival. Teddy was kind of a friend by default. I didn't have much interest in other kids and Teddy was kind of a doormat, so we hung out almost reluctantly, both just trying to get through the day. Stephen was my enemy in the way Norway was the enemy of Hitler: He was a brute and I was just in his way.

Toward the end of the school year, Stephen began amusing himself by tormenting me and Teddy as we waited for the bus. I had never been bullied before and it came as a shock.

Distraught, I decided to do something that would change the course of history: I decided to write Dan Majerle a letter, asking for help. He was my idol and I thought that, if anybody could help me, it was Thunder Dan.

Luckily, I wrote several drafts of my letter and I have retained a near-final version, presented below:

Dear Mr. Majerle, (impressed that I spelled your name right? In your Nike commercial, you made a joke about how no one spells your name right. But I memorized it. M-a-j-e-r-l-e. Don't pronounce the J.)

I'm a big fan of you. Your [sic] my favorite player. And I KNOW that one day we will both be playing as teammates on the Phoenix Suns. I know how to draw the logo and I'm a great dribbler.

But I am really in trouble right now and your [sic] the only one who could help me. Theres a kid named Stephen at school and every day he throws mulch at my head. And also at my friend Teddy's head.

Outside the school, there is a lawn and there are trees on the lawn and around the trees is mulch and Stephen hides behind the bushes and when me and Teddy are waiting for the bus, Stephen will throw mulch at are [sic] heads.

It doesn't usually hurt but sometimes it does.

Also Teddy's little brother, Dan has your birthday, September 9th. So he has the same name and the same birthday as you. That's cool and funny.

I thought that if you could come to the school (just at the end of the day when I'm waiting for the bus. You don't have to come for the whole day) and pretend like we're best friends and then when Stephen throws mulch, you can be like "Hey! Don't throw mulch at my best friend Jesse and his friend Teddy!" And then Stephen will be so scared (especially because your [sic] 6 foot 6 and 222 pounds and score 13.9 points per game) that he will stop throwing mulch at my head and then maybe he'll also think I was cool for having a friend like you, Dan Majerle, who is also my favorite basketball player. And then Stephen and I will become friends and I could finally stop hanging out with Teddy after school.

From you're [sic] number one fan, Jesse Eisenberg from New Jersey

It may not be immediately clear how this letter, so narrow in focus and seemingly benign in intent, led to collapse of the mighty Suns. But before addressing the vast historical impact of this letter, I'd like to first point out the naïveté and selfishness of its author:

I) The letter begins with me cheekily bragging that I know how to spell my favorite basketball player's name correctly ("impressed that I spelled your name right?") as though this is some great accomplishment.

II) The letter then assures the basketball star that I, a tiny nine-year-old boy, would someday play on the same team as Mr. Majerle, in part because "I know how to draw the [Phoenix Suns] logo" and know how to dribble. This is absurd for several reasons:

    a) I failed to spend ten seconds figuring out how old Mr. Majerle would be when I would be eligible to play in the NBA, as though I had a chance to begin with.

    b) I assumed that knowing how to "draw the logo" was a prerequisite for joining the team.

    c) I disrespect Mr. Majerle's skill set by touting my own "dribbling," as though "dribbling" is all it takes to play in the NBA. (Mr. Majerle, it should be noted, can shoot, dribble, pass, *and* play defense. Bragging to Majerle about dribbling is like bragging to Beethoven that I know my piano scales.)

III) I indulgently detail my problem with Stephen and assure Mr. Majerle that he is the "only one who could help me" when, in fact, I could think of several others who would be more qualified to help:

    a) my parents

    b) the school faculty

        i) the principal

        ii) a teacher

        iii) literally anyone else at school

    c) finding some inner strength and helping myself

IV) I mention that Teddy, my fellow victim, has a brother with the same name and birthday as Mr. Majerle, as though this tertiary-at-best connection nets me a best friend in Mr. Majerle. As though the equation for Best Friend includes

    a) having an already existing friend who has a sibling who has

        i) the same name as the new best friend.

        ii) the same birthday as the new best friend.

V) I freely admit that my main objective in asking for Mr. Majerle's help is so that I could get Stephen to think I was cool so I could be friends with him instead of Teddy. Shamelessly, I admit to throwing my alleged best friend Teddy under the bus so I could be friends with Stephen(!), who spent his ninth year on earth throwing mulch at my head!

VI) I leave several things unsaid that, in a way, are more egregious than what was said:

a) I implicitly ask Mr. Majerle to fly out to New Jersey to help me at school, but I never take into consideration his demanding basketball schedule, nor do I offer to pay for his PHX to EWR plane ticket.

b) At no point in my letter do I ask Mr. Majerle about himself. Nor do I wish him well in the ongoing basketball season or ask about his family.

c) I provide neither telephone number nor return address for Mr. Majerle to be in touch with me. I ask him for the world and assume he'll track me down.

My letter is infuriating even to me, its author. I can only imagine the anger it must have provoked in Mr. Majerle, a man at the height of his career, embarking on arguably the biggest moment of his life—the NBA Finals—when he was asked to fly to New Jersey to defend a scrawny, arrogant, helpless loser from mulch. It must have torn him apart.

In fact, I have often imagined Dan Majerle in the team locker room, reading my letter and stewing with a rage he didn't know he was capable of summoning.

(Majerle crumples the letter, throws it on the floor, and slams his locker in anger. Charles Barkley, coming out of a relaxing shower, is startled. He approaches Majerle.)

Charles Barkley: Dan, what's wrong? Are you OK?

Dan Majerle: No! I'm not OK! I'm furious!

Barkley: Why? What happened?

Majerle: This kid Jesse Eisenberg from New Jersey asked me to come visit him.

Barkley: What? Doesn't he know we're in the Finals?

Majerle: Apparently he doesn't even care.

Barkley: What?! Now I'm enraged, too!

Majerle: He thinks that just because he knows how to spell my name correctly—like that's some great accomplishment!—and his dumb little friend's brother has the same birthday as me, I should fly across the country at the most important time of my life.

Barkley: Does his friend's brother have the same name as you, too?

Majerle: Yeah, but still…

Barkley: Who does this kid think he is?

Majerle: I didn't even tell you the worst part.

Barkley: The worst part?

Majerle: Yeah! He wanted me to come visit him so I could defend him from some douchebag named Stephen who's throwing mulch at his head.

Barkley: Why doesn't he just ask Stephen to stop throwing mulch at his head?

Majerle: Right?!

Barkley: Or tell his parents? Or a school faculty member, like the principal, a teacher, or literally anyone else at school?

Majerle: Or just find some inner strength and help him*self*!

Barkley: What is wrong with this world? Why is Jesse bringing you into all his problems?

Majerle: He says I'm his favorite player.

Barkley: That's even *more* of a reason to *not* bother you during this sensitive time. It's the damn NBA Finals. I'm furious!

Majerle: And he didn't even ask me how I'm doing or offer to fly me out to New Jersey to save his life.

Barkley: Ahh! I hate Jesse.

(*The usually cool-headed coach Paul Westphal approaches.*)

Coach Paul Westphal: Charles, Dan, calm down.

Majerle/Barkley: We can't! / You don't know what's going on!

Coach Westphal: What's wrong?

(*Majerle fills Coach Westphal in on my letter.*)

Coach Westphal: What?! He wanted to use you to get closer to Stephen? What the fuck is wrong with this kid? I hate him! I can't think straight. How am I going to coach?

Barkley: How am I going to *play*? I'm paralyzed with rage!

Majerle: And I feel sick to my stomach. All because of this letter from Jesse.

Coach Westphal: Yes, this letter from Jesse all but assures us of a terrible Game 6 in the NBA Finals tonight.

And then I imagine the opposing team's locker room, where Chicago Bulls shooting guard John Paxson has just finished reading a fan letter:

John Paxson: (*smiling to himself*) Aww. Isn't this nice?

Michael Jordan: (*overhearing Paxson*) Isn't what nice?

Paxson: Oh, I was just reading this fan letter from a kid who just broke both his legs in a car accident.

Jordan: Oh yeah? What's it say?

Paxson: It says, "Dear Mr. Paxson, I'm currently in a wheelchair and I will probably not be able to walk for a very long time, but I just wanted to wish you good luck in the NBA Finals. From Jeremy, age 9."

Jordan: That is a nice letter.

Paxson: Yes, even though Jeremy's going through a tough time, he still has the tact to figure out his place in the world and wish me luck.

Jordan: Yes, and further, he doesn't burden you with asking for any outlandish favors like coming to his school to show off to his friends.

Paxson: Yes, this is how all fan letters should be written.

Jordan: Yes, I agree. And because of this child I feel ready to play at my best.

Bulls coach Phil Jackson: (*having overheard the conversation*) Yes, because of Jeremy, I feel like I'm in the best mind-set to coach.

Paxson: I think there is a growing consensus among us that this child and his sensible note will allow us to win Game 6 of the NBA Finals against the Suns.

And of course, they did win Game 6 of the NBA Finals against the Suns. John Paxson, bolstered by Jeremy's selflessness, would make his game-winning three-pointer with four seconds left. And the Phoenix Suns, their innocence punctured by my solipsistic note, would collapse.

And Phoenix's demise would not end with the 1993 Finals. As of the publication of this cathartic admission, they have yet to make it back to the NBA Finals—their final Finals moment, in 1993, extinguished by my poison pen.

Nor was the tragic fallout confined to the Suns. Michael Jordan, buoyed by Jeremy's life-affirming example, would win his third straight NBA championship and decide to leave basketball, apparently bored of or sated by the sport. If the Bulls had not won, I have no doubt that Jordan would have remained hungry, staying in the league and entertaining millions.

And worse than Jordan's departure was his questionable decision to play baseball. This move tarnished not just Jordan's athletic mystique but also the sport of baseball, which is America's pastime.

Therefore, by natural extension, Jordan's departure from basketball tarnished America, a country that in the immediate aftermath of the Cold War was at its unparalleled height.

Is it possible that, weakened by Jordan's hubris, which stemmed directly from my crippling fan letter, America was led to failed intervention in Somalia? Did the sour mood linger for two years, driving President Bill Clinton to act out sexually as a desperate balm to counteract America's diminished prestige? Alternatively, have we ever truly scrutinized the housing crisis of 2007 as an inevitable outgrowth of a wave of societal risk taking brought about by Michael Jordan's overestimation of his own abilities as a baseball player?

Is it possible that all of these American tragedies stemmed directly from my letter?

Yes. It is possible and it is likely.

Still, the question remains: Was I a butterfly, innocently flapping my wings in China, unaware of my disastrous ripples?

Or was I J. Robert Oppenheimer, aware of the destructive power of my letter and, at best, an amoral participant?

I truly don't know.

After the Suns lost, I moved on from basketball, developing an interest in obscure theater, where the damage I could inflict would have fewer consequences. Stephen now manages a hedge fund in Baltimore and has three kids who are likely severely damaged by his violent, immature tendencies.

Teddy is still in New Jersey, married with one son, who is likely unstable based on Teddy's wet-blanket approach to life.

The last I saw of my former hero was about a decade ago.

My sister and I were watching TV when Thunder Dan Majerle showed up, shirtless, in a commercial for deodorant. My sister said that I must be gay because Majerle wasn't wearing a shirt and I used to like him. I wanted to tell her, "No, I'm not gay! And liking a basketball player who's shirtless in a commercial doesn't make me gay!"

But I didn't say anything. I didn't fight back.

Because, in a way, this is who I've become. My letter and the subsequent nuclear fallout has turned me into a passive eunuch, too scared to ever fight back. I will sulk through life, getting hit in the head by the proverbial mulch.

My letter altered history exclusively for the worse. And so, I've put down my pen.

If history is written by the winners, I'd rather be a loser.

What If Wayne Gretzky Hadn't Been an Oiler?

Katie Baker

On his eighteenth birthday, Wayne Gretzky stood in front of more than twelve thousand admirers and signed a contract designed to last until he was nearly forty. It was January 1979, right before puck drop on a game between the Edmonton Oilers and the Cincinnati Stingers of the World Hockey Association, and Gretzky was inking a deal to play for loaded but loony Oilers owner Peter Pocklington for another twenty-one years.

Two cakes were shaped like the number 9. Gretzky's entire family was there. The flashy new contract ceremony was cause for celebration among the hockey-loving locals in central Alberta. Locking up the young phenom was a bargaining chip in the latest discussions between the rogue, doomed WHA and the establishment National Hockey League. And it was an agreement that would eventually lead to an Edmonton Oilers dynasty and have an enormous impact on modern hockey history, from salary caps to Stanley Cups.

Gretzky was used to this sort of fuss. Hockey's own Doogie Howser, he had been a remarkably precocious talent for his whole life, a savant who was forever leapfrogging his peers. As a six-year-old, he stickhandled around the ten-year-olds. At age ten, he scored 378 Pee Wee goals in one season. His team-issued jerseys were often several sizes too big, and he tucked one side into his padded pants so his stick wouldn't get caught in the fabric. (Over the years, that solution would turn into an iconic, trademark look.)

When he was sixteen, Gretzky played with guys as old as twenty in Canada's top major junior hockey league. He finished that season with 182 points in sixty-four games. Like any bored prodigy, he clearly needed a new challenge. Too young to enter the NHL Draft, which had a minimum age of twenty, he turned to the WHA instead.

Founded in the early 1970s by the same thirsty promoters behind the American Basketball Association, the World Hockey Association was an attempt to challenge the NHL's hockey supremacy. NHL stars were offered big bucks to jump ship to WHA organizations, even when the teams couldn't necessarily back up their offers. (When the league, at its inception, convinced NHL great Bobby Hull to join them to the tune of millions, almost every team in the league had to pool money to get it done.) Franchises were founded, relocated, and shut down on the regular. The hockey was not necessarily great. Nelson Skalbania, the owner of the Indianapolis Racers WHA franchise, told Sportsnet that the league "was quite cliquey—wild cowboy guys, who had a lot of fun in the business even though we were bleeding money."

Ultimately, the World Hockey Association was a wild experiment marked by antagonism, upheaval, some truly great team logos, and, in contrast to the NHL, a happy willingness to employ teens. On that January night in 1979, as Gretzky signed his newfound adulthood away, his opponents on the Stingers included Mike Gartner and Mark Messier, nineteen and eighteen years old, respectively. (They also included a twenty-two-year-old guy named Barry Melrose.) According to Bruce McCurdy, an Edmonton writer who was in attendance that night, the pregame program distributed to fans included an essay about Gretzky that drew reference to his youth. "Watching him play hockey," the essay said, "probably is a little like hearing Mozart play a piano at five or Einstein recite mathematics tables at seven."

This was why the entrepreneurial Pocklington had essentially purchased Gretzky from the Indianapolis Racers, the team that first signed him, just eight games into the 1978–79 season. Gretzky was Mozart, he was Einstein, he was box office bucks. To Pocklington, he was also the perfect trump card to hold while the NHL and WHA continued discussions about combining in some way, shape, or form. That conversation had gone on for years; in 1977, six WHA teams nearly joined the NHL, until the proposal was voted down by NHL owners. But the long-term lockup of one of hockey's most anticipated talents helped force everyone's hand.

The league agreed to turn four WHA teams—the Oilers, the Quebec Nordiques, the New England Whalers, and the Winnipeg Jets—into "expansion" NHL franchises. Several other teams, including the Stingers, closed up shop by the end of December 1979. And all the young players, like Gartner and Messier, were tossed into the superstacked 1979 NHL Draft, which had a new entry age of eighteen. Gartner was selected fourth overall, and Messier went in the third round. With the first pick, the laughingstock Colorado Rockies took defenseman Rob Ramage, age twenty. (Another defenseman, the eighteen-year-old Ray Bourque, was picked eighth.)

Through all six rounds of the draft, however, not one NHL team called Wayne Gretzky's name.

Wayne Gretzky was never drafted into the NHL—it sounds like the sort of thing you'd read about in an airport volume called *French Onion Soup for the Job-Seeking Soul*, alongside motivational anecdotes about the fledgling Beatles being advised "guitar groups are on their way out" or the *Kansas City Star* telling young Walt Disney his work "lacked imagination." How could Gretzky—who would still be the all-time NHL leading point scorer even if you removed every single one of his goals; who once recorded at least one point in fifty-one consecutive games; who led the NHL in scoring ten different times—not have been picked?

Because one of these disses is not like the others. Wayne Gretzky evaded the draft not because he was a wisp of a teen at 160-ish pounds (which he was) or because, if you were looking for weaknesses, he had an unexceptional-looking stride (which he did). He went undrafted because Pocklington designed it that way.

The contract Gretzky signed on his eighteenth birthday wasn't a standard player contract with the Edmonton Oilers. It was a "personal services" contract between Gretzky and the team owner himself. By structuring the agreement that way, Pocklington, who expected that a deal with the NHL might be on the horizon, opened a loophole. All young players on WHA contracts were draft-eligible once the WHA joined the NHL, but Gretzky's wasn't a WHA contract. As a result, the Oilers got to keep Gretzky, and the player who would come to be known as the Great One was never drafted by an NHL team.

But what if this tactic hadn't worked out? What if the league hadn't acquiesced to Pocklington's unorthodox plan and had forced Gretzky to live by their rules if he wanted to play professional hockey under their roof? Considering Gretzky's importance—not just to the Oilers but to the sport of hockey itself—the ramifications of his entering the draft and winding up elsewhere than Edmonton would run deep and wide. And it would begin, most likely, with the Colorado Rockies.

A common refrain on hockey fanatic message boards, when the subject of Gretzky in Colorado comes up, is: "The Rockies would have found a way to ruin it somehow."(Perhaps by exercising an option to trade picks with Montreal.) In their six NHL seasons from 1976 to 1982, the hapless Rockies never won more than twenty-two out of eighty games. They went through seven coaches, two sales of the team, and constant rumors that the franchise would be moved out of Denver. In 1982 the Rockies became the New Jersey Devils.

But when you have a gravitational force on your team, you're less likely to spiral out of control.

A player of Gretzky's caliber has a way of making everyone around him better, the same way LeBron James has in Cleveland. This includes management: When a once-in-a-generation player comes along, you can stop looking for him; your new job is to figure out how to build around his strengths, the way Oilers coach and general manager Glen Sather did. In the years after the Oilers joined the NHL, Sather drafted a number of the guys who would be crucial to Edmonton's dynasty, from Paul Coffey to Jari Kurri to goalie Grant Fuhr. He understood how to build a young, hungry team around his top star.

It's hard to know whether the Rockies would have been capable of doing the same. Ray Miron, the Rockies GM, told the *Denver Post* in 2010 that he constantly fought with his bosses over how to improve the team; he favored a true rebuild, while they wanted to bring in veterans for quicker results. And he was no fan of the guy the team brought in to coach the Rockies in 1979: one Don Cherry, in all his flashy glory. "He couldn't deal with young players," Miron told the *Post*, "and we had a terrible season." The Gretzky-less Rockies finished 19-48-13; Cherry was let go, and rather than continue coaching he got a hockey broadcasting job at CBC.

By all accounts, the bombastic, knock-'em-out Cherry probably would not have been an ideal coach for a player like Gretzky. Still, had Gretzky become a Rocky, it's likely that Cherry would have lasted for more than a year, at least, and who knows? Maybe in the simulation that followed, we would live in a world without Cherry's loud suits, and even louder opinions, on the exasperating, exhilarating, iconic "Coach's Corner." When it comes to impacts on the hockey world, it doesn't get any bigger than that.

What else would be different? Technically, Gretzky entering the 1979 draft would have changed everything, in a butterfly-effect sort of way: For one thing, the entire draft order—or at the very least, the majority of the first round—would have been reshuffled. Maybe Ray Bourque doesn't get picked by the Bruins and ends up, say, a Leaf! (More on Bourque in a bit.) Team records, league standings, draft order: It would all change. Would the Penguins have had the top pick in 1984, when they drafted Mario Lemieux? Would Brian Leetch be a New York Ranger? Probably not! (Although, knowing the Rangers, they would have eventually snagged him once he aged past his prime, perhaps just days before he slipped on ice getting out of a taxi.)

But without getting too deep into the impenetrable matrix of what-ifs, there are a few major story lines in NHL history that would have unfolded in very different ways.

For starters, the Edmonton Oilers would almost certainly not have won five Stanley Cups. (Yes, one of those championships came in 1990, after Gretzky was no longer on the team, but there's a big difference between the tail end of a dynasty and the beginning of one.) That would have been great news for top 1980s teams like the New York Islanders, who won four straight Cups in the early eighties before being defeated by Edmonton in 1984; the Philadelphia Flyers, whose young brawler of a goalie, Ron Hextall, could have been elevated to legendary status; and the Calgary Flames, who had the distinct misfortune of having to meet Edmonton again and again in the early rounds of the postseason.

There's also the question of what might have become of some of the players whose careers are inseparable from Gretzky's. Jari Kurri is a tremendous talent in his own right, and could have been a star player anywhere, but would he have become a Hall of Famer? More than half of Kurri's 601 career goals were attached to Gretzky assists, after all, and nearly 200 of his own career assists were on Gretzky goals. Would Messier be considered the greatest leader of all time? And what of Dave Semenko? He was a mostly unexceptional player—except for the fact that he was Gretzky's on-ice bodyguard, a role that earned him lasting, legitimate acclaim (and also, it should be noted, enabled Gretzky to thrive) and even paved the way for a 1983 exhibition bout against Muhammad Ali. It ended in a draw.

In 1988, after the Oilers had won their fourth Stanley Cup in five seasons, Pocklington made a tough choice. Gretzky's original contract had already been renegotiated upward once, in 1982, and further potential increases loomed in the coming years. Knowing that this would mean shelling out a lot more money in the near future, Pocklington, who was juggling different businesses and experiencing varying degrees of success and legitimacy, decided to unload Gretzky at a time when he'd yield the highest return. The result was a "trade" to the Los Angeles Kings in 1988 that involved a tearful press conference from Gretzky and $15 million coming back Pocklington's way. The move devastated the Oilers and their fans, made the Kings a splashy celebrity attraction, and helped Los Angeles get to the Stanley Cup

Final in 1993 (under the man who led the Cincinnati Stingers in penalty minutes during the 1978–79 season, Barry Melrose).

It also led to a significant increase in salaries league-wide. According to a *Sport* magazine survey of salaries in 1987, Gretzky that year earned the Canadian dollar equivalent of $717,250, not even enough to crack the top hundred salaries in North American team sports. And because he was indisputably the best player in hockey, Gretzky was also a de facto salary cap: Anyone asking for more than the Great One would seem out of their minds. But Los Angeles Kings owner Bruce McNall amped up Gretzky's paycheck, and by 1990 he was making $2,720,000, seventh in North American sports. Other salaries across the league rose accordingly.

Of the four teams that joined the NHL in the agreement with the WHA in 1979, the Oilers are the only one that still exists. The Hartford Whalers moved to North Carolina, the Winnipeg Jets went to Arizona (there's a Jets team today, but it's a new one), and the Quebec Nordiques wound up as the Colorado Avalanche. Which brings up another question: Would there even be a Colorado Avalanche? Arthur Imperatore Sr. bought the Rockies with the intention of moving them to New Jersey a year before the 1979 draft had even occurred. But it took a few years, and another sale of the team, for the league to allow a Rockies move. Gretzky could have brought enough prestige and success to convince ownership that sticking around Denver might not be so bad. And if that had happened, there would have been no Colorado Avalanche, and no Bourque asking to be traded there so he could win a satisfying, last-gasp Stanley Cup.

It's possible that Gretzky himself sometimes thought about what might have been. In February 1986, after he had already lifted two Stanley Cups with the Oilers and before he would win two more, Gretzky put on a light gray suit, parted his fluffy hair down the middle, and appeared on *Late Night with David Letterman*. (Connie Chung was the other guest; Jerry Seinfeld did standup.) Letterman asked Gretzky about the All-Star Game, cereal endorsements, and the necessity of hockey goons. And he also brought up a touchier subject: a lingering controversy between Gretzky and the nearby New Jersey Devils.

Two seasons earlier, in November 1983, the Oilers had defeated New Jersey, 13–4, and Gretzky was questioned about the lopsided margin. "Well, it's time they got their act together," said Gretzky, who finished that night with a hat trick and five assists. "They're ruining the whole league. They had better stop running a Mickey Mouse organization and put somebody on the ice."

It was an unusually savage comment coming from hockey's golden boy. Devils coach and GM Billy MacMillan was fired days later. For the Devils organization, the sting lasted for years, the way stings do when hard truths are involved. The next time the Oilers played in New Jersey, bitter fans wore mouse ears and held up signs that said things like GRETZKY IS GOOFY.

Gretzky sent an apologetic telegram to Devils owner John McMullen. But underneath all the commotion was the fact that he'd made a good point. And as he explained to Letterman, his motives were noble. All game long, Gretzky had been frustrated to see his buddy and former Oilers teammate Ron Low, a Devils goalie, being totally hung out to dry by his uninspiring New Jersey team.

Still, even if this was the impetus for Gretzky's remarks, it's difficult not to imagine that his strong tone probably also involved some bit of projection. Maybe seeing Low languish on a lame team, and this one in particular, struck a chord for Gretzky. After all, in one of an infinite number of alternate and yet not all-too-distant universes, Wayne Gretzky, the Great One, might have wound up playing somewhere in the swamps of New Jersey himself.

8

What If Major League Baseball Had Started Testing for Steroids in 1991?

Ben Lindbergh

The Question

The first thing you might wonder is, "Why 1991?"

Why not, for instance, 1988, when Oakland A's outfielder José Canseco denied steroid use when accused by *Washington Post* columnist Thomas Boswell in a televised CBS interview? Days later, MVP-to-be Canseco, who was winding down the first 40-homer, 40-steal season in baseball history, was serenaded with *"Stehhh-roids"* chants from the fans in Fenway Park. "I didn't mind at all," Canseco said postgame. "I just stood out there flexing." (That part, at least, seems to have been true.) Elsewhere that year, the International Olympic Committee repossessed sprinter Ben Johnson's gold medal after Johnson tested positive for stanozolol, and President Ronald Reagan signed the Anti-Drug Abuse Act of 1988, which outlawed the sale of steroids for non-medical purposes.

Or why not 1990, when Congress passed the Anabolic Steroids Control Act, which made steroids a Schedule III controlled substance, alongside opium, morphine, meth, and another baseball-clubhouse contemporary, amphetamines?

Either year would have worked for our purposes, since steroids trickled into baseball gradually rather than materializing en masse in one winter. But 1991 at least approaches plausibility, because that's the year Major League Baseball banned steroids.

The average fan didn't (and perhaps still doesn't) know that MLB banned steroids in 1991. Neither did many players, managers, or GMs, as later reporting revealed. But the MLB ban wasn't a what-if. On June 7, 1991, Commissioner Fay Vincent sent a seven-page memo to every team that declared, "The possession, sale or use of any illegal drug or controlled substance by Major League players or personnel is strictly prohibited." Later in the document, Vincent wrote, "This pro-hibition applies to all illegal drugs and controlled substances, including steroids," making explicit why he felt it was necessary to affirm that substances banned in the United States were, indeed, banned in MLB clubhouses.

MLB had banned steroids, but for all the attention teams paid to its text, the memo might as well have been an FBI piracy warning on a VHS tape. With no provision for regular or random testing, let alone lasting punishment, the ban was almost purely pro forma. Teams treated it accordingly, doing the equivalent of reflexively fast-forwarding and continuing about their business, which for an increasing number of clubs involved employing players who were flouting both baseball's ban and the law of the land. Vincent's successor, Bud Selig, recirculated the memo in 1997, but the text was nearly unchanged, as was the response. Baseball's new bodies bred suspicions, but not suspensions.

There's no easy way to concoct an alternate history in which MLB takes a much stricter stance early on. The so-called steroid era isn't something that could have been wiped away with a chain reaction started by some subtle action—maybe Barry Bonds "just saying no," or a drug shipment being delivered to Ozzie Canseco instead of José. As Jon Pessah, author of *The Game: Inside the Secret World of Major League Baseball's Power Brokers*, tells me, it's "hard to get past [the] fact that nei-ther players nor owners wanted testing or to stop steroid use." Pessah says that if a crusading commissioner *had* pushed for steroid testing at the time, amid the unrest and looming labor issues that led to the 1994 strike, "the union would have fought that battle and, more than likely, it would have won." It took time, belated reporting, a public backlash, and congressional hearings to bring an incomplete close to what most fans perceive to be baseball's most chemically compromised period.

So let's hand-wave away the precise steps by which we're saying steroid testing could have started earlier—imagine, if you like, a clubhouse whistle-blower, or a poignant plea by a baseball version of Lyle Alzado, the former NFL player who in 1991 attributed his incurable brain tumor to sustained steroid use, or Texas Rangers owner George W. Bush turning the steroid issue into a résumé builder. Whatever the mechanism, in this scenario steroid testing with penalties started thirteen years earlier than its actual inaugural season, 2004. How would baseball's next decades have looked different?

It's tempting to conclude that none of what followed—the high-offense seasons, the home run races, the hearings, the discredited records, the stigmas, and the exclusions from the Hall of Fame—could have happened with testing in place. But it's too simplistic to say that all the on-field performance and resulting off-the-field fallout we've seen since the 1990s stemmed from an absence of testing.

Dr. Charles Yesalis, a professor of health policy and administration at Pennsylvania State, has been researching and writing about the nonmedical use of steroids and other performance-enhancing drugs (PEDs) and supplements since the late 1980s. He tells me that some pro athletes, especially the star players, hire "teams of scientists, medical people, to make sure they don't flunk drug tests," adding that the idea that baseball's drug era is over is an illusion. Although tens of thousands of drug tests are administered every year in various sports, Yesalis reports that the positive-test rates are virtually always 1–2 percent. "I don't mean to be mean," he says, "but if you believe there's only 1 to 2 percent of elite athletes using drugs, God bless you, I think you have puppy-like naïveté."

No one knows how many major leaguers were using steroids before testing began. Even estimates by contemporary players diverge wildly: Canseco, perhaps seeking to juice (sorry) the sale of his in-progress manuscript about baseball's steroid problem, claimed in 2002 that 85 percent of players were using that year, which Chipper Jones, in his 2017 memoir, *Ballplayer,* called "completely ridiculous." Admitted steroid user Ken Caminiti put the figure at 50 percent, while his teammate Tony Gwynn guessed 20 percent. Perhaps those discrepancies reflect the phenomenon of transgressors overestimating the prevalence of misdeeds in areas from tax fraud to driving infractions.

What we can say with some confidence is that Canseco's 2002 assertion that "there would be no baseball left if they drug-tested everyone today" was, to use a technical term, bonkers. The next year, MLB *did* start conducting tests, which were intended to be anonymous (although some results later leaked). Only 5–7 percent of players tested positive, which suggests either that the problem wasn't as widespread as many had believed or—maybe more likely—that the tests weren't capable of flagging offenders.

MLB's efforts couldn't catch Bonds, who remained one of baseball's best hitters at age forty-two and, as far as we know, never tested positive for performance-enhancing drugs in his five seasons after some form of testing started. "Had they started [testing] earlier," Yesalis says, "they would have caught some careless people." But many players, he believes, would have simply switched to growth hormone or designer drugs for which no test existed. Testing, he tells me, doesn't eliminate steroid use, as baseball's 2013 Biogenesis scandal confirmed; it "drives it further underground using more sophisticated drugs, arguably perhaps more dangerous drugs." The NFL has been testing for steroids since 1987, and not even puppy-like naïveté could convince football fans that testing has kept that league chemically clean.

Moreover, we can't prove that unrestricted steroid use was directly responsible for the bulk of the home-run-rate spike that started in the 1990s and lasted well into the 2000s. After all, pitchers were presumably injecting themselves also, and not every juicer bulked up; the first player suspended under the steroid policy in 2005 was slight center fielder Alex Sánchez, who averaged two dingers per 162 games in his five-year big-league career. I know, I know—I saw Sosa, McGwire, and Bonds get bigger, too. But even in 2006 and 2007, years after testing was implemented, teams were still scoring more runs per game than they had in, say, 1998 or 2001. And baseball's highest-ever rates of home runs on contact actually came in 2016 and 2017, *twelve to thirteen years* after testing was instituted, when 4.4 percent and 4.9 percent, respectively, of non-strikeout at-bats ended in homers. Those topped the rates in the sport's previous peak home-run-rate seasons, 1999 to 2001, which finished at 4.1, 4.2, and 4.1, respectively.

The Computations

Those 2016–17 home run rates prove one of two things: that players are still getting the same artificial enhancement they were in 1999, or that the previous high in home runs wasn't solely the product of steroids. Either interpretation casts doubt on the idea that earlier steroid testing would have meaningfully altered an era. In baseball, so many nonchemical factors can influence scoring and home run production: changes to balls or bats, strike zone expansions or contractions, shifting field dimensions (and, particularly in the case of the Rockies' Coors Field, elevations), and more. (Indeed, extensive research has revealed that the recent, unprecedentedly rapid rise in home run rate is at least partly attributable to changes in the ball's size, seam height, and bounciness.) Sudden, dramatic differences in offensive environment were part of the sport long before anyone was whispering about steroids. How can we tell whether this difference was, well, different?

Here's one way: If steroids boosted offense, we would expect to see more performance variation in the population of players, as some hitters took steroids and reaped the benefits, while others stayed relatively clean. We can check that by examining the standard deviation in offensive performance among qualified hitters each year—essentially, a measure of how closely all players are clustered around the mean. Let's call it the Superman Score. The more variation in results (as measured by Weighted Runs Created Plus (WRC+), a park- and league-adjusted rate statistic that captures a hitter's overall output at the plate), the more far-flung the outliers and the greater the Superman Score.

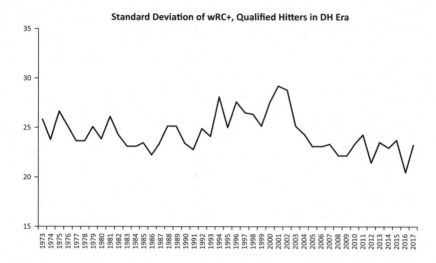

Sure enough, we *do* see abnormal variation during the period from the strike through 2002, the last year with no testing. Nor does this spike in the Superman Score appear to stem from franchise expansion watering down the player pool, since there was less variation in the three expansion seasons during this span (1977, 1993, and 1998) than in the years immediately preceding them. The effect is even more obvious if we look at the difference between the average Home Run / Plate Appearance of the top five home run hitters in each year (i.e., the most extreme Supermen) and the league-average HR/PA in the same seasons.

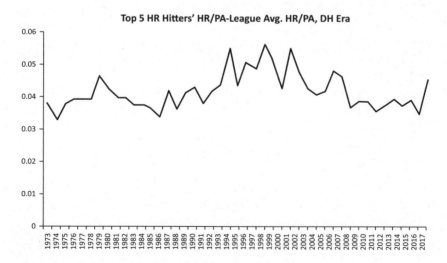

As one would expect, the home run leaders during the so-called ste-roid era were separated from their peers to an abnormal degree. In fact, the top five home run hitters in 1998 (including McGwire, Sosa, and Canseco) and 2001 (including Bonds, Sosa, and Alex Rodriguez) were the greatest outliers not only of the DH era, but also of the live-ball era that began in 1920. That seems like solid evidence that something superhuman was happening.

We know that one other apparent characteristic of the steroid era was the tendency of hitters to remain productive—or become even better—at ages when we would normally expect them to decline. So for one last piece of corroborating evidence, we can examine each sea-son's average hitter age weighted by Wins Above Replacement (WAR), a holistic stat that estimates a player's overall value relative to a theoreti-cal, freely available "replacement player." Let's call *this* stat, which we'll graph below, the Methuselah Measure. In the Methuselah Measure, the more valuable a hitter is, the more heavily his age is weighted in the calculation of the seasonal average.

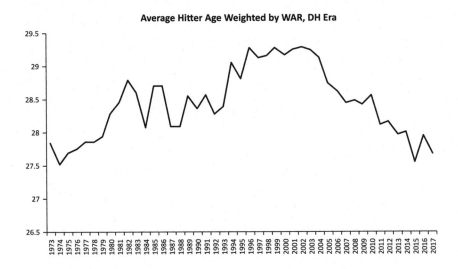

Average Hitter Age Weighted by WAR, DH Era

It looks like we've found a pattern. Again the steroid era stands out, this time for having hitters who avoided decline at advanced ages. The DH era's ten highest WAR-weighted ages all fell between 1994 and

2004, and in the whole live-ball era, only the years around the end of World War II, when many players in their prime were still in the service, can match or exceed the top steroid-era seasons.

The Consequences

In theory, at least, an aging league favored big-market teams that could afford to pay expensive older players, which has some intriguing implications for our fewer-steroids scenario. If testing had come more quickly, then competitive parity—which eluded the league in the 1990s and was one of Selig's priorities before he decided to do something about steroids—might have, too, because it would have been harder for high-payroll teams to spend their way to success. With fewer established players lingering at a high level, teams might have looked overseas for new talent sources sooner, accelerating the sport's international expansion. Additionally, with younger, poorly paid players producing a greater proportion of the value in the league, the sport might have seen a movement to amend the arbitration system and get younger players paid, instead of dramatically restricting their earnings before free agency as baseball's collective bargaining agreement still does today.

Despite his skepticism about the current game being "clean," Yesalis does draw a distinction between today's cheaters and those of untested times. "They were totally unfettered in their use," Yesalis says. "[Testing] would've quite possibly eliminated the extreme outliers that we saw."

In other words, there's solid statistical backing for the intuitive sense that with earlier testing, we wouldn't have seen the standout seasons that define that era in modern fans' minds—particularly those by Bonds, McGwire, and Sosa. Those players probably would have aged out of the game earlier or failed to post stats that defied credibility. Which likely means that the home run records of Roger Maris and Hank Aaron would still stand, instead of Bonds's single-season and career marks looming over the sport like the now-regarded-as-unbreakable women's track times that suspected steroid users Florence Griffith Joyner, Jarmila Kratochvílová, and Marita Koch recorded in the 1980s (although that trio *was* tested). While other factors might have made the mid-to-late nineties and early-to-mid aughts a high-offense era regardless, testing could have compressed the range of individual stat lines such that the sport would have looked more like 2016, when the league as a whole hit tons of home runs but only seven players topped 40 (and the leader hit 47).

Without the disillusionment caused by those instinctively asterisked 60- and 70-homer seasons, more recent outlier years wouldn't have prompted as much skepticism from fans and writers. It's also possible that fewer players would have sought out PEDs, not only because testing could have functioned as a partial deterrent, but also because clean players would have felt less pressure to keep up with their blatantly performance-enhanced peers, as Bonds reportedly did after seeing the fanfare that greeted McGwire's and Sosa's home run heroics.

If steroid use elevated some players, it had to have hurt some who stayed clean. In a world with stricter testing, some of the success that went to the Supermen might have been bestowed on unknowns like Eric Knott. Knott is a former major league pitcher who got into sixteen big-league games with the 2001 Arizona Diamondbacks and 2003 Montreal Expos, then hung on for years at levels just below the big leagues without ever breaking back in. He's exactly the sort of fringe major leaguer whose career could have been curtailed by the PEDs other players were taking; although he admits to taking amphetamines, he says he didn't use steroids, and he believes that that decision cost him service time and salary.

Knott notes that if testing had made the easy way out more onerous, teams and players might have been more motivated sooner to look for mental and physical benefits in other areas. "It would have accelerated the advancement of performance science [nutrition, weight training, sleep studies, mental training, etc.]," Knott says. "An athlete is always looking for an edge. Taking those advantages (steroids, amphetamines) away earlier would have only sped up the advancements the game has made in performance science."

In that less tainted timeline, Bonds, Roger Clemens, and suspended PED violators Rodriguez, Rafael Palmeiro, and Manny Ramírez would be in the Hall of Fame, although if we're subtracting the drugs-fueled performance of PED-aided players, McGwire and Sosa still wouldn't be. Other unconfirmed-but-suspected users, including Jeff Bagwell, Mike Piazza, and Iván Rodríguez, would have enjoyed more direct routes to Cooperstown plaques, as would some non-PED suspects who've been hurt by the ballot's backlog of statistically qualified but ethically compromised candidates. With greater certainty about who did what when—false certainty, in some cases, but probably better than the hazy suppositions and reasonable suspicions we fall back on now—the sports world would be spared at least some of the perennial moralizing, lamenting, character-clause parsing, and back-acne chronicling that accompanies Hall of Fame voting today.

But before we anoint the earlier-testing time line as a PED panacea, let's consider the costs. Would baseball be significantly worse off in any way without its notorious PED past?

The Costs

A perception exists that the 1998 McGwire-Sosa home run race saved baseball, bringing fans back to the ballpark after the exodus caused by the 1994 strike and preventing contraction of the Minnesota Twins, Montreal Expos, or other franchises. It's true that baseball needed help at the gate, with per-game attendance down 19.5 percent in 1995 compared to the previous year. It's also undeniable that the steroid-fueled duel drew print and TV attention to the sport, or at least to the two sluggers' pursuit. That must have had value. But it seems like a stretch to say that the game wouldn't have recovered regardless.

For one thing, per-game attendance recovered much more in 1996 (+6.5 percent) and 1997 (+4.5 percent) than in 1998 (+2.9 percent). In 1999, with the memory of a thrilling record chase fresh in fans' minds, it barely budged (+0.3 percent). Per-game attendance actually dropped (as did the economy, which might have more to do with attendance) in 2001, and again in 2002 and 2003. Not until 2006—well into the testing era—did MLB bounce all the way back to its 1994 attendance pace (which probably would have tailed off had the '94 schedule been completed). MLB's total revenue also increased more from 1995 to '96 than it did from 1997 to '98 or 1998 to '99, and the league's revenue surpassed its 1993 level by 1997. The data don't really fit the idea that McGwire and Sosa played a pivotal role in assuring the game's economic well-being, and that's even before accounting for the loss of any fans who were driven away when baseball's steroid problem became common knowledge.

The economic literature doesn't offer unanimous support for the "steroids saved baseball" hypothesis, either. Although a 2014 journal entry by Young Hoon Lee and Seung C. Ahn concluded that in recent decades, home-team slugging percentage did "influence attendance significantly," and a 2008 article by David Gassko at the *Hardball Times* calculated that each additional home run hit by a team translates to two thousand extra fans in attendance over the course of a season, a 2009 study by Robert Lemke, Matthew Leonard, and Kelebogile Tlhokwane found that home runs per game hit by the home team wasn't a significant factor in predicting 2007 attendance, and a 2012 paper by Cameron Grinder concluded that "increased home runs appear to have a negligible effect on attendance in most cases as well as a negligible effect on MLB revenue."

Prior research has shown that sports strikes tend not to have long-term effects on attendance, and while the cancellation of the 1994 World Series may have made that strike more damaging than most, the wounds probably wouldn't have been permanent. Baseball's roots run deep, and even without steroids, MLB would have grown rich on skyrocketing regional broadcast rights, the growth of digital/mobile powerhouse MLB Advanced Media, and the ballpark-building boom spurred by the Baltimore Orioles' opening of Camden Yards (itself a home run enhancer) in 1992. The McGwire/Sosa narrative seems like as much of a myth as the widespread belief that Babe Ruth's home run hitting saved baseball after the 1919 Black Sox scandal, another neat notion that's not consistent with the facts.

There's one more potential testing casualty to consider: sabermetrics. In the high-offense, high-homer pretesting era, the ways in which teams were throwing runs away were more obvious. Because runners were more likely to score once they reached base, walks were worth more. And because outs were more costly, sacrifice bunts were especially ill-advised. Without that nudge, it's possible that the team best known (and semimythologized) for walking and avoiding the bunt, the Oakland Athletics, wouldn't have embraced Bill James's philosophies, signed Scott Hatteberg, and inadvertently helped make Chris Pratt a superstar. And if they had deployed the same strategies, they might not have worked as well.

Is it actually conceivable that the lack of testing kick-started the ascent of analytics? Well, let's take the 2000 A's, the first playoff team run by Billy Beane, whose specific strategies worked best in an environment of high-octane offense. Those A's, winners of ninety-one games, drew the second-most walks in the majors—154 more than the average non-Oakland American League team. Roll baseball back to the 1992 run environment, when offense was down and any runner was less likely to score, and the same number of free passes would have been worth one or two fewer wins. As it happens, the 2000 A's won the AL West by only one game in the loss column. Take away one or two wins, and maybe the A's don't make the playoffs, maybe Michael Lewis isn't intrigued by their underdog, do-more-with-less story, and maybe *Moneyball* never spreads the gospel of finding inefficiencies to every team and sport that hadn't already subscribed.

Except that if the A's had just missed winning the West that year, they still would have won the wild card. And they *wouldn't* have missed winning the West, because the only team to walk more than they did was the Seattle Mariners...who finished second in the division to the A's. If walks had been worth less, those A's would have won by an even wider margin.

Sabermetrics would have won, too, even if offense hadn't exploded via the bats of beefy sluggers. James wrote his *Baseball Abstracts* long before the steroid whispers started. They were waiting to be popularized. And with technology advancing, revenues and franchise values rising, and larger sums at stake, it was only a matter of time until owners and front offices started running baseball teams like real businesses instead of relying on unexamined assumptions and going with their guts.

On *Effectively Wild*, a baseball podcast I cohost for FanGraphs, listeners regularly submit far-fetched hypotheticals: What would Mike Trout be worth if he always had to run backward? What if the grounds crew planted a tree between the mound and home plate? What if a team took away outfield fences? In 2014, a listener named Vineet poked fun at this kind of question by boiling it down to its essence: "If baseball were different, how different would it be?" Surprisingly often, when we work through a response, we conclude that the game would find an equilibrium, and that what sounds at first like a setup for radical change leads to an unexciting answer: "Not that different."

In the process of (possibly) preserving a storied record or two, earlier testing could have changed what we *think* about baseball. Maybe that matters, because it's our belief that sports are important—and more or less on the level—that gives games their meaning. Baseball's deep history and obsession with stats make it the sport that most celebrates a sense of continuity with long-ago greats, which steroids threatened to sever. But baseball is still standing, and it wouldn't be standing much stronger (or weaker) if it had adopted a more proactive PED policy in 1991. Once you have three strikes, four balls, bases that sit ninety feet apart, and a league that's open to anyone, most questions concerning the degree to which a century-and-a-half-old game would be different can be answered the same way: not that different at all.

9

What If Bucky Dent Hadn't Homered over the Green Monster in 1978?

Stefan Fatsis

Kojak called as soon as the games ended.

He'd already checked the train schedules and everything. We'd meet in front of the high school at 7:30 the next morning—Kojak (got a buzz cut in fourth grade), Fonzie (said "Whoaaaaaa" unironically once in sixth grade), the Cannon (JV soccer coach complimented a penalty kick), and me, Bean Juice (no one knew why, even the kid who stuck me with it in fifth grade). First bell was 8:23, but we'd tell our parents we had a Spanish club meeting or jazz band rehearsal or whatever.

It was a ten-minute walk to the Pelham train station. Half-hour ride on the 8:07 to Stamford. Half-hour wait for Amtrak. Three and a half to Boston. The T to Kenmore. Scalp four tickets and find our seats in the belly of the beast in time for first pitch at 2:30. The Yankees would win the one-game playoff in Fenway—and then a third straight American League title and second straight World Series—and we would book back home, a Murderers' Row of lies tucked in the pockets of our Levi's cords. Our parents wouldn't know a thing.

And even if they dragged it out of us—if we missed a connection and evening turned to night, or night turned to midnight, and they called each other, or the cops—how could they be mad? They were the enablers. Bought us yearbooks and plastic helmets and pennants that still hung on our bedroom walls. Took us to Bat Day and Cap Day. Dropped us at Dyre Avenue and let us ride the 5 train, covered in graffiti like some Christo installation, to Grand Concourse and switch for the final two stops uptown to the Stadium. They saw us in the backyard, focused like monks, perfecting the stances of our preteen idols: Horace Clarke's legs spread wide as the Lincoln Tunnel; Roy White's pigeon-toed precision; Bobby Murcer's looping, laconic practice swings. They watched us lob Folly Floaters against the garage, which we would then deploy on the stickball court.

But those old Yankees sucked. These new Yankees ruled. Chambliss in '76, tears of joy, my immigrant father in his La-Z-Boy, smoking his pipe, unaware that my life was, at that precise moment, at its apex. Then '77, Reggie signing for the unholy sum of $3 million over five, "the straw that stirs the drink," the tête-à-tête with Billy in the dugout. Son of Sam and the blackout. But also the young Guidry, Mick the Quick, Thurman, Sparky, and Sweet Lou. I was there for Reggie's three home runs in the sixth and final game of the World Series at the Stadium. That's a lie—I was there for the first two. The family friend who wangled the tickets wanted to beat the traffic, so I heard the roar of number three as we walked to the fucking garage.

I never forgave him, or my oldest brother, who lived in the city and stayed behind and delivered to me a hunk of sod he'd ripped from the trampled field, as if that would fill the bottomless hole in my soul. (I planted it in the backyard. It died.) But we won, the Yankees won, and we'd be champs for a long time. I was sure of it. We were all sure of it. Even during the Bronx Zoo of the following summer, we were sure of it. It was just theater. Reggie, in July, pissed at being asked to bunt with the winning run (Thurman) at first, fouling off the first pitch, blowing off the new sign, and bunting foul twice more; Billy losing his shit and demanding that Steinbrenner suspend Jackson for the rest of the season (the rest of the season!); the team falling fourteen games behind the Red Sox at the end of the day; the tabloids maxing out on point sizes. Six days later, Billy said of Reggie and George (respectively): "One's a born liar and the other's convicted." And then resigned in tears.

The thing everyone forgets? Between Reggie bunting and Billy self-destructing, the Yankees won all five games they played. The fourteen-game deficit was down to ten. By September 1 it was six and a half. And on the tenth of September, Year of Our Lord 1978, the Boston Massacre was in the books—the greatest sweep ever: 15–0, 13–2, 7–0, 7–4—and the New York Yankees and the Boston Red Sox were tied for first place in the East Division of the American League of Major League Baseball. We went up three and a half on the sixteenth and should have locked the damn thing down. I can't say the Yankees blew it. They won six of their last eight games. Boston happened to win all eight.

On the final day of the regular season, Luis Tiant shut out the lowly, tatterdemalion Toronto Blue Jays, while Catfish lost to Cleveland.

We made it without a hitch. Our jowly European history teacher, Mr. Smith—Froggy—wondered what the hell we were doing at school so early, but he didn't break stride. At the station, Kojak and Fonzie scanned for commuting dads while the Cannon and I bought tickets. We told the conductors we had the day off—teacher meetings, Kojak said. Upon arrival in Boston, I found a pay phone and called my other brother, who was on an eight-year plan at MIT. He asked what the fuck I was doing here, and then said he was too stoned to join us.

Fenway Park was a dump—even fifteen-year-old me knew that. But I understood that it was mythic, too, that "lyric little bandbox of a ballpark," in Updike's words, which I wouldn't read for another decade. It was impossible to deny the history of Fenway, just as it was impossible to deny the history of the Stadium (the original, not the renovated one). Carlton Fisk waving that home run fair in 1975 sure was something—especially because they lost Game 7. And the rivalry had turned feral: Munson and Fisk brawling at home plate in '73; Chambliss getting hit in the arm by a dart—*an actual dart*—thrown by a fan in '74; Piniella and Fisk and then Nettles and Lee brawling in '76, Lee separating his shoulder. Sprinkle *that* on your pancakes, Spaceman.

We paid twenty bucks apiece for the seats. Face was $5.75. That was nuts, but we were teenagers in Yankees caps, easy marks. Our cash reserves from a spring and summer of mowing and umpiring were nearly depleted. But we'd bought round-trip tickets, and could survive on hot dogs and adrenaline. And holy shit: third row, just to the right of the Pesky Pole in right field. All that green—the seats, the grass, the Monster. It was beautiful, hell and heaven all at once. We were going to see history.

Just not the history we expected.

I'm switching to the present tense here because, forty friggin' years on, it feels every bit like right this second. Guidry—24-3 on the season—is pitching. For Boston, Mike Torrez; after less than a year in pinstripes, he and the World Series ring we gave him defected in free agency. Advantage us. But Yaz homers in the second and they scratch out a run in the sixth. Two–zip Boston; they have as many runs as we do hits.

Then the seventh, so full of promise. With one out, Chambliss singles to left and Roy White singles to center. Jim Spencer, batting for Brian Doyle, flies out. Two down. Bucky Dent, choking up like an undersized Little Leaguer (me), takes ball one. Flail and a miss, one-and-one. And then Bucky skies one down the left-field line. Like Fisk three years earlier, Dent tries to will the ball fair. Wave. Wave. Wave. But it doesn't cooperate. Strike two. And then he takes strike three. Mighty Bucky has struck out.

But Rivers walks to open the eighth, and Munson lashes a double off the Monster, scoring Mickey. Then Reggie, not suspended for the rest of the season, hits a mammoth homer to straightaway center off Steamer Stanley. Just like that, we're winning, 3–2. Goose Gossage one-two-threes and we're three outs away.

Through the first seven innings, the score ensured we could avoid the attentions of our hosts. Munson's wall ball and Reggie's blast ended that. We've been whooping and bouncing and low-fiving since—and the natives have noticed. Our noisy group hug after Reggie's homer triggers a cascade of peanuts. When Butch Hobson K's to end the eighth, Kojak screams, *"Fuck yeah! Let's go Bombers!"* to which the locals—co-opting our "Boston sucks" chant, invented in the bleachers at the Stadium a year earlier—reply with a chorus of *"Yang-kees suck!"* and a sea of index fingers identifying the infidels. It was, in retrospect, probably a bad idea for me to answer with a different digit.

Gossage gets Dwight Evans to start the ninth. But then he walks Boston's Dent-like shortstop, Rick Burleson, bringing to the plate Boston's Dent-like second baseman, Jerry Remy. Remy is five nine, one-sixty-five. Even Bucky has more home runs (four) than he does (two).

Occasionally now, in a conjoined display of masochism and nostalgia, I'll watch the at-bat on YouTube. "There's the tying run there at first base," Bill White tells his WPIX viewers. "One out, Jerry Remy's the batter."

The left-handed Remy takes a ball, then fouls the next pitch off of his right instep. The Red Sox trainer sprays it with ethyl chloride to numb the pain. "That's only temporary relief," White says. "Sometimes I wonder whether it's relief at all."

In right field, our hearts are racing, but we are quiet as parishioners, aware that things might not end well, and that we are outnumbered by a lot.

"The count's one and one," White says. "One out and one on, the Yankees lead at 3–2 in the ninth inning here at Fenway...Deep to right! Piniella...can't see the ball! He's back to the wall! It's...off of Piniella's glove and...off the Pesky Pole and into the seats! It's a home run! And the Red Sox win!...The final score, the Red Sox 4, the Yankees 3, and the Red Sox win the 1978 American League Eastern pennant."

Oh, look, there I am: the ball deflecting off of Piniella, doinking the Pole, bouncing off the head of some Masshole—they didn't call them Massholes back then—right to me. Easiest catch I ever made. I go fetal, and the pummeling begins. A fist to the kidneys, meaty male hands twisting my wrist and prying my fingers. Kojak and Fonzie pull off Massholes; the Cannon plays human shield. When the Bostosterone abates, I stand up, raise the ball aloft like the severed head of a vanquished soldier, and in the rawest, most impulsive and animalistic moment of my young life, wind up and hurl that piece of shit whence it came. The ball, signed by AL president Lee MacPhail, cuts a slow, graceful arc through the late-afternoon sun before skittering to a stop near second base. I had an arm.

Kojak, Fonzie, the Cannon, and I roar in celebration of my audacious taunt. I'm Timmy Lupus at the end of *The Bad News Bears*; shove it straight up your ass, Boston. And then we spy the gathering army and bolt for the turnstiles. My beloved NY cap is ripped from my beloved NY head. The Cannon swats away double-barrel birds thrust in his face. A full cup of beer showers the Fonz.

We sprint up Lansdowne Street, a menacing chorus of *"Yang-kees suck"* ringing in our teenage ears.

Hub fans bid kids adieu.

We made it home, were found out—Kojak's dad saw me catch the homer; oops—and were grounded for the rest of October, during which, of course, the Sox swept the Royals in the American League Championship Series and the Dodgers in the World Series. Covering it for the *Baltimore Evening Sun* was a twenty-five-year-old son of Groton, Massachusetts, named Dan Shaughnessy. Forget the *Globe* and the *Herald*. Shaughnessy's Game 4 gamer is the one that endures:

> BOSTON—Was there ever any doubt?
>
> Sure, there were bumps on Jersey Street, slogs as muddy as the original Fens, ifs piled high as the Green Monster. If Ted had played in '46, if Lonborg hadn't faded in '67, if the Spaceman hadn't blistered in '75. If, if, if.
>
> You can bury the ifs and the almosts under the Citgo sign. Ask Father Geoghan to say a prayer for the departed past— and then go buy a round at the Eliot. The Boston Red Sox are champions of the world.
>
> Not that the Fenway Faithful didn't believe. It's not as if the Red Sox were cursed. It's not as if the fate of the franchise was sealed a long, long time ago, as the poet said, when Harry Frazee of Boston traded Babe Ruth of Baltimore to the Yankees of New York.

> They don't write books about curses. That's not how sports work. That's not how life works. What's 60 years between titles anyway? Not even a lifetime.

Shaughnessy was hired the next week by the *Globe*. He broke the news of the trade—bitter Reggie straight up for bitter Jim Rice—and covered the dynastic second, third, and fourth titles in '79, '80, and the strike-shortened '81, wooing readers and players alike with his positivity and goodwill. Then, "tired of all the winning," Shaughnessy announced he was leaving the *Globe* to write fiction. (His dystopian 1984 novel, *The Curse of the Bambino*, depicted a world in which the Red Sox never—ever—win the Series. Reviewing the book in the *Globe*, Boston superfan Stephen King called it "a tale of horror too unspeakable to commit to print—and one too preposterous to credibly imagine.")

The Miracle of Pesky's Pole, as it was dubbed, transformed the penurious and racist Red Sox ownership like some baseball *Christmas Carol*. Boston spent truckloads of money and signed or traded for more black players in the next three years than it had in the previous twenty—Joe Morgan in '79, Dave Winfield in '80, and, Reggie, re-signed, in '81. "Twenty-five guys, one Green Line car," Reggie proclaimed. The Red Sox healed the wounds of a divided city.

Then, at the peak of their power and leverage, the Yawkeys overreached, as you knew they would. Complaining about undersized, rat-infested Fenway and threatening to move to Hartford, the owners pried from the city that sweetheart deal: the sports megaplex in Southie, one stadium for baseball, one for football's laughingstock New England Patriots. The Red Sox played their final game in Fenway on October 6, 1985, and moved into Prudential Stadium on April 14, 1986. Just-retired Jerry Remy threw out the first pitch.

I know, the fuckers won it all again that year, thanks to World Series MVP Bill Buckner's 13-for-32 batting (that's .406 for the historians out there) and his slick fielding at first base. But Shaughnessy was right—all that winning, and that discordant big hatbox of a stadium, 330 down the lines, 400 to dead center. There was nothing lyric left to love, and, after '78, '79, etc., nothing for fans to moan about the way they once did. The Red Sox were a corporation, as dominant and as personable as IBM.

The wrecking ball took its first cut at Fenway on the day after the '86 Series, stirring the poltergeists below. And in 2016, on the thirtieth anniversary of Boston's last championship, Shaughnessy emerged from the basement office of his Newton home, reconsidered his '78 deadline proclamation, and made a triumphant return to nonfiction sportswriting with the best-selling *The Curse of the Green Monster.*

And us? Well, with hindsight like Ted Williams (20-10), I maintain that the Yankees' loss on October 2, 1978, was a blessing. Reggie's departure let Thurman stir the drink. Munson didn't win another ring, but those next four All-Star seasons led to that touching Cooperstown ceremony where he sprinkled a vial of Stadium dirt on his rumpled suit. Martin left the torment of the Bronx for good. Managing in Milwaukee, he found a therapist (who would become his third and final wife), stopped drinking, started meditating, and was a beloved mentor to scores of young players: "Uncle Billy," they called him. When Steinbrenner hired some Whitey Bulger babbo to plant cocaine in Reggie's Fenway locker in '84, and Bowie Kuhn, in his final decision as commissioner, banned the Boss from baseball for life, the Bronx actually cheered.

Yeah, we have our own curse, the Curse of Pesky's Pole. It's been *forty* years for us, and we're still waiting. (Those singsong Fenway chants of *"Nine-*teen *seventy-*seven!" do sting.) But there's honor in futility, joy in the hunt. The Yanks are lovable, sometimes losers, sometimes not, and who could ask for more? No one can take away those Division Series appearances in '96 and '97, when that Jeter kid looked like the real deal. (Shame about his knee; he never should have gone skiing with that model.) And the close call in 2009, when "The Captain," True Yankee David Eckstein, gritted the plucky Bombers all the way to Game 6 of the ALCS. Good times.

Without the Pole, the Yankees wouldn't be the Yankees. Without the Sisyphean struggle, without the walk in the desert, there's no Sons of Kevin Maas, the online bar where Kojak, the Cannon, Fonzie, and I relive our youth, politely bemoan the present, and wait 'til next year. There's no *Good Vinnie Hunting*, the movie about Yankees fan and Hunts Point Meat Market janitor Vince Hunting (Leonardo DiCaprio), whose math genius is unlocked by a therapist at Columbia (Lorraine Bracco) who missed Game 6 in '77 because she had to "see about a guy." And there's no way a kid from Great Neck who turned nine a week B.R.—Before Remy—experiences enough heartbreak to make New York a journalistic totem of obsession and pathos, and to reinvent sportswriting. If the Yankees somehow manage to win it all again, Bill Simmons just won't be Bill Simmons anymore.

Don't get me wrong—I'm not happy about '78, whatever good it spawned. But tragedy is memory, too, and I'm grateful for that moment seared in my consciousness. I can still smell the beer on the Fonz's Yankees windbreaker, and still the *Fuck you*s echo in my brain. I can see Jerry Remy's batted ball carving the Back Bay sky, and taste the sweet exhilaration of my bold rebellion in front of 32,925 people, myself included.

I'm going to switch to the present tense again for this last little pentimento, or whatever it is (to quote Salinger), because, though it happened a couple of years ago, it too feels like today. My son is fifteen, like me back then. Time for some closure. I take him to a Red Sox–Yankees spring-training game in Fort Myers. (You know where those corporate shills play? JetBlue Park at Fenway South, I shit you not.) We get to the ballpark early, before batting practice even. Remy, who does TV for the team, is on the field chatting with Pedroia, who's playing catch with Bogaerts. "Jerry!" I shout. "Over here!"

I've waited four decades for this moment, and I'm prepared. I tell him the whole story. Skipping school, the train to Boston, the seats in right, catching his homer, and heaving it back. He laughs and thanks me for the ball—says he always wondered who threw it, never saw anyone do that before, always assumed it was an act of kindness by a Red Sox fan.

Not so, Boston. It was a primal howl born of crushing disbelief, a delirious response to an unthinkable horror, a spontaneous, cathartic release. From my backpack I pull a print of the black-and-white photo that ran on Page 1 of the *Times* the next morning—Piniella, the Pole, the ball, me—and extend a Sharpie.

"*Jerry Fucking Remy*," he writes, and winks at me and walks away.

10

What If Jerry Tarkanian Had Beaten the NCAA and Liberated College Basketball?

Jonathan Hock

A transcript of the Hall of Fame Induction speech given by Jerry Tarkanian, delivered in Springfield, Massachusetts, on September 8, 2013:

Senator Johnson, Commissioner James, Governor Calipari, Distinguished Members of the Hall, and Fellow Inductees—

I'm sorry my voice sounds so weak. I feel OK, but when I was away I didn't talk for long periods of time, and now I sound like this. I'm sorry if it's hard to hear me. [*applause*]

First, I want to thank my presenters, John Thompson and John Chaney, my cofounders of the NAABP, the National Alliance of All Basketball Players. It's been twenty-five years since the Supreme Court decision that—as we used to say in those early days—"set our people free." It was your stalwart vision of fairness and justice in the face of money and power; your unflinching commitment to the rights of young people; and your unwavering support for me during my time away—all that you did carried us. You changed the course of history, both American history writ large and my own humble American history.

And I am so proud to be an American, the eldest son of an Armenian immigrant. My mother was just a girl when she fled her homeland on horseback after her father and her brother were beheaded by Turkish soldiers. Humbly she raised me; humbly, but unafraid.

My father died when I was thirteen, and after that, whenever I'd screw up, my stepfather would tell me I'd amount to nothing. But my mother gave me unconditional love and more second chances than I could count. "This whole country is a second chance," she'd tell my stepfather in her wonderful, thick accent. "I shouldn't give one to my own son?"

As a coach I believed in second chances, and we won a lot of games with rosters full of screwups who made their second chances count. I loved those players and their refusal to be beaten down by a world that can be so ugly. All those kids that had the deck stacked against them.

So now you can picture me back in 1988, a child of immigrants, standing a little straighter than I'm standing here today, humble and unafraid as my mother raised me... before the Supreme Court of the United States.

Years earlier, I had brought the case against the old NCAA when they forced UNLV to suspend me without due process of law, which, we may remind ourselves, even the lowliest immigrant son is entitled to in America. The Nevada State Court ruled for me and told the NCAA it couldn't prevent me from earning my living by coaching. And that should have been that. But the NCAA wouldn't let it go. They kept appealing, realizing that if they had to give this ugly Armenian guy due process, they'd have to give all the other people due process, too—the black people, the women, everybody. And they weren't going to let that happen. You know why? Because once you give people rights, the next thing they're going to demand is money. [*laughter*] Stop laughing—this is how they used to think. Give the powerless their rights and before you know it they're going to want their fair share of the money, too. And money, honored guests, is why the NCAA existed. Money was where the NCAA always drew the line.

When I was coaching at Long Beach State, it was UCLA's time, they won the championship year after year after year. Long Beach State was never at their level, but we got pretty good. In 1971, when UCLA was about to win their fifth in a row, we played them in the Regional Final. We lost by two points. So what was our reward for getting almost as good as mighty UCLA? A knock on the door. It's the NCAA, and they want to come in and ask a few questions. Soon they're saying we were doing this and that, while everybody in the country knows Sam Gilbert is giving cars and whatever to Kareem Abdul-Jabbar and Bill Walton, but no, the NCAA is sniffing around Long Beach, not Westwood. So I write an essay for the paper in Long Beach, the *Press-Telegram*, and I say, Why are they picking on us? Why do they pick on little guys like Centenary, in Louisiana, who you never heard of, when the big SEC schools were buying every player they could? And why are they investigating Western Kentucky? Kentucky did more cheating in a day than Western Kentucky could do in a year, I said.

So I leave Long Beach State and go to Nevada Las Vegas. The NCAA snoops followed me and say we did thirty-eight things wrong at UNLV, and ten of those things are my fault. UNLV disagrees, and we even had a guy from the NCAA lying on tape to one of my kids, but the NCAA said it didn't matter and they were going to put the program on probation and they'd make the punishment worse if the university didn't suspend me for two years. They didn't show us evidence or anything, just said we had to do it. At that point, UNLV had a choice. They could accept that the NCAA has the power to tell them what to do, or they could pull out of the NCAA because they think the ruling is unjust, and they couldn't comply with an unjust ruling. UNLV takes choice one. They accept it that the NCAA can tell them—Nevada Las Vegas, an institution of the sovereign state of Nevada—they *accept* it that the NCAA can tell them what to do.

So they suspend me. I sue the NCAA. I win. [*applause*]

It turns out that in the United States, a private concern like the NCAA is not allowed to act with the power of the state. When the NCAA forced the University *of the State of Nevada* Las Vegas to suspend the coach, that's what they were doing, acting like *they're* the state. The Nevada court said so.

But like I said before, the NCAA doesn't let it go. They keep appealing the case, and it goes all the way to the Supreme Court.

At the Supreme Court, the NCAA argues that all they did was "recommend" to UNLV to suspend me, and that even though they threatened sanctions that would kill the program forever if they didn't suspend me, they actually had no power at all. It was not only gutless, but pure baloney. And you know what? The Supreme Court of the United States wasn't buying baloney that day. Four of the justices, Scalia and his boys, did say the NCAA was right. But five justices, led by Justice Byron "Whizzer" White, said no, that was nonsense, *of course* the NCAA had the power and they were absolutely telling the state what to do. So the Court shut it down. I keep Justice White's opinion framed, kept it with me all through prison, all those years, it's beautiful. He wrote, "The key...as with any conspiracy, is that...the parties agreed to take the action." He called it a "conspiracy" [*"yeahs" and "amens" from the crowd*]—he *did*, which is what it was, by the way. [*applause*]

Had the Court ruled for *them*, the players would still be generating billions of dollars and getting not a dime of it. And the guys running the NCAA and their bosses, the presidents of the universities that used to belong to the NCAA, would still be making millions. But the Court ruled for *me*. And thousands of young Americans were given the full rights of participation in this great country of ours. Including the right to make a living. [*applause*]

Here's what happened next: After the ruling, it took about three minutes for Coach Thompson and Coach Chaney to find me. Big John was waiting for me in the lobby of the Georgetown Marriott where I was staying, grabbed me by the arm, and told me that Chaney was already on the Amtrak from Philly and we needed to talk. "Do you realize what you did today, Tark?" Big John asked me. "Yeah, I won," I said. [*laughter*] Big John laughed, too. He laughed a laugh so big the whole lobby shook. "Let me explain to you just what it *is* that you won."

By the time Chaney arrived, I'd begun to understand what these guys had already figured out—what they'd been *waiting for*. Once the NCAA could no longer tell the schools what to do, there *was* no NCAA. We were all free agents. We could pay the kids their fair share of whatever money came in from our program. If a few of us joined forces, paying the kids to play, what kid would still go to a school that enforced some nineteenth-century idea of "amateurism"? Sure, we'd have to create our own schedule and cut our own TV deals, but with the best kids, that was gonna be easy.

And it *was* easy. Within a couple of weeks, we had a plan. Big John got Jim Boeheim and Syracuse to join us first, he was the easiest to convince. Then came Louie Carnesecca at St. John's and Rollie Massimino at Villanova and Jim Calhoun at UConn. Chaney went down to Raleigh and talked Jim Valvano into it at NC State, and that kid who'd just been hired by UMass, John Calipari—I know today you call him "Governor" here in Massachusetts, but then he was still a loudmouth kid trying to be a coach—Cal called Chaney and begged that we let him join, too. Chaney liked his spunk and said yes. Big John worked for weeks on Dean Smith, but it just wasn't going to happen. I know a lot of us can still remember when they were a big-time program at Carolina and it's a shame to see them reduced to basically an intramural team these days. But once Duke came on board in our second year, there just wasn't room for a third Carolina team, and when Dean told Big John he'd reconsidered and wanted in, Big John had to tell Dean that we were sorry, but he was out.

In the West, Lute Olson brought in Arizona, and I didn't have to twist Larry Brown's arm to bring in Kansas. Then came Billy Tubbs and Oklahoma, Jim Harrick was a layup at UCLA, and when Phil Knight threw Nike in behind it with the Oregon schools, we were in business. With that we scooped up Louisville, Memphis, Cincy, and the entire Metro Conference—*they called us!* My wife, Lois, came up with the name after she read a piece in the paper about it, calling it the "NAACP" league because it was Thompson and Chaney's idea. "The N double-A B P," she said. "The *B* is for 'basketball.'" "What's the rest for?" I asked. "You figure it out," Lois said. So I did. And the National Alliance for All Basketball Players was born.

ESPN was new then, and they put us on TV almost every night. During our first regular season, we had 250 games on national TV; the NBA had forty-five. Before long, we just had so much more money than they did, they didn't know what hit 'em.

Since we didn't have a draft—free agency was an article of faith for us from the start—anyone who wasn't already signed to an NAABP school was free to sign with any team in our league. Recruiting became wide open and *honest.* Nobody had to hide anything from anyone—we didn't have to get a friend or a booster to hit off a kid's uncle or high school coach anymore. If you wanted a kid, you made him an offer. If you needed more money to get him, you called a friend or sold another sponsorship and tried to meet his price. We liked it, the kids liked it—it worked. Sure, some of the schools in the old Big Ten, now the Big—what are they down to? Five?—held out, Bobby Knight just couldn't bear it; but that's fine. To each his own: Indiana still plays our guys from Butler in exhibitions; sometimes the Hoosiers even get within single digits.

We caught a lot of grief at first from writers who said that our players were thugs and dropouts, dumb kids who couldn't pass the SAT and even get into college. But no, they were just young men who thought they should be paid money if the school they worked for received money to showcase their talent. And many of the kids did go to classes, if they wanted to, and we've got a bunch of college graduates in the room tonight who never would have earned—I said *earned*, not *been given*—a degree if not for the NAABP. [*applause*]

But the point is, you don't have to be a choirboy to have rights, and we weren't pretending they *were* choirboys. But no longer could anyone else pretend that they didn't have *rights*.

It was the future governor himself, John Calipari, who first realized we could poach players from the NBA. During the 1989–90 season, he read an article about how Patrick Ewing was being booed in New York by Knicks fans. Cal thought this was a terrible thing, which it was, and it was probably making Patrick depressed. So he called Big John and told him to call Patrick and tell him to come back to Georgetown. Our first commissioner, Sonny Vaccaro, called Phil Knight and asked him to cover the contract, which Phil agreed to without hesitation, as long as we didn't publicize where the money was coming from. Patrick left New York that afternoon. David Stern sued us the next day, but since there was no non-compete clause in Patrick's NBA contract, and the United States has antitrust laws, the judge said that Patrick was free to pursue his profession at Georgetown. And that he did, leading Georgetown to the NAABP title in his first year, his first of five. You were huge for us, Patrick—he's sitting right there, next to Big John and Governor Cal—a natural-born champion. Thank you for believing in us. [*applause*]

Worldwide Wes, where are you? [*applause*] Over there. [*more applause*]

The NCAA and the NBA treated you like a criminal, but you were a natural as CEO of the NAABP. After Michael quit in 1998 and the NBA was about to go under, you brought David Falk, David Stern, and Phil Knight to the table—tell me who else would have come up with the solution that William Wesley did? David Stern steps down as NBA commissioner to become chief counsel at Nike, Michael comes out of retirement to become the first player/commissioner of the NBA, and we throw them a lifeline with Super Series I, our champion versus their champion for the All Ball title. It took the NBA a few years to catch up and win one, but we were willing to share revenues and level the playing field to keep as many good basketball players employed as possible. Young people being paid what the market will bear to play basketball— that's what we've always been about. [*applause*]

In our first year, the NBA tried to save so-called college basketball by creating the "One and Done" rule, requiring people to be nineteen years old before they were allowed to be paid to do their jobs [*laughter*]—don't laugh, there was a time not that long ago when this was allowed in America, I'm not talking about North Korea here, no disrespect, Ambassador Rodman. Kobe Bryant's here tonight, KG, great players and students of the game...Can you guys imagine that they would have had you go to St. Joe's and Maryland for free? Greg Oden, sitting over there? Remember those great seasons at Syracuse before the injuries, the MVP season in '07? Would you have given that all away for nothing? I just want to lay that out there for the young kids here who don't know how it used to be.

Once they instituted One and Done, all the best high school players flooded the NAABP. In '89 it was Shaq and Kenny Anderson—man, remember when they both came to New York together, and later Chris Mullin and Walter Berry jumped from the NBA to go back to St. John's, and they won it all? What a team that was, huh, Louie? In 1990 it was Grant Hill and Ed O'Bannon; '91 brought us the "Fab Five"—I was so glad when you all decided to come to Vegas together, and when Phil Knight agreed to increase our payroll to bring you all in. Chris Webber, when you offered to come off the bench behind our star player, Larry Johnson, and Jalen Rose, when you told me you'd be OK being on the second unit with C Web if we'd pay you more—and you were *right* to ask for it—I knew we had guys committed to winning. Finally, the way you all embraced Swee' Pea, Lloyd Daniels, when he came out of rehab to join our team. Both times he came out, you embraced him. The second time the program took. Swee' Pea got in shape, and started playing great ball on the second unit with Jalen and Chris. The night we upset St. John's in the Final game, right there in our old gym in Las Vegas, to win our first title, you guys didn't laugh at me when I cried. And I cried because I was living my dream, and my mother's dream. She had escaped genocide and come to the Land of Second Chances for her last shot. She had supported my dream and taught me to believe in the dreams of others. And it was those other dreamers—Shaq and Kenny and Mully and Walter and Jalen and Chris and Swee' Pea—who made me a champion for the first time. I didn't think it would be the only time. But you never know what's around the next corner in life, who's waiting for you, and whether they're waiting with an outstretched hand…or a clenched fist.

My troubles started the next year, 1992, and I didn't see them coming. Maybe you know the story already; I suppose you do. We were approached in Vegas about a combination twenty-five-thousand-seat arena and casino complex. The guy who pitched us was something of a reclamation project himself, a casino operator and developer coming off three bankruptcies, but he was confident and charming, and I couldn't resist a guy looking for a second chance. He offered the team a cut of the money from what he called luxury suites, which was a pretty new idea at the time, plus profits from the casino, so the players would make extra money if the casino made money. I would, too.

I said yes.

That next season, we started getting visits from all these so-called VIPs from Atlantic City who wanted to own the luxury suites and wanted to shake my hand. I didn't know these guys and I didn't care to know them. Maybe I should have paid more attention. We sold luxury suites to all of these guys.

Next thing I know, I'm invited to attend a trial in New Jersey with a bunch of these guys for racketeering and money laundering—as a co-defendant. Turns out the luxury boxes were a scam to launder money, and they said I was the linchpin. They sent me away for twenty years.

Big John and Chaney made it down to Montgomery to visit a few times, but Alabama was far and you guys had busy jobs—I understood why you stopped coming. Louie wrote letters to me every week—I love you for that, Louie, and for the cannolis you brought when you visited, even though the guards wouldn't let you bring them in. Mostly it was quiet, and I kept mostly to myself. I was happy when I saw Ohio State was given a franchise and a sixteen-year-old named LeBron James joined them. I'd watch all of his games on ESPN in prison, and even though you never won a title, LeBron, you grew into a great leader, and when you became player/commissioner at age twenty-three, I cheered for you. Commissioner James, stand up and take a bow for me. [*applause*] I know you've played thirteen years and you're getting frustrated, but you're still not even thirty, so keep trying, you deserve that title.

I admit I stopped watching games after a few years. I even missed the Ohio State–Knicks Super Series when Jeremy Lin led the Knicks to that miracle win. It just hurt too much to be out of it, feeling forgotten.

Then one day I was asked to come into the warden's office. I had a visitor. It was Senator Johnson. "Hello, Senator," I said. "Call me Earvin," he said. "I'm here because I want you to know that we've been thinking about you, all of us players from both leagues. We know it's wrong that you're in here. So me, Coach Thompson, Coach Chaney, and a bunch of guys went to meet President Obama a couple of weeks ago. You know, he's a big Bulls fan—so he was an NBA guy—but he remembers when you had Shaq and them and won it all. And he told us he'd ask Attorney General Eric Holder to look into your case. If it looks good, they're going to give you a pardon." He smiled at me. "I think it looks good," he said, laughing. I just cried.

A week later, Senator Johnson, my beautiful wife, Lois, Big John, and Chaney all showed up in a limousine to take me home. Now, two years later, I stand before you to accept the greatest honor in our great game. And I stand today as I have always stood, humbly but unafraid. Happy that I'm not forgotten. And proud of every kid who ever had it in him to live out his destiny in America, to be as big as it was in him to be . . . even if he needed a second chance to do it.

Thank you. [*standing ovation*]

11

What If Football Were Reinvented Today?

Nate Jackson

"I believe in rough games and in rough, manly sports. I do not feel any particular sympathy for the person who gets battered about a good deal so long as it is not fatal."

That was President Teddy Roosevelt in 1903—the year that nineteen American boys died from their football injuries. Although popular, the game of football had become too brutal for many—a "death harvest," the *Chicago Tribune* called it. But Teddy Roosevelt was trying to save it, championing a philosophy he called the Strenuous Life—a declaration of manliness intended to thicken American skin.

The football carnage was owed to several factors. Medicine was unevolved, so many injuries—especially those involving internal bleeding—became infected. And since antibiotics had yet to be discovered, a child could die from a deep bone bruise or a punctured lung. But the limits of medicine were exacerbated by the rules of the game itself, and the style of play that they encouraged. It took only five yards to gain a first down and the forward pass was illegal, so offenses created predictable mass formations that chewed up just a few yards at a time. Not much misdirection and no downfield action. Every play was shot from a cannon. Football looked like a kamikaze scrum.

Roosevelt understood that tough speeches would not be enough.

The game needed reform. So he convened a football summit at the White House, attended by leaders from football powerhouses Harvard, Princeton, and Yale. As a colonel in 1898, Roosevelt had led the Rough Riders in the Spanish-American War. As commissioner of the New York Police Department he had a legion of officers under his command. And now, as president, Roosevelt had designs on a nation of scrappers—men who could pull the trigger and take a punch. And he thought football was just the game to do it.

The summit produced several rules changes, allowing the forward pass, abolishing mass formations, creating a neutral zone between offense and defense, and doubling the first-down distance to ten yards. Many coaches were flummoxed by the new rules and decried what they saw as the softening of American toughness. Cartoons depicted football players in tutus. *This* isn't football, they said. But the new rules spread out the action and made the movement of the ball less predictable. The athletes adapted, as they always do. Fatalities decreased and the game survived.

Walk softly and carry a pigskin.

Through two world wars and a great depression, the United States has been defended by hardened men who, by participation or proximity, prepared for battle on the gridiron—all of us products of the strenuous life. Perhaps we owe our very freedom to the game of football and the bloody lessons it taught us. Without it, we are France.

So let's fix what's broke, which isn't much. We already have a pretty great game on our hands—complex, strategic, explosive, carnal. It scratches a lot of itches for us. But we can't ignore what we now know about the human brain and what the modern game of football does to it. Sunday's symphony of smashing helmets causes a degenerative brain disease called chronic traumatic encephalopathy, or CTE—along with the ubiquitous broken bones, torn ligaments, snapped tendons, and degenerated joints. Football, in many cases, equals pain and suffering. It always has.

Many fans would like to avoid this little distraction and focus instead on something less sad, like touchdowns and Super Bowls. But as a former NFL player, I must live with the consequences of repetitive violence and trauma—we all must. This chapter is not for the fans. It is for the players whose minds and bodies have been broken playing this game. And for the children who will meet the same fate; more than a million kids play high school football in America—not to mention youth football participation. If the result of this reimagining is a more exciting game for the spectator, good. But if the long-term health of the athlete is ignored in favor of the consequence-free entertainment sensibilities of those on the sport's periphery, then I will have failed here.

That said, the structure of the game is fine just the way it is. I see no reason to change it. Football is exciting. That is one thing we all agree on. And the violence is part of that excitement. We are not trying to remove the violence from the game. We are, like Roosevelt's summit, trying only to make the violence less predictable. And I believe that a few minor tweaks will go a long way. So for the sake of the experiment, here's what stays:

- same size field
- same scoring system
- same movement system—four downs to get ten yards
- same time-keeping rules
- same tackling rules
- same blocking and hitting rules

No cause for alarm, purists: All football rules remain. Let's look instead at playing *style* and *strategy*, and how they make the game particularly dangerous, especially for the brain. The point of football is to attack the enemy and take over his territory—just like war. War is America's most lucrative spectator sport. Football was created in its image, which explains the overlap in terminology—blitz, shotgun, flanker, trenches, gunner, ground attack, defense, offense, and so on—and the military presence at our football games. Fighter jets buzz the stadium as we hold our hands over our hearts and sing the national anthem, honoring the sacrifices of those who came before us, and whose deaths afforded us the opportunity to die for something, too.

That's the way we look at it on the field, sadly. We prepare for battle. We are under attack. We see ourselves as warriors. There is a very real undercurrent of *willingness to die*, which is unspoken but apparent in the style of play. What you see out there—bodies colliding at full speed—is a total disregard for self-preservation. It is human pack hunting. It is tactical assault combined with gang warfare.

And while it is anonymous soldiers who create good football *teams*, anonymity doesn't sell jerseys or ink endorsement deals, and it won't improve television ratings. For show business, we need *superstars*. Guys we can sell. Enter the Football Quarterback. In our modern football saga, the Football Quarterback is the main character—and, in this writer's opinion, his role has made things more dangerous for everyone else. We will attempt to flatten the influence of the quarterback. Not because we do not like him, but because protecting him gives us brain damage.

"Football Quarterback is the most difficult position in all of sports," says the former Football Quarterback. Our football storytellers are usually former quarterbacks, which shapes much of the conventional wisdom around the game of football, but a simple eye test will tell you that Joe Namath, Joe Montana, and Tom Brady—while charming—are some of the least dynamic athletes on an NFL football field. They are slower, weaker, and softer, generally speaking, than the rest of the players. They also have the longest careers. It makes little sense that the hardest position in sports can also play the longest. He can play until he's forty, if things go right for him. Why? Because no other player has a bubble of protection created for him—which is called the pocket. The pocket is the epicenter of football carnage. Too many big men too close together.

Most NFL offensive linemen weigh more than three hundred pounds. And the defensive players they are matched up against are just as big. Why encourage the creation of these outsized bodies in sport, knowing that they face grave health risks in life? And why root them into the ground in the middle of the field and force the man with the ball to stand behind them—held hostage by their immobility?

In fairness, the practice of overprotecting the quarterback was born of necessity. The pocket was created when no one *could* throw; when the forward pass was not legal. When ball skills were suspect. When you wanted as few men to touch the ball as possible—because they could not be trusted to hold on to it. Now we have Odell Beckham Jr., snatching uncatchable footballs with his pinkie. And he can throw! Just as well as any NFL quarterback. That's a fact that the Football Quarterback crowd has to accept. A good arm is no longer a novelty. The modern athlete *can throw*.

I say set him free. Allow him to evolve. Let them all use their rocket arms. Consider the American basketball player's evolution: For decades the point guard was the only man who handled the ball in the backcourt, dribbling and passing with rigid technique. Now there are mold-breaking guards and forwards and even centers who handle the ball and create unique scoring opportunities and mismatches that make the game more explosive and artistic—and more entertaining to watch. The blurring of positional lines allows the athlete to do whatever he does best.

This freedom is not afforded to football players. Certain players with certain numbers are ineligible receivers. A guard cannot, all at once, line up as the quarterback, take a snap from the running back, and throw a pop pass to the center, who has just become the tight end.

Nay. The tight end is the tight end. His jersey number denotes it. Any evolution happens within the genus of each position. The tight end, for example, classically featured a somewhat mobile bruiser who was relied on mostly for blocking. Now the most celebrated tight ends are skilled pass catchers who can stretch formations and take advantage of defensive weakness down the field.

In many ways, the modern quarterback is stuck in his mold. His is the most rigid—and the most marketable—so his evolution meets the most resistance. And it's not only what he does on the field, it's everything—what they call optics. Showbiz. The search for the next American Hero; and the producers have a certain look in mind. How does he carry himself? Does he have a beard? Does he date a stripper? Does he laugh when he's losing? What's he like on the field? Is he faster, stronger, and springier than his football-throwing predecessor? His athletic impulses may tell him to run; to move to the open spaces; to create—do the things that Joe Namath and Terry Bradshaw couldn't—but he is trained to stay in the pocket. So he stays put, inside the tornado of hammers—while three-hundred-pound bodies get chopped up around him.

Tradition is the enemy of progress.

In the effort to prevent the brain damage and diabetes that collects around the pocket—here is an idea:

> *All offensive players* are now eligible receivers who may run, throw, and/or catch the ball, within the existing rules of ball movement. Therefore, there is no such thing as an "ineligible man downfield."

AND

> *Offensive players* may line up *anywhere* along the line of scrimmage, from sideline to sideline, so long as *seven* of the *eleven* men are on the line of scrimmage.

Pockets would still exist, but not as predictably, and would likely result in different attack patterns, which, I believe, would result in fewer injuries, improving the quality of play and the longevity of the players. Injuries end careers and cause teams to fall apart. Football injuries put me in the hospital. Fewer injuries are good for business. Football injuries are the cause for multiple lawsuits against the NFL. This is a problem for the sport. Anyone watching a professional football game will observe, on nearly every other play, behemoth men writhing on the turf. Football players get hurt *constantly*. Why? Are they fragile? No. They will eat your grandma. It's that their required skill set has become so narrow that they are not adaptable athletes. They are trained for a specific set of predictable movements. Outside of those movements, they are vulnerable.

I know this vulnerability from experience. Growing up I participated in soccer, swimming, basketball, tree climbing, Red Rover, and so on, and never got hurt. Not until college, when I played football only, did I start having injuries. Specialization *causes* injury. Injuries are costly to teams and the individuals who comprise them. So how do you de-specialize the game? Dismantling the pocket is not enough.

We must make the game faster—not the action of the game, but the forty seconds between each play. This forty seconds allows specialized choreography to be set up. It also lets players catch their breaths, thus making their hits more powerful. Who knows, a shorter play clock may even make football more entertaining. All of the starting and stopping and long pauses between action are often confusing to new eyes. The average NFL game lasts over three hours. TV timeouts, huddles, commercials, measurements, reviews, challenges, yellow flags, red flags—*yawn!*

> **Proposed rule change:** 20-second play clock, 30 seconds after a first down, 1 minute after a score, 1 minute after a change of possession

With less time between plays, the huddle would become impractical, and the game would be more like a permanent two-minute offense. Specialization would decrease because there would be no time for a punt team to replace the offense on a fourth down. No matter. There are ten guys on every team who can punt nearly as well as the punter—all they have to do is practice punting. Those same offensive players might stay on the field and run down to cover the kick. More running equals less obesity. *Good-bye, stubborn belly fat!* Smaller men hitting each other from different, less direct angles: *Good-bye, CTE?*

But the blurring of positional lines would shake the establishment. Conventional wisdom would evaporate. Experts would become obsolete. The Football Quarterback would be sad. But the transition would be fun. So would the uncertainty. The athletic ability and raw power of American boys would be unchanged—therefore the game would still be attractive. Just put it on TV and watch the money roll in. It's the ball in flight that they fancy. They'll always come to watch us collide.

During my rookie training camp with the San Francisco 49ers, in 2002, in between practices we were all directed to a room to take our passport photos and fill out a new passport form. Three weeks later, at the end of a bloody training camp, we got our brand-new passports. The next day, we flew to Osaka, Japan, to play in a preseason game against the Washington Redskins. My passport was stamped "Entertainer" as I passed through customs. Although I more often felt like a "Warrior," in truth an NFL team is closer to a touring company of *Les Misérables*.

As of this writing, the league makes $14 billion a year. ESPN pays the NFL $1.9 billion per year for the privilege of broadcasting one NFL game per week for seventeen weeks a year, plus the playoffs. There are new hands reaching in every season, squeezing out more and more money from professional football. Fans aren't going anywhere. Neither are the networks. Nor are the advertisers. We're all hooked.

The professional game will live on. But what about the kids? Over a million teenagers play full-contact, head-smacking high school football in this country. And many more much younger boys play Pop Warner. All of them are watching football on Sunday. The NFL is making sure of it. Dads are coaching their Pop Warner kids to play just like Ezekiel Elliott, like Cam Newton, like J. J. Watt. And the kids know exactly what's expected of them.

Today the majority of high schools in America have a football team. It is as much a part of education as math and science. It's also fun—*really* fun! And it hurts, *really* bad! And still we keep playing it. There is something instructive in that. Football is so much about pain and the control the human mind has over it. This is something we need in America. This toughness that is born on the football field often protects our shores. We need warriors. We need soldiers. We need to know who is cut out for the martial arts and the strenuous life. But we need their brains intact.

Little kids don't need to be smashing skulls. For every five good football coaches, there is one who only wants blood, every day repeating violent hitting drills all practice long—trying to build his own little army. There is no way to weed out these coaches. So this reinvention will ban tackle football for boys under the age of fifteen. High schools can have varsity tackle football teams if they'd like; but a child must hit puberty, we'll decide, before we let him assault his contemporaries under our supervision. After that, strap up and go for it, boys. But, remember, *every* offensive player is an eligible receiver now. And the play clock is shorter; only twenty seconds. Eyes up. Look alive.

So how about it? Can we handle some new *optics*? I think we can. This is America. We won our name in war. We polish it with football.

12

What If There Had Always Been Sports PR Flacks?

L. Jon Wertheim

Public relations has always been a murky line of work, camped some-where in that gray area between journalism and advertising. Sticking with the color scheme, in the 1956 classic *The Man in the Gray Flannel Suit*, Gregory Peck's character conceded, "I don't know much about public relations." His colleague responded: "Who does? You got a clean shirt, you bathe every day, that's all there is to it."

In sports, the PR type used to play offense. That is, before sports became an entire industrial complex, its own sector of the economy, the publicists used to actually, well, publicize. Their job entailed drawing attention—and by extension fans—to teams and events and athletes.

We're talking about guys like Andy Furman of the Oral Roberts University athletic department, who came up with Satan Worship Night. When Oral Roberts played the DePaul Blue Demons in bas-ketball, self-proclaimed devil worshippers were allowed entrance at no charge. In New York, Irving Rudd was famous for purposely instruct-ing workers at the racetrack he repped to erect a gigantic sign read-ing YONKERS RACEWYA. Passersby had a good laugh over the error—an eighty-four-foot typo, as it were—but few forgot the name.

In 1952, Pete Rozelle started a job as a public relations specialist for the Los Angeles Rams. Within five years, he was the team's general manager. His sales and marketing skills were such that by 1960, he would begin a reign of almost thirty years as the NFL's commissioner and become one of the most powerful and enterprising figures in the history of sports.

At some point—correlating with sports' graduation from divertissement to big business—sports PR became something else entirely. And the practitioners began playing defense. The job was less about promotion and more about protection. It wasn't about attracting media so much as it was about evading those armed with cameras and notepads and recording devices. Facilitation turned to obfuscation. Members of media relations departments preferred that said relations were of the arm's-length variety.

Sports PR types began issuing wondrously bland press releases and limiting access and controlling damage. They started subjecting athletes to the blight that is media training, an exercise intended, commendably, to help athletes sidestep controversy but which has the effect of bleaching away personality.

There are, of course, entirely valid business justifications for all this. What corporate entity worth nine or ten figures, as sports franchises are, *doesn't* have a tranche of operatives making sure that key employees stay on message, that representatives don't sully the brand, that media does more fawning than ferreting? (More conspiratorially, all this PR has the effect of homogenizing athletes, which erodes their power in collective bargaining. That is, if the athletes become bigger brands than the teams themselves, the labor market changes considerably.)

Anyway, it's enough to make the sports media nostalgic for the days when access was less restrictive. It makes fans nostalgic for the days when sports figures were, collectively, more outspoken and charismatic, less concerned with running afoul of company policy or corporate messaging. It makes the mind race, imagining if today's defense-minded publicists had always been part of the sports firmament.

———

Lou, I'm loving the intro to your speech! Such powerful stuff! You are amazing, brah!! I've made a few suggestions in track changes and am happy to discuss. Text me whenever convn't!

Fans, for the past two weeks you have been reading <u>and hearing on the Yankees radio network</u> about the bad break I got. Yet today I consider myself a lucky man ~~myself the luckiest man on the face of this earth~~. I have been in ballparks for seventeen years and have never received anything but kindness and encouragement from you fans.

> **Pinstripe PR LLC**
> May be a touch arrogant
>
> **Pinstripe PR LLC**
> Deleted: er
>
> **Pinstripe PR LLC**
> Worry this might offend fans who believe the earth is flat
>
> **Pinstripe PR LLC**
> and Yankees team sponsors as well as our tv and radio partners.
>
> **Pinstripe PR LLC**
> Any use of this speech without prior consent is strictly prohibited

---

"At yesterday's press conference, Coach Vince Lombardi was quoted as saying that 'Winners never quit and quitters never win.' This line was taken out of context and misconstrued by some media members. Nevertheless, Coach Lombardi apologizes to any quitters he may have offended. This will be his only statement on the issue."

"We've been clear about expectations for our players on and off the field. Ty Cobb's continual involvement in incidents that run counter to those expectations undermines the hard work of his teammates and the reputation of the Detroit Tigers organization. His status with our team will be addressed when permitted by league rules. We will have no further comment at this time."

"My prediction for this upcoming Super Bowl? Whichever team has the most points on the scoreboard after the fourth quarter. Seriously guys, it's Jets policy not to issue forward-looking statements."—Joe Namath

---

"Four, four, four."—Moses Malone's postseason prediction, as relayed to the team reporter for 76ers.com

———————

"The Pittsburgh Pirates management is aware of the alleged situation involving Dock Ellis and the circumstances surrounding his recent no-hitter. We are in the process of gathering facts and determining the appropriate internal action."

———————

Reporter: What do you think is happening to the team?
Micheal Ray Richardson: We just need to keep playing hard and trusting in ourselves and our system. Now's not the time to point fingers.
Reporter: Insofar as this team is a ship, would you deem it seaworthy?
Richardson: I challenge the premise of your question.
Knicks public relations official: That's it. Interview's over.

———————

"I can only speak for myself. But, personally, I find the Viet Cong wholly unobjectionable."—Muhammad Ali

———————

"If you come to a fork in the road, make whichever decision you think will be more advantageous, given your personal situation at the time."—Yogi Berra

———————

@Yankees:
    Join @TheRealBabeRuth to strike out scotch!! He will be speaking to Woman's Christian Temperance Union tomorrow in Utica. #trydry #boozersarelosers

———————

Through his publicist, Alexandra Morse, Mr. Barnes declined comment. Morse, did, however, request that the public cease referring to Barnes by the nickname "Bad News." Said Morse:

"Marvin is not about negativity. We don't know how this started but, candidly, it is offensive and it must stop."

———————

LETTER TO MY YOUNGER SELF

by Bob Knight
Players Tribune Contributor

I have always felt that the most important word in basketball, if not life, was this. Respect. Respect for your team, for your boss, for your country, for the tiny island territories and protectorates of your country. Respect. I remember the glorious 1975–76 season. So many smiles, laughs, it's hard to believe I was paid to coach this wondrous game.

"Where My Hoosiers At?" That was the first question I asked the team as we boarded the bus on the way to the biggest game of our lives....

———————

"Am I the greatest? That's not for me to say. I consider myself a skilled practitioner. I just want to give 110 percent."—Muhammad Ali

13

What If...Title IX Never Was?

Mary Pilon

In another disappointing showing, the United States came in fourth in the medal count at the 2024 Summer Games.

The Games, held in Paris, struggled to garner attention from American fans and drew only a few hundred athletes. Because no network has yet to show interest in acquiring the broadcast rights, stateside fans hoping to catch a glimpse of basketball, cycling, or weightlifting clung to erratic online streams and inconsistent dispatches from a few errant reporters who were in France. Many Parisians, when asked how they felt about the storied international sports competition held in their backyard, merely shrugged.

In the medal table, Team USA was far behind stellar Olympic performances from China and Russia, and barely ahead of the Germans. The Americans had particularly lackluster performances in track and field and swimming. As always, their men's basketball team was the class of the world, but their women's team did not make it into the medal rounds. The same was true for all the women's team sports— volleyball, water polo, field hockey, and soccer; American women failed to advance, if they qualified a team at all. They even failed to field a full team for gymnastics. The dreary showing compounded the buzzkill of the 2020 Tokyo Games, along with the 2016 Rio Games, when, again, Americans failed to crack the overall medal count, finishing seventh and fifth, respectively.

"We just can't seem to get results," said Billie Jean King, eighty, a U.S. Olympic Committee board member and the sole woman in sports executive leadership. The frustration for King comes nearly fifty years after the tennis star defeated Bobby Riggs in the "Battle of the Sexes" exhibition match, an often-overlooked moment in sports history. "We did recruit a few dozen women to Team USA this go-around, which is an improvement from last time. But it's still so hard to conjure up any interest."

Among King's crusades that continue to fall flat: introducing a women's marathon to the Olympics, getting women to join local swim teams, and finding sponsors for athletes such as Simone Biles, a gifted gymnast who is back in Texas waiting tables due to a lack of sponsorship interest. "Tennis taught me a lot about patience," King said. "But this feels like watching sloths."

The hypothetical scene laid out above is not a far cry from that of the 1972 Munich Games, held the same year that Title IX was passed. In those games, the 84 American women won 23 medals compared with 71 medals for the 316 American men.

Title IX, the law stipulating that institutions that receive federal money must provide equal opportunities regardless of sex, is now forty-five years old, and it has completely transformed women's—and men's—athletics by providing countless opportunities for new generations of athletes. The fortunes of American women have reverberated elsewhere in the world, as some sporting events such as the Olympics are bankrolled by U.S. television dollars.

While Title IX is revered today by feminists and sports enthusiasts, the truth is that the change in law was something of an accident, and in fact almost didn't happen at all. In fact, the NCAA was taken by surprise when informed of the law's implications and then attempted to weaken its scope and impact.

The NCAA's astonishment can be at least partly understood in the context of the law's original intent. Sports was never meant to be its focus. The idea for a federal statute mandating gender equality in federally funded institutions started with Bernice "Bunny" Sandler, an academic who sought out a faculty position at the University of Maryland for which she was more than qualified. In spite of her doctorate in counseling and personnel services, Sandler was told she came on "too strong for a woman" and failed to advance. She began to draft legislation that would bar sex discrimination in institutions such as the University of Maryland that receive federal funds, her hope being that other female professors wouldn't share her fate. Nowhere in the regulations, or in Sandler's early pleas, is there anything about the track team, or the rowers, or the right for little girls to kick around a soccer ball. In fact, Sandler would later admit that she hadn't really considered the implications for sports at all.

What little fanfare accompanied President Richard Nixon's signing Title IX into law came in the form of rather dry and dutiful reporting deep inside newspapers.

Soon, Washington would be swallowed up by Nixonian news of a far grander scale, and this little-understood law that could have been mistaken for a chapter of the tax code was further relegated to the inside pages.

In 1972, women's sports were largely considered to be a novelty, if they were considered at all. In 1972, only 294,000 girls participated in high school sports, compared with 3.7 million boys, according to the National Coalition for Women and Girls in Education. Many of those who did were teased for doing so and were subject to worn-down equipment, coaches, and a patchwork of inconsistent officiating.

What physical activities did exist were recreational in nature rather than competitive. Think hoop dancing, jumping jacks, twirling in place, maybe some gentle tossing of a ball or baton. Even the rules for established sports such as basketball were rewritten for females, lest they be too physically taxed. In spite of women being able to perform strenuous physical activities such as, say, giving birth, the notion of the weaker sex was pervasive. If a sweat was broken, so, too, was the belief that women were delicate, floral, and deserving of a powerless position in society.

Wealthy women fared somewhat better, particularly those who had access to stables and equestrian courses, or who continued to benefit from the bicycle boom of the nineteenth century. But even for more progressive advocates of women's sports, exercising, particularly during menstruation, was considered taboo. Dr. Edward H. Clarke twisted already false science to create the notion that women were slower and dumber when they got their periods. He wrote in his 1873 tome *Sex in Education; or, A Fair Chance for the Girls,* "Both muscular and brain labor must be remitted enough to yield sufficient force for the work." "The work" being menstruation.

In spite of the attitudes at the turn of the century, and with little financial or political support, women started to form recreational sports leagues for more competitive endeavors such as tennis, croquet, and archery. They were largely barred from full membership to country or athletic clubs that offered access to necessary facilities, and joining was virtually impossible for women of color. Into the 1920s and 1930s, some intramural sports were offered in colleges, but mostly in the form of "play days" or inconsistent sorority competitions. Meanwhile, men's collegiate sports only began to bloat, with critics decrying as early as the late 1920s that the amateurism ideal in college sports had eroded. Attendance at the Rose Bowl surged to 72,000 in 1930, more than double the 35,000 fans who had watched the game a decade prior. The fear of exploitation also kept many women's coaches from organizing intercollegiate competitions between female athletes. When they did occur, publicity, funds for travel, and awards were limited under the guise of protecting women from the commercialism overtaking college sports.

Although World War II brought an unprecedented number of women not only into the workforce but into traditionally male-dominated occupations, the message from 1945 onward was that Rosie the Riveter had had her fun and now should make her way back to the kitchen. And she certainly didn't belong on a soccer field or basketball court (Rosie the Pivoter?). Some progress was made in 1957 when feminists successfully lobbied for the Division for Girls and Women's Sports to allow college programs to...exist. In the late sixties, schedules and leagues for female collegiate athletes formed, but the emphasis was still largely on participation, a contrast from the more competitive, win-at-all-costs messaging that their male counterparts received from the NCAA. The NCAA at the time felt that including women in its ranks would threaten its financial success with men's sports. For years the organization fought with great success to keep women, literally, on the sidelines.

A policy fix on a national scale was required. But what if Title IX hadn't been passed? Imagine if the status quo of the early 1970s hadn't been budged by legislative fiat. The effects would've been far-reaching. With fewer women exercising, for instance, the market for sporting goods and apparel today would look more like its barely existent incarnation then. Perhaps the fitness explosion of the 1980s doesn't have the same magnitude without the female athletics explosion of the 1970s. Maybe the Phil Knight of Title IX–less 2017 is the CEO of a midsized running shoe company, living in an Oregon cabin and grumbling that he never had the chance to take his company public. Maybe Nike is the shoe of choice for lanky male distance runners, but it never expands beyond its niche.

Cast your mind forward to 2024. The country, still in thrall to traditional attitudes that Title IX helped chip away at, has yet to produce a viable female presidential candidate, let alone a donor base for one. All this is to say nothing of the obesity statistics that show women are disproportionately more likely to be overweight than men. Consequently, they're living shorter, unhealthier lives, keeping infant mortality rates stubbornly high. They're still not cracking corporate boards at all, accessing startup capital, and are a rare sight in law and medical schools. Domestic violence rates rise and the teen pregnancy rate continues to climb up, as researchers scratch their heads.

By 2024, a handful of women try to fight back, building on the work of seventies icons such as Gloria Steinem. But keep in mind that women's suffrage came seventy-two years after the Seneca Falls Convention, and the public is largely unreceptive to the argument that sports for girls means something other than posing in a bikini on the cover of *Sports Illustrated*, which now has a weekly swimsuit centerfold.

A future devoid of Title IX would be almost the same as a future with it in one way—the vast majority of girls who start kicking around a soccer ball or tossing a basketball in a hoop won't make it to a World Cup final or the WNBA (which wouldn't exist). But if achieving the pinnacle was the purpose of athletic participation, sports would be a waste for almost all children. Even the slightest amount of sports participation among young men and women instills a sense of self-esteem that is applicable to other arenas. Though without Title IX, you can strike the "and women" part from that last sentence.

"I don't see what the big deal is," said Mo'ne Davis, a twenty-three-year-old who had been barred from participating in the Little League World Series as a child. "I think I could have handled playing baseball with the boys just fine."

The dispiriting thing about this thought exercise is that the dystopia isn't as remote as we might wish it to be. Even with Title IX, inequality remains. And a federal law cannot ban the retrograde attitudes of some male sports fans, as underscored by the recent #CovertheAthlete and #MoreThanMean movements. Both used videos and social media to confront audiences with the degrading questions and comments fielded by female athletes and female sports reporters alike, merely for doing their jobs. The U.S. women's national soccer team, whose 2015 World Cup victory was the most-watched soccer game (male or female) in U.S. history, recently sued its governing body, demanding equal pay for equal work. (FIFA's total payout for the Women's World Cup was $15 million, compared with $576 million for the men.) Not long ago, members of the U.S. women's national hockey team, ranked No. 1 in the world as of this writing and winners of six of the last eight world championships, revealed they were paid the grand sum of $1,000 a week for the six months leading up to the Olympics. Access to sports still remains a struggle, particularly for women of color and poor women.

These days it's popular to pay lip service to feminism. Let's call it fauxminism. Many fathers would nod their heads at affirmations of their daughters' worth and agree they should have equal opportunities.

Executives would agree that women deserve more attention for their athletic endeavors, but few actually back up the lofty sentiments with real money or actual policy.

Without the force of law lofty sentiments would stay sentiments, not necessarily out of sexism so much as inertia. A "What can you do?" attitude pervades human experience, and there is little that the good will of man, and woman, can do absent the interventions of institutions to compel behavior. Even among the most progressive and well-intentioned of sports leaders, absent Title IX the checks wouldn't have been written, the games not attended, the athletic complexes not built. There would be no question of bankrolling women's sports, because women's sports wouldn't exist in any meaningful way.

James Naismith is the father of basketball, William Morgan the father of volleyball, and Abner Doubleday has been called (erroneously) the father of baseball.

Women's baseball, volleyball, and basketball don't have different fathers. But they do all have one mother. Title IX.

With a little help from Richard Nixon.

14

What If Tom Brady Hadn't Stepped In/Taken Over for an Injured Drew Bledsoe?

Steve Kornacki

DREW BLEDSOE HURT AS 0–2 PATRIOTS LOSE TO JETS

Bledsoe wasn't able to come out for the final series, because at 4:48 of the fourth quarter he sustained a brutal sideline hit by Mo Lewis, which knocked Bledsoe unconscious for a few seconds.

—*Boston Globe*, September 21, 2001

PATRIOTS WIN THRILLING SUPER BOWL, RESTORE PRIDE TO NEW ENGLAND FANS

A last-place team one year ago . . . they jelled under the leadership of coach Bill Belichick and the quarterbacking of Brady. They won their final nine games, and last night's shocker ranks as the second-greatest upset in Super Bowl history.

—*Boston Globe*, February 4, 2002

The referee held up his hands a few inches apart, and the Ericsson Stadium faithful—what dozens of them remained—let out something meekly resembling a cheer. The visiting New England Patriots were just short of the marker, and now head coach Bill Belichick had a choice. It was fourth down and they were sitting at their own forty-five, with just inside of two minutes left, both in the game and in this dispiriting season. If nothing else, dignity was at stake here. The book said to punt—pin the Panthers, themselves losers of fourteen straight, and dare Chris Weinke, the error-prone twenty-nine-year-old rookie, to lead the kind of clutch drive that had eluded him all year. Instead, Belichick looked out at Drew Bledsoe and told his quarterback to stay on the field. Why not just put an end to it with one play here?

On the CBS telecast, the announcers perked up. They'd been sentenced to the runt of this Sunday's litter, a contest of also-rans airing in the Boston and Charlotte markets and nowhere else; at least now they'd bear witness to some genuine suspense. "Belichick wants to roll the dice!" play-by-play man Don Criqui exclaimed. "There's coaching to win and there's coaching not to lose," Steve Tasker chimed in. "This is coaching to win."

The crowd was positively audible as Bledsoe lined up under center Damien Woody. There were two backs behind him. The formation was tight. A QB sneak or a handoff? Or were they trying to draw the Panthers off? Woody snapped it to Bledsoe, who stepped back, started to turn, then felt the ball slip from his grasp. He saw it hit the ground and pounced: a recovery for a loss of a yard. Turnover on downs. You knew what was coming next. Weinke, who'd thrown twice as many picks as touchdowns all season, suddenly morphed into John Elway, firing off three straight completions, and when John Kasay's twenty-seven-yarder sailed through the uprights as time expired, the Panthers had their first win since Week 1—and the Patriots had yet another defeat grabbed from the jaws of victory.

The CBS camera showed the coaches converging at midfield and shaking hands. Staring at the ground, Belichick resisted George Seifert's attempt to offer a word of encouragement, yanking his arm away and shambling off toward the locker room. "A very frustrating end to the 2001 season for Bill Belichick," Criqui said. "And a sight that Patriots fans have grown accustomed to."

The loss meant a 6–10 record for the 2001 Patriots, who were spared only by the hapless Bills from finishing in the AFC East cellar for the second straight season. A year that had begun with optimism that the team had finally absorbed Belichick's system had ended almost exactly where the last one had. The Patriots, a rising NFL power in the late nineties, were now indisputably a franchise in decline. And their coach, brought in with considerable fanfare before the 2000 season, now looked to be the latest example of the genius coordinator who just couldn't cut it as the head man. Belichick's Patriots record now sat at 11–21. His career mark, adding in his five seasons as the Browns coach, was just 48–67. He had now completed seven full seasons as an NFL head coach, and in six of them his teams had posted losing records.

Not that his job was in jeopardy—yet. The Patriots and their owner, Bob Kraft, had invested too much in Belichick to give up so soon, surrendering a first-round draft pick to free him from a contract with the Jets. The owner's pride was at stake, too. When Kraft bought the team in 1994, saving the franchise from a move to St. Louis, he inherited Bill Parcells as his coach. There was success on the field but turf wars, power struggles, and bruised egos off of it. After leading the team to the Super Bowl in January 1997, Parcells abruptly resigned, complaining that Kraft had overruled him on key personnel decisions. "If they want you to cook the dinner, at least they ought to let you shop for some of the groceries," he explained. He moved to the Jets, taking Belichick with him as his defensive coordinator. Together, they revived one of the league's worst franchises, leading Gang Green to the cusp of a Super Bowl appearance and transforming the New England–New York rivalry into a blood feud. Belichick was given credit for the stout defense, but it was his mentor who got the glory.

Kraft, meanwhile, turned to the anti-Parcells, Pete Carroll, who oversaw a steady descent into mediocrity. When the 1999 season ended in futility, Kraft set his sights on Belichick, who leaped at the chance to escape his boss's Hall of Fame shadow. The owner and coach shared the same motivation. They both wanted to prove they could win without the Tuna. The results were far from encouraging so far, but Kraft wasn't ready to admit he'd whiffed on another coach—especially not when he knew how much it would delight Parcells.

Besides, for all the losing, the Patriots really didn't seem that far off. They were competitive in virtually every game and almost never got blown out—just five of the twenty-two losses under Belichick had come by double digits. There were weapons on both sides of the ball— Lawyer Milloy and Ty Law in the secondary; Willie McGinest at line-backer; Antowain Smith in the backfield; Troy Brown, David Patten, and Terry Glenn catching passes. And, of course, there was No. 11 himself, the best quarterback in team history. What was holding this team back, it seemed, was subtler. They blew leads, they missed open-ings, they made the wrong mistakes at the wrong moments.

Was it possible it was because of Bledsoe? You'd hear it every now and then from callers on Boston sports talk shows, and the columnists and TV talking heads would sometimes bring it up, usually delicately, aware that what they were suggesting didn't seem to make sense. After all, Bledsoe wasn't just a premier NFL quarterback; he was the franchise savior.

When they chose him with the top pick in the 1993 draft, the Patriots could barely be described as a professional sports enterprise. They were coming off a 2-14 season and had lost fifty of their previ-ous sixty-four games. The aluminum bleachers in their home venue, a glorified high school stadium, would at best be half filled. Game after game would be blacked out on local television. In the early nineties, you were more likely to see kids in the Boston area walking around with Cowboys gear on than anything with the hometown team's logo on it. That was life before Drew. In his second year, Bledsoe threw for 4,500 yards and brought the Patriots to the playoffs. By his fourth, they were in the Super Bowl. Even after the Parcells divorce, he still made the Pro Bowl. His stats were more pedestrian in 2001—3,300 yards, 19 touchdowns, and 15 picks—but the Pats had won big with him before. Surely they could again. Right?

One of the doubters, secretly, was the head coach. To Belichick, Bledsoe was a naturally gifted quarterback who was simply too inconsis-tent. A game against the Jets early in the '01 season neatly encapsulated his frustrations. Trailing 10–3 with five minutes left, Bledsoe scrambled on third and long and, confronting New York's Mo Lewis just before the sticks, delivered a stiff-arm that forced the linebacker out of his way and brought the home crowd to its feet. Armed with a fresh set of downs and a sudden burst of momentum, Bledsoe immediately threw an interception, and the rally was over. As the losses mounted, Belichick had begun pondering what a Patriot offense without Bledsoe might look like.

Here his mind wandered back to his Browns days, and what had so far proven to be one of the defining decisions of his career. After struggling for a few seasons, Belichick concluded that the incumbent quarterback, Bernie Kosar, was past his prime, so he benched and then cut him. But Kosar was a local hero, a Youngstown kid who'd won a national title in college then come home to play pro ball. With his move, Belichick certified himself as a reviled figure in Cleveland, haunting him for the rest of his tenure. The lesson: If you're going to get rid of a beloved quarterback, you'd better be sure you have a better option in place—and that you win right away.

As he considered Bledsoe now, Belichick quickly realized there was nothing he could do. For one thing, Bledsoe was locked in. Just before the '01 season, he'd signed a ten-year, $103 million contract. The quarterback was also one of Kraft's favorites, someone the owner regarded like a son. And after two dismal seasons, Belichick's political capital had all but evaporated. If there was a problem with Bledsoe, the consensus held, it was an indictment of the coach and not the quarterback.

It might be different, Belichick realized, if there were some highly regarded prospect on the roster behind Bledsoe. Maybe then fans would be curious to see what this young gun could do. But the Patriots' backup was an obscure sixth-round pick named Tom Brady, who'd thrown all of seventeen passes in his two seasons with the team. Belichick was intrigued with Brady and managed to insert him for most of the fourth quarter in a late-season blowout win over the Browns. Playing in garbage time, Brady was unremarkable that day. It was trades and free agents and draft picks that the Bledsoe critics talked about—not Tom Brady.

As he looked toward his third season, Belichick could see that he was boxed in. It was going to be a make-or-break year for him and he would have no choice but to stake his coaching career on the arm of Drew Bledsoe.

They came out of the gate fast in 2002. In the opener against Jacksonville, another franchise desperately trying to combat decline, Bledsoe completed thirty-four of forty-seven passes for 357 yards, three touchdowns, and no interceptions. The Pats won easily. They handled Miami the next week, then disposed of the Lions. A 3-0 start. First place in the division. A rejuvenated quarterback sporting a 114.8 passer rating. "It took them long enough," *Boston Globe* columnist Dan Shaughnessy wrote, "but Bledsoe and Belichick look like they've finally figured each other out."

No one panicked when they fell short in Oakland in Week 4, but then came the Sunday night meeting with the Jets. Both teams were 3-1, and the early edge in the AFC East was on the line. The Pats' brand-new stadium, filled beyond capacity for the biggest game in several years, shook with excitement as the home team jumped out in front 14–0. But the Jets chipped away, and the New England offensive machine ground to a halt. When Curtis Martin scampered into the end zone with six minutes left, the visitors grabbed a 21–17 lead. Now it was up to Bledsoe to rescue his team. He regained his sharpness, leading them from their own twenty into the red zone in just eight plays. Then the other Drew reared his head, badly underthrowing Troy Brown. Interception. He got another chance when the Pats' defense forced a three-and-out, taking over at midfield with forty-two seconds left. Two plays later, he threw it away again, and that was that.

Five more losses followed in succession, then finally a win, then two more defeats. They were 4-9 now. The playoffs were out of the question; yet another losing season now assured. It was as if something about the Jet loss unmoored the entire team, and especially its quarterback. After Bledsoe put up MVP numbers to start the season, his interceptions were now outpacing his touchdown passes. There were other problems, too. Belichick was openly warring with Glenn, the star wide receiver. Belichick had wanted to release him the year before, but

Kraft, reasserting himself in personnel choices as the losses piled up, told his coach to make it work with Glenn.

Worse, the fans were now in full-fledged revolt. Officially, every game at Gillette Stadium was sold out, but as December arrived there were seas of empty seats. In the home finale against the Bills, a group of fans unfurled a giant homemade banner that read: WE MISS THE TUNA. Kraft was refusing to answer questions about his coach's future, which by itself amounted to an answer. The swan song came in Miami, where early in the second quarter Bledsoe was knocked out with a concussion. Tom Brady, the little-used backup, trotted onto the field. In theory, it was an opportunity for him. After Brady held a clipboard for three years, his contract was coming up. The Pats were likely done with him, especially with Belichick on his way out, but a competent performance here would perhaps convince another team to take notice and bring him in as a backup. In reality, the Dolphins were fighting to make the playoffs, and the Patriots had already quit. Brady never had a chance. He threw for fifty-eight yards and two interceptions as Miami rolled to a 34–7 win.

Belichick was fired the next day, one of three head coaches to get the boot on Black Monday. He was 53-78 for his career, and the consensus was universal. "There can be no shame, none whatsoever, in being a defensive genius," the *Globe*'s Bob Ryan wrote. "That is what Bill Belichick is. He was a defensive genius when he helped Bill Parcells win two Super Bowls with the Giants. He was a defensive genius when he reunited with Parcells here and brought the Patriots to the Super Bowl in 1997. And he was a defensive genius when he followed Parcells back to New York and, miracle of all miracles, made the Jets not just relevant, but something approaching dominant. He is, was and always will be a defensive genius. What Bill Belichick most decidedly is not, however, is a head coach."

It had now been six full seasons since their run to the Super Bowl, six seasons since Parcells left town. In that time, the Patriots had gone 44-55 with just one playoff victory. It had now been four seasons, and counting, since they'd even made the postseason. They were becoming an afterthought in their own town. The dwindling fan base was fragmented. A faction had remained loyal to Parcells after his exit and now they were louder than ever, and winning converts. Once upon a time, Kraft had been a celebrated figure throughout New England, the diehard fan with deep pockets who'd stepped up to stop the team from fleeing to St. Louis. Now he was a talk show punching bag, the meddlesome owner whose ego had driven away the best coach in NFL history and ruined what should have been a golden age of Patriots football.

Meanwhile, the legend of the Tuna was only growing. Other coaches had won more Super Bowls, but Parcells's feat somehow seemed more impressive. He had resuscitated not one, not two, but three moribund franchises, pushing each to the top of the league, or at least close to it. The Jets were 1-15 the year before he took over. In his first year, he lifted them to 9-7. In his second, they went 12-4 and made it to the AFC title game. All of this while the Super Bowl–caliber team he had left to come to New York sputtered in his absence. He'd stepped away from the sidelines and was now an ESPN analyst, but word was starting to get around: At sixty-one years old, Parcells believed he had one more run left in him.

The Boston media wondered if Kraft might turn to Tom Coughlin, a Parcells disciple just fired by Jacksonville, or maybe Steve Mariucci, a quarterback specialist who'd just been let go by the Niners. Kraft talked to them and to a series of hot-shot coordinators, but he hesitated to pull the trigger. He'd blown two coaching hires, and his franchise—and his reputation—had paid dearly for it. This one had to work. And there was only one thing that he knew would work. He picked up the phone and made the call he had sworn for six years he'd never make.

"Bill," he said when the familiar voice answered, "I was wrong."

They smiled and said the right words at the press conference. "I feel really good about this," Parcells said. "I want to emphasize that I have a lot of respect for Bob after the conversations we've had." He would be the coach and the general manager. "Will they let you shop for the groceries this time?" one of the reporters asked him. Kraft jumped in. "As far as I'm concerned, he can have the company card." Bledsoe was on hand, too. He'd been happy when Parcells left for New York, believing the coach was too overbearing and stifling, and he'd said so in public.

Now, he expressed his own regrets. "What I've come to appreciate is that he's a winner and has a gift for making everyone around him winners, too"

From Providence to Bangor, Patriot Nation erupted in euphoria. Season ticket requests poured in; overnight, the wait list ballooned to five years. Gleeful callers shared their joy on the radio shows. The *Herald* ran a special eight-page section under the title HE'S BACK! The mayor of Boston, Tom Menino, declared a "Bill Parcells Appreciation Day." The D'Angelo chain announced a special deal in honor of the returning hero—half off all tuna sandwiches. "It must be said," Bob Ryan wrote, "that Bob Kraft deserves credit for swallowing his pride."

Empowered like he wasn't before, Parcells set about stuffing the roster with his type of player—gritty, intense, loyal. Richie Anderson and Dedric Ward, Parcells guys both, came aboard early. So did Vinny Testaverde, replacing Brady as Bledsoe's backup. More would follow. (Brady would spend the next several years casting about for an opportunity in the NFL and Canada before returning to his native northern California and becoming a high school coach.) Terry Glenn, publicly mocked by Parcells as "she" during his first run with the Pats, showed up to training camp in the best shape he'd been in for years. "That old Parcells attitude seems to be back," the *Globe* reported.

Under Belichick in 2002, they'd won five games. In 2003, the Patriots passed that total by Halloween. They clinched the division on the last day of the season, gutting out a 13–10 decision over the Jets. They were 10-6, their best mark since 1997, and were rewarded with a home playoff date with the wild card Denver Broncos. Just before kickoff, the NFL announced that Parcells had been voted its coach of the year. His team then proceeded to validate the decision, dismantling Denver 28–6. All sixty-five thousand fans stayed to the very end, savoring their return to the league's upper echelon. A "We love Bill!" chant started near the home end zone with a few minutes left. By the time the final seconds ticked off, the whole stadium had joined in.

They lost the following week in Kansas City, in a sequence Pats fans would scream about for years to come. Down 23–20 and facing a fourth-and-two from the Chiefs forty-three with just over three minutes to play, Parcells elected to punt. "If you can't trust your defense, you can't trust anyone," he'd later say. When Toby Gowin's boot pinned Kansas City inside the one, the Tuna's call looked plenty wise. But on first down, Trent Green connected with Johnnie Morton, who read the New England coverage perfectly and took it all the way to the house to seal the game. Maybe too perfectly, it turned out: Months later, it was revealed that a low-level Chiefs employee had been clandestinely videotaping the Pats' hand signals. It had been, the Chiefs claimed to a league-appointed investigator, the brainchild of defensive coordinator Romeo Crennel—who, in turn, said he'd gotten the idea from his time on Belichick's Patriots staff. Irate Patriot fans demanded that the game be vacated retroactively, to no avail. "There's a word for what the Chiefs did," Kraft said. "Cheating."

But for all the weird drama of the game that bounced the Patriots from the playoffs, the season was nothing short of an unqualified success. Bledsoe even returned to the Pro Bowl for the first time since '97, throwing for 3,812 yards and twenty-nine touchdowns on the season.

The Tuna had done it again. Four coaching stints and four stunning turnarounds. "I don't want to say he's better than Lombardi," *SI*'s Peter King wrote, "but he just might be." The Patriots were back. They won the division again the following year, made two more wild card appearances, then after a down season in 2007 came storming back in 2008. With an 11-5 record, they again won the division and this time advanced to the conference championship game, oh so close to another Super Bowl. It was right there for them, too. Trailing 21–20 in the final minute, Bledsoe brought the Pats inside the Steeler ten, and Parcells called for a field goal. It would be a chip shot, but there was a twist. His backup had suffered a freak wrist injury in the locker room at halftime, so Bledsoe would have to serve as the holder. When he went to field the snap, the ball slid straight through his hands. As Heinz Field erupted in joy, CBS announcer Jim Nantz turned to his lead analyst and asked what might go through a coach's mind in a moment like this. "Beats me," replied Bill Belichick, who'd blossomed into a self-deprecating broadcasting star. "The good thing about having the kind of record I had is that I never had to deal with a situation like this."

But Parcells did have to deal with it, and he just couldn't shake the loss. A week later, he announced his retirement. His second run with the Patriots hadn't produced a Super Bowl, but it had revived an entire region's football spirit. With a 61-45 record and five playoff appearances, it marked the most successful six-year run any Patriot coach had ever enjoyed. Kraft announced that the field at Gillette Stadium would be named in Parcells's honor and gave him the title of head coach emeritus. "We maybe didn't appreciate him like we should have the first time he was here," the owner said. "But then we learned through painful experience just how lucky we'd been to have him. We've never had it better than we did these past six years—and I'm not sure we ever will."

15

What If the 1999 U.S. Women's National Soccer Team Had Lost the Women's World Cup?

Louisa Thomas

Brandi Chastain caught the ball tossed by the referee and placed it on its mark. She did not look at the goalkeeper, nor around her at the shrieking crowd. The moment was tense, the stakes high. If she made the penalty kick, the U.S. women would defeat China to win the 1999 Women's World Cup. There were more than ninety thousand people— including the president of the United States—in the stadium watching, waiting, wishing, and they were loud. Millions more Americans were watching at home, the largest American audience ever to watch a soccer game—men's or women's.

More than the result of a tournament seemed to turn on this shot. It was treated as a test of whether a woman's team sport could capture the imagination of the American public—and then keep it. Chastain knew it. "We're at the epicenter of a big rock being thrown into a huge pond," Michelle Akers had said as the team prepared for the final. "We just don't know what the ripple effect will be." Win, and the ripples would spread; lose, and they seemed likely to recede and leave little in their wake.

Chastain waited for the whistle that would signal her shot. The odds were in her favor; penalties are successful around 70 percent of the time. But there were crosscurrents against her. Earlier that year, in March, Chastain had hit the crossbar on a penalty kick against China's goalkeeper Gao Hong at the Algarve Cup. China had won that game—and the title. Before selecting the players to take the extra shots at the Women's World Cup, the American coaches hesitated over whether to choose Chastain for the critical fifth slot. They worried that her PKs had become too predictable for goaltenders. Perhaps the Algarve Cup—or the own goal that Chastain had knocked into the American net during the quarterfinals—was also on their minds. Just before the penalty kicks began, the U.S. head coach, Tony DiCicco, came over to Chastain and told her that she would take a shot, but she had to take the kick with her left foot. She agreed that she would. There was only one catch: She had never taken a penalty kick left-footed in a game before.

The whistle came, and Chastain started her run. She struck the ball sharply, and it flew sharply off her laces.

July 10, 1999: China wins the Women's World Cup 5–4 in a penalty shootout. The Americans' loss gets a headline on all the front pages, along with a picture of Chastain, crumpled on her knees, hiding the tears on her face with the hem of her shirt. She is the goat—but only for a moment. Quickly, she is forgiven, and then, as quickly, she is forgotten. So, for the most part, is the team. The U.S. women's national team's strong run is applauded, and the unbelievable turnout and support is noted as a harbinger for the growth of women's sports, but attention returns to where it had been: the NFL, MLB, NBA, college football and basketball, the stray NHL playoff series.

In the ensuing years, success at the World Cup level continues to elude the national team. At the Olympics, the Americans bring home gold medals, but the team does not monopolize the American public's attention. There are rivals, not only male athletes but female stars, mostly gymnasts and swimmers. During the Olympics, the team is one among many notable stories, perhaps at a disadvantage to competitors in individual sports, who are easy for networks to follow and feature.

The country's attention does refocus on women's soccer every four years for the World Cup in the dead days of summer, when the basketball and hockey playoffs are over, baseball is in a summer lull, and football is still far off—though the off-season activities of football players still often lead the news. Winning might change that, but the U.S. can't quite seem to pull it out. Four years after its disappointing defeat to China, at the 2003 World Cup, the U.S. team loses to Germany in the semifinals, and four years after that gets blown out by Brazil at the same stage. The team generates significant buzz, but not quite at the level it had attracted in 1999, and outside the World Cup and, to a lesser extent, the Olympics, it fades again. Interest resurges in 2011, when the U.S. records a stunning win over its rival Canada during the semifinals. But it isn't until 2015 that the U.S. women finally win the Cup, sixteen years after the heartbreak in Pasadena. That team, led by a new generation of skilled, powerful, outspoken stars, redeems and fulfills the legacy of the 1999 team. It becomes a powerful symbol for women's empowerment, not only in sports but all walks of life.

Still, women's soccer fails to capture the public attention in a day-to-day way. Hoping to capitalize on the huge television audiences and the hundreds of thousands of people that had flocked to games across the United States during the Women's World Cup, a women's professional soccer league is formed after the 1999 World Cup, featuring not only American stars but players from international teams. Despite offering modest salaries to players, the league folds after three years. A few years later, another league is formed, but again, small crowds and little mainstream coverage can't sustain it, and it, too, folds after three years. Finally, a league is formed with significant support from national federations instead of relying on private financing, advertising, and ticket sales. It manages to survive and attract a fiercely loyal fan base, but it is hardly the juggernaut that men's major professional leagues are—or even Major League Soccer. Average attendance is in the low four figures (compared to twenty-one thousand–plus for MLS), and many of the salaries are not enough for players who are not members of the national team to live on. Even the stars from the national team do not make anywhere near the kind of money usually associated with professional sports—or even as much as their male counterparts. Several of the biggest stars of the victorious 2015 team sign contracts with European clubs.

Participation levels for women's soccer continue to rise, a trend that began not with the 1999 team but long before. The 1990s had seen an explosion of interest in the sport, not so much as a result of the women's victory in the inaugural Women's World Cup in 1991 but mostly due to the effects of Title IX, passed in 1972. In the late 1970s, there were only a few thousand women playing soccer in high school. By 1991 there were more than 120,000, and by 1999 that number had more than doubled, to 250,000. After 1999, there was a slight slowdown of the sport's growth—perhaps understandably—before it picked up again. By the time the American women win the World Cup in 2015, the sport has grown another 50 percent, to 375,000. But women's soccer still ranks below basketball and volleyball in popularity, and only just above baseball/softball.

There are major gains, of course. By 1999, athletes who are women are, in general, no longer regarded as freaks. They are not the curiosities that they were in the 1980s and early 1990s, when those sports that drew on the youth and femininity of their participants—figure skating, gymnastics, even tennis—produced the most popular female athletes. Women's sports are more often discussed in tones of respect. Young girls grow up wanting to be soccer players and basketball stars, not only ballerinas and princesses. Broadcasters find that there are consequences for sexualizing their subjects or treating gender as comic relief. This trend continues despite that difficult loss in '99. Still, even these gains are not uncomplicated. It takes ten years after the U.S. women's loss for ESPN, the self-proclaimed Worldwide Leader in Sports, to focus on women's sports. It does so by creating a sister site to ESPN.com, espnW, but its focus and tone are different from the flagship site; its layout has a decidedly more feminine style, and its tone is sometimes more celebratory than reportorial. One of its stated missions is to "inspire."

Commentators may speak of women's sports more respectfully, but they rarely do it enthusiastically—and they rarely do it at all. In fact, after 1999, the percentage of coverage devoted to women's sports on network affiliates and ESPN's flagship *SportsCenter* actually falls. A

USC study finds that the percentage of airtime devoted to women's sports actually dropped by more than 50 percent between 1999 and 2014 and by 10 percent on *SportsCenter*. The fall wasn't from great heights. Fifteen years after the women's national soccer team lost in 1999, *SportsCenter* features female athletes only 2 percent of the time. Instead of covering women's soccer (or any other women's sports), networks run segments on the question of whether an NBA player recently traded from the Los Angeles Lakers to the Minnesota Timberwolves will be able to find a burrito in Milwaukee, or the heartwarming story of a stray dog that finds its way into the Brewers' stadium, and whom fans and players call Hank.

Soccer, despite the promise of the game's growth in the 1990s, the popularity of the 1999 team before its loss, and the consistently high performances on international stages, struggles to get a regular purchase in the sports ecosystem outside the Olympics and World Cup—even among women's sports. Women's basketball receives by far the most coverage, with tennis second and golf third.

The women's national team, despite its overall sustained excellence near the top of the game, is routinely treated—in terms of coverage, crowds, and federation pay—as inferior to the men's team, even though the men historically have achieved far less success. The women make less money than the men (a pay gap that reflects the overall wage gap between men and women in the United States). They receive smaller per diems and bonuses. They are, at times against their will, forced to play on turf instead of grass. Finally, buoyed by the success of the 2015 team, the national team takes legal action and threatens to strike. After years of conflict, a new bargaining agreement is implemented, and the women's pay is substantially increased—but, reportedly, not all the way to the level of the men.

It is hard not to wonder how different the situation would be, for women's soccer and women's sports more generally, had Chastain made that goal.

Of course, in reality, Chastain *did* score. The ball slid just inches inside the goalpost, past the diving Hong's outstretched hand. The crowd detonated, the sound of the screams a high-pitched explosion. Chastain—as she had seen so many male soccer players do in triumph countless times before—ripped off her shirt as she whirled around and slid on her knees, flexing her arms and letting out a cry, exultant. A photograph of that moment—Chastain in her white shorts and black sports bra, abs amazing, muscles flexed, her blond hair disheveled by effort, her head tossed back in a triumphal roar—would be on the cover of *Newsweek* and *Sports Illustrated*. In 2014, *SI* readers voted on that cover as the second-most iconic in the magazine's history, after only the famous "Miracle on Ice" photograph during the 1980 Olympics.

That victory made the U.S. women more than household names, more than superstars; it immediately made them symbols of the progress of women's sports and women's empowerment.

Here's the thing: The scenario I just sketched out if the U.S. team had lost is exactly what happened when they won.

Two professional leagues failed. Coverage of women's sports changed in tone and nature but did not increase. The women's national team struggled to achieve the economic parity that it—and many—believed it had earned.

But of course, this account leaves out something critical, something that isn't immediately obvious. For starters, startling advancements are rarely immediate; the path of progress is long. More important, for thousands and thousands of people—perhaps in ways they are not entirely aware—the 1999 Women's World Cup victory had profound and enduring effects, even if they were effects that can be hard to measure.

For millions of Americans watching that game—especially young women—the women's national team represented something they had never seen. For starters, it was a *team*—a collective, not a compelling personal story that could be set to strings and aired as a sob segment on NBC, but a unit of women bound by training and skill. Individual female athletes had become stars before, but no women's team had ever commanded such a big stage. Rooting for a team was different from rooting for an individual. You could wear a jersey; you could debate strategy; you could follow as if you were a fan of the Lakers. It seemed to have the same legitimacy. More than that, there was a kind of echo effect. I, like many women, was never compelled to buy tickets to any of the women's pro league games. But as a high school student myself when that team won, I internalized the idea that female athletes deserve respect. And, perhaps even more important, it made me want to be physically and mentally strong; it made me want to play games.

Symbols matter. The famous photograph of Chastain clutching her shirt said something more powerful than any motivational speech about women could have. Women could be muscular, proud of it, and show it. Women could be cool under pressure. Women could be winners. There was something sublime about watching a group of women, working in concert, display their strength and skill. There was something cathartic about the moment when the ball sailed into the back of the net. I will bet that those who watched it, those millions, will never forget it.

It may be that if the 1999 U.S. women's national soccer team had lost, another women's team would have come along soon after and had the same emotional, cathartic, galvanizing impact. But it seems to me unlikely. There was so much drama in that moment, that single shot. Winning never matters as much as it seems it should. Still, it was a moment that was primed for them, and which they seized.

16

What If the Olympics Had Never Dropped Tug-of-War?

Nate DiMeo

Tug-of-War was introduced as a team sport in the Summer Olympics of 1900 as part of the track and field competition. During the next five Olympiads, teams of five, six, and eventually eight men faced off, each team with the goal of dragging the other six feet to victory. A list of medal winners from the earliest days of Olympic Tug-of-War reflects the improvisatory nature of the modern revival of the Games, with its first gold medal going to a team comprised of both Swedes and Danes. St. Louis, 1904, saw all three medals awarded to teams of Americans, with the gold going not to "the United States National Team" but to the Milwaukee Athletic Club. Hometown fans in London watched two teams representing competing police athletic leagues facing off in the final in 1908. Tug-of-War had its last Olympic hurrah in 1920, after which it, along with thirty-three other sports, was culled from the competition.

But what if it stayed in?

"TUG-OF-WAR"

From: *The Big Book of The Olympics: Your Comprehensive Guide to the History, the Stories, the Scandals, and the Glory of the Games,* Expanded 5th Edition, with new foreword by Bob Costas, Inter-Corp GlobalMediaProperties, 2014.

Men's Tug-of-War

It is nearly impossible to imagine how different the world would have been were it not for the results of a simple game of chance. The scene: the sun-drenched breakfast room of a resort in Lucerne, Switzerland. The time: the summer of 1921. The game had something to do with two sprigs of lavender, a pocket knife, and a ribald cartoon featuring the then crown princess of Denmark. Not much else is known about the rules of this contest but its outcome was clear: The loser, one Dieter Hrempf, a member of the International Olympic Committee's Competition Committee's Rules Subcommittee as well as a leading light among Bavarian paddleboat manufacturers, reluctantly cast the deciding vote that kept Tug-of-War a part of the Games. As has been noted many times,[i] it is rather ironic that the results of such an apparently convoluted game of chance yielded the preservation of this most primal of sports. Tug-of-War has been famously hailed by Sir Winston Churchill as "endeavor, distilled," by Stephen Ambrose[ii] as "the knotted thread of history in our century," and, unforgettably, by the man who defined the possibilities of the game by parlaying his two Tug-of-War gold medals at Montreal in 1976[iii] into a successful political career, Vice

i. Our favorite treatment of Herr Hrempf and his famous vote is in ESPN's 30 for 30 Short, "War-of-Tug," directed by Alex Gibney. For younger audiences, do seek out "Has Anyone Seen Doktor Kostelwiscz' Glass Eye? Not Doktor Kostelwiscz!," written and illustrated by Mo Willems.

ii. We would be remiss not to note Dr. Ambrose's monumental *Band of Tuggers: Forty-Three Seconds That Shocked the World* and the sixteen-part HBO docudrama that it inspired.

iii. Simpson's immortal "Scamper," which of course earned the U.S. Six-Man team a shocking victory over the heavily favored Soviet team led by Tug legends Vasily "the Red Hammer" Yurgev and Ivan "the Monolith from 2001" Skelnikov, was voted number 17 in *Sports Illustrated*'s "100 Greatest Sports Moments of the Century." It remains, as of this printing, the second-most-watched Tug-of-War highlight video on YouTube after the infamous video of Pierre-Yves Arneault, anchor of the fourth-place French Six-Man team from 1996, losing three fingers. (The video features Al Michaels's legendary call, "Something happened! Something happened! Something happened! God, how can one man bleed so much? There's just so much blood...Mr.

President Orenthal J. Simpson, who gave us the immortal phrase, "It's just a man, and probably some other men, against some other men just, like, tugging," during his address to the Republican convention in 1988. For it is surely its simplicity—men (and since 1976, women) just, like, tugging—that accounts for much of its appeal. As the 100-meter dash is to the individual sports, Tug is certainly to team games. It is fitting then, that it was the entanglement of those two events that brought the sport to the center of the Games.

Finding Its Footing: 1920–1932

Looking back at the earliest days of Olympic Tug-of-War, perhaps we shouldn't be too hard on those IOC members who nearly ditched the sport one summer morning in a gentiles-only resort in the Swiss Alps. Its first decade featured lackluster competition between lackluster athletes. This was the time of figures like Petey "Six Pints" Kendall, the British cement mixer turned three-time Olympic captain, so nicknamed after his prematch ritual. Tug-of-War was the purview of police athletic clubs, fraternal organizations, and Harvard (or Princeton or Oxford) men who couldn't quite cut it on the track or in the pool or the boxing ring. There was very little tactical innovation to speak of during this period, with teams spending most of their weight allotment on massive anchors like the aforementioned Six Pints. A series of controversies known collectively as the Footwear Wars led us to our current, barefoot state in time for the Games of 1932. But beyond tinkering (Two-Man and Solo Tug added and dropped in 1928; the mud pit added to the center of a demonstration Ten-Man Tug event in 1924), there's little of interest in the so-called Dead Tug era for fans of the game today. It did, however, catch the imagination of one notorious sports fan.

Vice President, I think I might be ill," which was voted number 2 in *Sports Illustrated*'s "100 Greatest Sports Calls of the Century.")

The Pull of the Game: 1936–1988

The scenes are so familiar. They have been etched into our collective consciousness by the black-and-white newsreel footage shown in history class and edited into montages before Olympic broadcasts—Adolf Hitler's glare of contempt, the shocked German team detangling themselves from the pile as the Americans walk away, Jesse Owens laughing on the steamer homebound for New York, wearing Glenn Morris's gold medal. They have been brought to life so many times on stage and screen[iv] that the story of the 1936 Six-Man Tug-of-War final is part of our cultural DNA. But, with apologies to the screenwriters, novelists, playwrights, and book-report-writing schoolkids who've found inspiration again and again in this remarkable tale, your authors humbly offer this too-brief synopsis:

Prior to the 1936 Olympics, Hitler was, perhaps literally, Tug-of-War's biggest fan. Biographers have documented his abiding fascination with the sport, tracing it to seeing preliminary matches in his native Austria prior to the 1920 Antwerp Games. But the fever had taken hold by 1925, as evidenced by several Tug-based metaphors in *Mein Kampf*, published that year. And in 1936, in his role as German chancellor, Hitler exerted his influence over the Summer Games in Berlin, seeing them both as an opportunity to demonstrate the rising power of the Third Reich and to promote his ideas of racial supremacy. He insisted that his beloved Tug-of-War be elevated to the premier event of the Games. In marked contrast to all previous Olympiads, which shunted off Tug to minor arenas, the Six-Man Tug-of-War final was scheduled as the last event of the Games in Hitler's pride and joy, the hundred-thousand-seat Olympic

---

iv. The 1936 Olympic Tug-of-War final is the only historical event to result in a collective "EGOT," by inspiring works that have earned performers Emmys (both Billy Dee Williams and Lee Majors for *Jesse and Glenn*, 1980); a Grammy (Crystal Gayle for "Heartstrings" (Love Theme from *Tug of Their Lives*), 1976); Oscars (for Lead Actors William Holden, *The Glenn Morris Story*, 1944, and Jamie Foxx, *Jesse*, 2005, Supporting Actor Paul Winfield, *Tug of Their Lives*, 1976, and Supporting Actresses Halle Berry, *Jesse*, 2005, and Meryl Streep for her immortal, forty-three-second cameo as a stoic Eva Braun in *Fun und Games? Nein!*, 1986); and a Tony (Best Choreography in a Revival, Tommy Tune, *Tuggin'*, 1983).

Stadium. While this decision alone surely did much to introduce the public to the glories of Tug, it was a second, more crucial decision that would come to place it permanently at the center of the international stage.

Hitler held the now uncontroversial view of Tug-of-War as the ultimate team athletic endeavor. But he went further, believing that it would be the ultimate demonstration of Aryan physical superiority. So convinced was he that an Aryan-German team would humiliate all comers, he sought to ensure that the inevitable German victory would be free of all second-guessing. He wanted a pure, undeniable validation of Teutonic racial virtue. He successfully pressured the IOC to alter the rules of competitor eligibility, such that the team could be formed by any men already representing any nation in any sport. Swimmer, weight lifter, hammer thrower, or yachtsman—the best athletes from a given nation would represent that nation in the Six-Man Tug-of-War. Furthermore, those athletes could be selected until the day of the competition. His idea was that the Games themselves should clarify the coach's choice—as heroes emerge within the course of the Olympic fortnight, those heroes should tug for their country.

Jesse Owens, of course, changed all that. The story, long thought to be legend but recently confirmed by a team of German and American scholars, goes that Hitler, having watched each successive Owens track and field gold medal victory with rising fury, in short, lost it when the American Tug team with Owens in the two spot won its semifinal match against Sweden in a then-record 31 seconds. A combination of threats and rumored bribes led to an unprecedented midstream rule change that prohibited members of team events from participating in the medal rounds of the Tug-of-War. As a gold medalist in the 4×100 relay, Owens was thus prohibited from the final against the home nation.

The Americans were outraged.

There are conflicting stories about who was behind their world-historic response the next day, though the likely apocryphal midnight speech of Decathlon gold medalist Glenn Morris (delivered famously by William Holden in his Oscar-winning performance as Morris)—"Jesse's an American as much as you or me or Roosevelt, so let's show 'em who Americans are!"—is the version that has had so much enduring influence. By any rate, the newsreel footage is undeniable: Two all-white teams approach the pulling area in the center of the Olympiastadion while both Jesse Owens and Adolf Hitler watch from the sidelines. The teams get into set positions, the first judge raises his arm and then lowers it to commence tugging, and the Americans… drop the rope. The ensuing images—the German team a-tangle on the ground, the Americans walking stoically away, and the later footage of der Führer, stunned and seething, Morris giving Owens his Decathlon gold medal—are among the most indelible in American life. And, of course, the image of President Franklin D. Roosevelt a month later in the Rose Garden, with his right arm around Morris and his left around Owens, grinning with his cigarette holder clenched in his teeth, is one of the most iconic of the twentieth century; it was revived during the civil rights movement and has been revered and parodied[v] in equal measure.

What could have been a more dramatic introduction for most of the world to the sport than that?

Tug was not only thrust to the center of the sporting world where it remains today, it became an echo of and proxy for international politics. The history of postwar Tug-of-War is nearly inextricable from history writ large. Again and again, the Olympic final was a contest between the United States and its Western allies and the Soviet Union and the Eastern Bloc. The U.S. and Soviet Union faced off in the final no fewer than six times between 1948 and the dissolution of the USSR in 1990.[vi] But even with boycotts, the Soviet doping scandal of 1988, the joys of Vice President Simpson's "Scamper," the "weighted rope" controversy of Mexico City, Earl Campbell's gruesome compound fracture in the

---

v. Perhaps most famously by actor Charles Durning, portraying Roosevelt, while embracing Sir Paul McCartney and Stevie Wonder at the end of their music video for "Ebony and Ivory."

vi. Then governor Bill Clinton's joking remark on NBC's *Meet the Press*, in reference to the breaking news of the fall of the Soviet Union: "While there are those who will point to economic instability or the aging Politboro, or American military superiority, clearly they didn't want our boys to clean their clock in Tug a couple years from now and break that tie."

'76 semifinal, and the remarkable victory of the Seven Dwarves[vii] in the quarterfinals in '52, there is certainly no more significant Cold War Tug than the one that took place in 1966.

American GIs and East German soldiers faced off in a televised Tug with the Berlin Wall as the center line. Though the U.S. was at a clear advantage throughout the match's 2:42 duration, a tie was in the cards, having been engineered through weeks of negotiations between U.S., Soviet, and East German authorities (that also resulted in the secret exchange of three American spies, one Belgian diplomat, an erstwhile Canadian tourist, and four Eastern Bloc spies, and the opening of the Baltics to exporters of Wisconsin hard cheeses). Viewers at home were annoyed and uplifted in equal measure.

While the Americans and Soviets were waging their Cold-Tug-of-War near top of the podium, this era also saw tremendous growth of Global Tug. As Che Guevara noted in his Congo diaries, "To topple the oppressor, first one must rise, but with tug-of-war, men rise by moving laterally. It is a paradox of liberation, yes, but the working peoples should turn to Tug as a tool to topple the oppressor. To pull the world leftward, we must tug." So it is that developing nations have used Tug—often pouring the majority of their athletic development and Olympic team budgets into identifying prospects and training them in the tugish arts. And though the superpowers on the world stage reigned for nearly three decades as the superpowers of the game, the Olympics repeatedly saw notable performances from smaller and less economically advantaged countries, notably by bronze medalists from Togo, Senegal, New Zealand, and Trinidad and Tobago; silver medalists from Tunisia and Sri Lanka; and, of course, the shock gold medal win by the legendary "Flying Foxes" of Fiji in 1972.

It should further be noted that fans of Global Tug consistently maintain that the Olympic tournament is an inferior product to both the

---

vii. Prior to the standardization of Six-Man with the 1962 Olympics, Tug teams were merely required to weigh less than a collective 1,500 pounds. And so the legendary Seven Dwarves faced off with the Four Giants and won, though contemporary analysis points to an undiagnosed Achilles' tear in Soviet anchor Yevgeny Vertov, rather than the long-accepted narrative of Eisenhower Era scrappiness.

African Championships and the Copa de Guerra quadrennial tournament in South America.

The World's Game: 1992–the Present

Since the fall of the Soviet Union, Olympic competition has opened up. The United States has continued its dominance, with three gold medals, one silver, one bronze, and a shocking fourth-place finish in 2012.[viii] Beyond the American program, the past two decades have seen remarkable parity among nations, with only the German, Russian, and Australian teams managing more than a single medal since 1992. Further, the global dominance of American media has made American tuggers international superstars since the days of prepolitics O. J. Simpson, Bruce Jenner, Jim Brown, Franco Harris, Pete "Charlie Scramble" Rose, and Ed "Perfectly Proportioned" Jones.

Today, even as a kid growing up in Senegal might look up to Papiss Cissé and a young German child might try to master Marcel Schmelzer's stutter-step lunge, they are wearing the T-shirts of American stars like Rob Gronkowski and LeBron James and Frank Gore. They are drinking Coke Zero and wearing the Under Armour Tug gloves advertised by Blake Griffin and LaDainian Tomlinson.

Postscript: Whither Professional Tug

Despite its primacy in the Olympic Games, Tug-of-War remains a minor professional sport around the world, save for the obvious

---

viii. Forever known as "the Slip," the 2012 stumble occurred during the semifinal match against eventual gold medal winners Australia. The U.S., bumped into the bronze medal match, could not rally past the injury to their captain and Five, LeBron James, and fell to that year's Cinderella, Burkina Faso. Though James is perhaps his generation's most gifted tugger, the Slip is seen by many pundits and historians of the game as a mark on his legacy. He has been dogged by questions about his "heart" and competitive desire, while critics point to other Olympic heroes like gold medalist Kobe Bryant and two-time gold medal–winning anchor Bruce Smith. Further. James's height and natural athletic gifts have meant "What if LeBron James had played basketball instead of Tug-of-War?" has become one of the Games' great what-ifs.

exception of the Brazilian Super-União do Extratores, where the twenty-five-man-per-side elevated spectacles, famous for the flashy costumes, scantily clad cheerleaders, and shark tanks, bear little resemblance to the traditional sport. This despite endorsement deals that place every member of the U.S. Tug team in *Forbes*'s annual list of the highest-paid athletes. Yet, as Morgan Freeman, known as "the Voice of God" for his authoritative Tug calls over the past thirty-two years, wrote in his inspirational 2008 memoir, *Close to the Line: A Life in Tug*, "The American landscape is littered with the detritus of the dying dreams of failed tug-of-war leagues."

Today, the current iteration of the World Tug-of-War Federation operates an awkwardly aligned bracket of five league-owned franchises, all but one of which are in North Ontario. Its rival, if it can be called that, is the moderately successful Women's Bikini Tug Confederation, which has ridden its "Jugs-o'-War" model to modest success in recent years, adding franchises in Daytona and San Padre Island. These leagues are but sad imitations of the 1970s heyday of North American Tug-of-War when the pre-merger/pre-bankruptcy American Tug-of-War Association and the pre-merger/pre-coke-trafficking-bust/pre-trademark-infringment-ruling American Tug-O-War Association half-filled arenas across the country.

17

What If Billie Jean King Had Lost to Bobby Riggs?

Wayne Coffey

It was the most watched tennis match in history, and the tawdriest, an event with all the subtlety of the Vegas Strip, and enough circus-like antics to give circuses a bad name. The first entrant was Billie Jean King, the twenty-nine-year-old champion of Wimbledon and the champion of female athletes everywhere; she was carried into Houston's Astrodome on a gilded Egyptian litter, a latter-day Cleopatra, with each of the four corners manned by a beefy, half-clad member of the Rice University men's track team. Next up was Bobby Riggs, a fifty-five-year-old tennis hustler and former Wimbledon champ himself, a self-avowed male chauvinist pig who was carted in on a rickshaw, the lifting being done by four amply endowed young women.

"My bosom buddies," Riggs called them. He shared this description shortly after he declared that women's tennis "stinks" and that women "belong in the bedroom and the kitchen, in that order."

Helen Reddy was on hand to sing her hit single "I Am Woman" live for King's entry. Riggs's choice of walkout music was "Conquest," a march from an old Tyrone Power movie. Howard Cosell called the match in a primetime ABC telecast that drew an estimated worldwide audience of ninety million viewers, with thirty thousand more people in the building, among them artist Salvador Dalí, who presumably was waiting along with everyone else to see whom heavyweight champion George Foreman would be handing the $100,000 winner's check to. The loser would get nothing.

Deep in the heart of Texas oil country, the night of September 20, 1973, was billed as the Battle of the Sexes, played out on a seventy-eight-by-twenty-seven-foot hard-court rectangle. Tacky trappings notwithstanding, King and other activists in the burgeoning feminist movement viewed the evening as much more Athletic Armageddon than made-for-TV sideshow.

A young broadcaster from Louisville, Kentucky, said she had so much vested in the outcome she could barely stand to watch.

"I remember being so nervous I had to pace," Diane Sawyer told ABC News. "I was so scared for [Billie Jean]—and for all of us."

King herself didn't even bother to pretend that it was just another match. She would complete her career as a thirty-nine-time Grand Slam champion in singles and doubles, universally regarded as a competitor with few equals over nearly one thousand career matches. Not one of them was even close in import to the Battle of the Sexes.

"I just felt I had to win," she told Robin Roberts of ABC. "Emotionally, I felt like it was like life and death."

The best-of-five match in Houston came amid significant changes in the realm of women's sports. A year earlier, Congress passed the landmark legislation that became known as Title IX, which prohibited discrimination based on sex in any educational program or activity receiving federal funds. King, meanwhile, was consumed with making the fledgling women's pro tennis circuit a viable entity, an unyielding pursuit triggered in part by her disgust when she learned in 1970 that an event called the Pacific Southwest Open was going to pay its male champion $12,500 and its female champion $1,500. The promoter wouldn't budge, so King and eight other top players called for a boycott, and found a new sponsor, Philip Morris's Virginia Slims brand of cigarettes, for a separate women's tour.

"You've come a long way, baby" became the slogan of the tour, and yet King knew better than anybody that there was a much longer distance to go. In 1972, the leading male tennis players had formed a union, and King believed the women would benefit from the same sort of collective voice. During the Wimbledon Championships in 1973, King convened with the other top female players at London's Gloucester Hotel, and in a matter of hours they agreed to the basic principles that became the foundation of the Women's Tennis Association.

"We finally all came together as one voice and having the power of one—you know, just one group," King told CNN years later. "It made such a difference."

It didn't take long for the new group to score its first victory. Threatening to boycott the 1973 U.S. Open if the women's winner was not paid the same as the men's winner, King and her racket-wielding sisters won the standoff, making the Open the first Grand Slam tournament to pay players equally. The immediate beneficiary was Australia's Margaret Court, who won $25,000 for her victory at the 1973 Open—or $15,000 more than King earned for her 1972 title at the same tournament.

Still, the new tour was a fragile enterprise in those days, fighting for legitimacy and even-handed treatment, and the cause was not helped any by the so-called Mother's Day Massacre in 1973, when Riggs, having been spurned in his attempts to play King, convinced Court, the top-ranked female player in the world, to accept his challenge. In the hills outside San Diego, Riggs, a master of mind games and tennis trickery, presented Court with a Mother's Day bouquet, then routed her 6–2, 6–1, in fifty-seven minutes, before immediately angling for what he knew could be a much bigger payday than the $10,000 he got for beating Court.

"I want [Billie Jean King], the Women's Libber leader," he said. "She can name the place, the court, and the time, just as long as the price is right."

King watched the Riggs-Court match unfold in abject horror. The world's preeminent female player had just been humiliated by a man twenty-five years her senior. What did that say about the quality of women's tennis? Who was left to shut up the patronizing Neanderthals who thought it was cute that women wanted to play sports, so long as they got out of the way when the real competition began?

"I knew at that moment that I had to play him," King said.

Apart from being a ten-time Grand Slam singles champion, King was the daughter of a fireman, a public-courts kid who braided her serve-and-volley gifts with a blue-collar grit, fortified with a toughness and resilience people might not have seen behind her glasses and her tennis dress.

"The male is supreme. The male is king," Riggs said before the match. He praised King for being a good serve-and-volley player, "for a woman," before openly mocking the quality of women's tennis, and promising to jump off a California bridge if he could not beat her. The $100,000 prize was set. Sides were taken. The nation's most celebrated oddsmaker, Jimmy "the Greek" Snyder, made Riggs a 5–2 favorite.

Ever on the lookout for revenue streams, Riggs signed a deal to wear a yellow SUGAR DADDY outfit, and presented King with her own SUGAR DADDY lollipop before the match. Not to be outdone, King handed Riggs a squealing piglet.

"It was so cute," she said.

"I can't remember any kind of event in any other sport that brought out the emotion in people as that match did," Chris Evert, then an eighteen-year-old prodigy on the way to a Hall of Fame career, told a reporter.

King's psychological pattern was to become beset by nerves well before a match, then calm down as time got closer. It was no different this time. When her longtime doubles partner, Rosie Casals, visited her not even a half hour before she entered the Astrodome, King told her, "I am going to win."

Eschewing her vaunted attacking serve-and-volley game, the five-foot-five-inch King realized early on the best thing she could do was to lengthen points, not shorten them. She fell behind early, and then started running Riggs this way and that way. When he tired, King spanked a winner past him. It happened over and over. Riggs double-faulted to drop the first set, and soon a PR person for the women's tour was handing out invitations to the "Bobby Riggs Bridge Jump." Riggs didn't fare much better in the next two sets, either. The final score was 6–4, 6–3, 6–3.

When Riggs dumped a backhand volley into the net on match point, King threw her racket into the air. Riggs used his remaining energy to hop over the net.

"I underestimated you," he told Billie Jean King.

King's victory over Riggs (reported on the front page of the next day's *New York Times*) was that much more remarkable considering the pressure—virtually all of it self-inflicted—she was under. She was the most vocal and ardent advocate for the cause of all female athletes, a person full of righteous outrage at the idea that her triumphs should be worth less than those of her American contemporary Stan Smith, or any other male player, for that matter.

Moreover, she was someone who had committed her whole life to using sports as a means to achieve social change.

"I thought it would set us back fifty years if I didn't win that match," King told a reporter. "It would ruin the women's tour and affect the self-esteem of all women."

Would the women's tour, in fact, have been horribly diminished if Riggs had won in the Astrodome? Would the sweeping changes brought by Title IX, giving millions of young girls competitive opportunities that were never there before, have been less impactful?

Would King have become the face of gender equity? Would she have been awarded the Presidential Medal of Freedom, the nation's highest civilian honor, and would the National Tennis Center, home of the U.S. Open, have been renamed in her honor?

And, as someone who would one day become one of the world's most prominent homosexual athletes, what of her stature as a champion of gay rights and the LGBT movement? Would she have been seen as a less influential voice?

For his part, Riggs, nothing if not a shameless huckster, would absolutely have done everything possible to keep the fat checks coming. One can imagine an alternative scenario set off by a Riggs victory, which might have been chronicled this way:

> Minutes after trouncing Wimbledon champion Billie Jean King in the Astrodome last night, Bobby Riggs, still wearing his Sugar Daddy T-shirt and surrounded by the four "bosom buddies" who escorted him into the arena, was quite content

to pile on the indignities. "Billie Jean was kind enough to present me with a pig before the match, and then I went out and did what men have always done in the world, and that is bring home the bacon," Riggs said. "Billie Jean is a nice girl and a nice player. Maybe in a couple of decades when she is my age I will give her a rematch."

Riggs then issued a challenge to any other top women's players, including Chrissie Evert and Martina Navratilova—or "that big Czech chick," as Riggs called her.

"How about it, Chrissie? Margaret and Billie Jean took their shots. You think you can beat the old man?"

What would the consequence of this challenge have been? You can imagine Chris Evert, then just eighteen, demurring. Evert had yet to win a Grand Slam event at that point, having fallen that year to Margaret Court in the finals at the French Open and Billie Jean at Wimbledon. It would seem unlikely that Evert would allow the promising course of her career to be diverted by participating in a tawdry, Riggs-conceived sideshow. Navratilova? She was a Czech teenager, not yet seventeen years old, when the Battle of the Sexes went down in Texas, and even with her formidable serve-and-volley weaponry, was still not yet ready for such an excruciatingly public challenge. While the competitor in her might well have wanted to shut Riggs up—and while Riggs probably would've pounced on the chance to turn the showdown into a jingoistic carnival with ample Cold War rhetoric aimed at the green-card-carrying kid from behind the Iron Curtain—Navratilova likely was too young and too new to the spotlight to embrace a gender-driven circus. The fact was that Riggs needed King's stature and fame to assure the Battle would yield the audience, and the money, he was looking for.

Just as certainly, opponents of Title IX and armchair sociologists would've weighed in on the innate physiological advantages that male athletes have over female athletes, and used Riggs's victory as a way to diminish the value and quality of female athletics. After all, almost sixty-five years after Roger Bannister broke the four-minute-mile barrier, there has still not been one woman who has equaled the feat (the women's mile record is 4:12.56, by Svetlana Masterkova of Russia, set in 1996). The male gatekeepers of the Olympic movement had such little regard for female endurance that they didn't even permit women to run 5,000 meters until 1996—or eighty-four years after males started running that distance in the Olympics. A King defeat also likely would not have been any sort of boon to the push for equal prize money, emboldening promoters to take a hard line against the threat of a boycott or the power of the infant women's union.

It seems likely, too, that King's enduring image as the ultimate competitor would've taken a hit, and so would wider societal "permission" for women to want to win as much and compete as hard as men do, without apology.

For all the exemplary tennis Billie Jean King played over her career, a loss to Riggs would've—at least for a period of time—knocked her down a rung on the tennis ladder, but also within the pantheon of great female athletes.

But for how long would she, and women's sports, have been stunted?

Mary Jo Kane is the director of the Tucker Center for Research on Girls & Women in Sport at the University of Minnesota. She remembers the Battle of the Sexes well, and fondly.

"Billie Jean King did what she did on so many occasions. She rose to that occasion," Kane said, adding that it was an "iconic moment that changed the master narrative that women couldn't beat men."

And yet, for all of her profound respect and admiration for King, Kane does not agree that a Riggs victory would've set back women's sports a half century.

"I would never want to diminish [King's] contributions, but the train [of the women's sports movement] had already left the station, and that's because of Title IX, one of the most impactful pieces of civil rights legislation this nation has ever passed. No longer were we at the mercy of the good will of an athletic director or school president if we wanted to play sports. Now supporters of Title IX had a big stick; they could sue you in a court of law. Title IX fundamentally and forever altered the landscape, and the timing was perfect for Billie Jean King to become the role model and icon she has become."

Kane believes that while a Riggs victory would've slowed progress to a degree, and lowered the WTA's profile for a period, the massive increase in the number of girls who now had the opportunity to compete in sports would've mitigated the harmful repercussions.

"In two generations, we as a society have gone from young girls hoping there *is* a team to hoping that they *make* a team. That is the legacy of Title IX. If Billie Jean King hadn't won, that still would've happened. [Her victory] just accentuated that growth, making her an even bigger role model with an even greater platform."

Had Riggs won it's quite likely his next contest would have been a rematch with King herself. Given King's competitive wiring, it is completely inconceivable that had she lost to Riggs, she would've just gone away. King ended her Hall of Fame career with the thirty-nine Grand Slam titles and universal acclaim as one of the greatest pure competitors on the planet. One of her signature quotes was, "Champions keep playing until they get it right."

She would've kept up the fight. She would've been in the face of every tournament promoter who tried to tell her that women didn't deserve the same treatment, and pay, as men. She would've railed about the hideous hypocrisy of treating people differently because of gender, race, or sexual orientation.

She would've said what she did say at a stop on the WTA tour once: "Everyone thinks women should be thrilled when we get crumbs, and I want women to get the cake, the icing, and the cherry on top, too."

Billie Jean King's hallmark, both as a player and as a social crusader, was highly skilled, unrelenting aggression. She kept pushing, kept coming at you. She cared passionately about winning and doing her best, and if things didn't go as she'd hoped, she was going to come back and get it right.

It is what champions do, after all, and that's why it's hard to imagine her as anything other than the champion, of both tournaments and causes, she became.

"I have often been asked whether I am a woman or an athlete," Billie Jean King said. "The question is absurd. Men are not asked that. I am an athlete. I am a woman."

18

What If Mike Tyson Had Beaten Buster Douglas?

Jeremy Schaap

For those of us who were old enough to appreciate the shocking news from Tokyo on February 11, 1990, it remains a "Where were you when you heard?" moment. I happened to be in Hanover, New Hampshire, to cover a college hockey game. In vain, I had searched for a hotel or bar that had HBO, which was carrying the fight on its regular service. Instead, I went with two friends to a party on the Dartmouth campus and was informed, by a stranger, that the unthinkable had taken place.

Knocked out?

Really?

By a guy named Buster Douglas?

The same Buster Douglas who'd quit on his stool against Tony Tucker? Impossible.

It really is almost impossible now, nearly three decades later, to convey the degree to which Michael Gerard Tyson was considered invincible in early 1990.

He was twenty-three and undefeated. He'd entered the fight 37-0, having won thirty-four by knockout. Of those thirty-four vanquished opponents, exactly half were dispatched in the first round.

Tyson knocked out Michael Spinks in ninety-one seconds in June 1988 in Atlantic City. He'd unified the heavyweight title while barely suffering a scratch. Most opponents seemed to lose control of their bodily functions at the mere thought of climbing through the ropes and coming face-to-face with this brutal destroyer of worlds.

And who was Buster Douglas?

Nobody. That's who. In his biggest previous fight, he'd had Tucker on the run—but inexplicably seemed to lose interest just when one of the heavyweight titles was in his grasp. He was big, strong, quick—but notoriously devoid of the fire and drive that champions typically possess.

Tyson had run into trouble with bigger heavyweights who could jab—guys, on paper, who resembled Douglas—but Douglas was such a nonentity in the minds of most observers that only a handful of American news outlets considered it worth their while to send anyone to Tokyo to cover the fight.

One of those who was assigned, Ed Schuyler of the Associated Press, delivered the ultimate bon mot on the legitimacy of the proceedings. At customs in Tokyo, Schuyler was asked, "What is the nature of your visit? Business or pleasure?"

"Business," Schuyler said.

"And how long do you expect to be working here?"

"About ninety seconds," Schuyler said.

The bookmakers were in the same camp. Las Vegas set early odds at 12–1, then 27–1, then 32–1 without many takers. By fight day Tyson was a 42–1 favorite.

In the entire history of the heavyweight division, stretching back nearly a hundred years, to John L. Sullivan himself, to Jack Dempsey, Joe Louis, and Rocky Marciano—despite all the stiffs and bums of the month who got their shots—never had the odds on a heavyweight title fight been more lopsided than 8–1.

Until Tyson-Douglas.

There is no need here to recapitulate the details of the upset. Suffice it to say that Douglas rose to the occasion, which is like saying David rose to the occasion against Goliath. But Buster had no slingshot. True, in the eighth round Douglas was knocked down by Tyson and benefited from a long count, but he did rise to his feet to go right back at the champ.

Douglas called upon all his talent, finally marshalled for the occasion, and he was determined, in the wake of the recent death of his mother, Lula Pearl, to honor her with a performance worthy of her and his gifts.

That morning in Tokyo, Buster Douglas was a force.

But what if? What if there had been no upset? What if Tyson had done what he was expected to do?

Well, everything would be different in the world of boxing, that's fairly certain, and maybe the sport, which has lost so much of its appeal—in the United States, anyway—would still truly matter. Maybe Mike Tyson would never have gone to prison for rape. Maybe instead of later starring in the *Hangover* films, he would've cemented his legacy as one of the great champions of the heavyweight division.

For obvious reasons, the domino effect is much stronger in boxing than in other sports. In the major team sports, each season is its own, separate and distinct. In the other major individual sports, tennis and golf, the big events roll around each year on the same place in the calendar. The effects of the previous iterations of the Masters or Wimbledon are limited. But in boxing, there is no calendar, per se. Matches are made specifically based on the outcomes of previous bouts.

So let's assume that Tyson had triumphed in Tokyo to remain undefeated. In that case, he would next have fought Evander Holyfield, who was in Tokyo as an observer, keeping a close eye on the proceedings and promising to be an enticing entrée for any pay-per-view customer who was watching this presumed appetizer of a fight on HBO. If Tyson beats Douglas, Evander is up next—and tens of millions of dollars are in the offing. In real life, Holyfield would defeat Tyson in 1996—and then again in 1997, after losing a small chunk of his anatomy to Tyson's bicuspids. But that was a different Mike Tyson—older, slower, changed by three-plus years in prison after a rape conviction, and, most important, stripped of his cloak of invincibility. If they meet later in 1990, Tyson defeats Holyfield.

What would that mean?

It would mean that instead of the thrilling trilogy of Holyfield bouts against Riddick Bowe, we might have gotten a thrilling trilogy of bouts between Tyson and Riddick Bowe.

The other heavyweight champion of the era from Brownsville, in Brooklyn, Bowe was a big, strong heavyweight who knew Tyson from childhood. He won two of his three megafights against Holyfield, and probably would have won the other had it not been interrupted by an attention seeker with a fan attached to his back who flew into the ring just as Bowe was laying it on.

If Holyfield doesn't get a reprieve from Fan Man and come back to beat Bowe in Las Vegas on November 6, 1993, he doesn't reclaim the world heavyweight title, which means Michael Moorer can't take the title from him in his next fight, on April 22, 1994, which means that Moorer doesn't become the first southpaw heavyweight champion of all time. More significantly, it means that Moorer—another Brooklyn native—doesn't get knocked out seven months later, in the tenth round of his first title defense, by a former champion named George Foreman, who at the age of forty-five reclaims the belt he lost twenty years earlier in Zaire to Muhammad Ali. In other words, if Mike Tyson had beaten Buster Douglas, *you* might have eaten your burgers off a conventional grill during the late nineties and early aughts.

But in boxing terms, the actual path of the Heavyweight Championship went: Tyson-Douglas-Holyfield-Bowe-Holyfield-Moorer-Foreman.

Had Douglas not won that night the title likely would have been Tyson-Tyson-Tyson with perhaps some Holyfield and Bowe interregna.

This hinges on another consequence of a Tyson victory in Tokyo. If Buster Douglas succumbs, Tyson's itinerary for the foreseeable future is upended. It's fair to ask if Tyson would have been in Indianapolis in July 1991 as a judge at the Miss Black America pageant. Perhaps his impulses, character, and attitude were such a volatile combination that he was on a collision course with some sort of transgression. But it is accurate to say that a victory against Douglas could have resulted in a set of circumstances other than the ones that saw him serving time at the Indiana Youth Center prison—a misnomer, as it was an adult facility—until March 25, 1995.

If Tyson doesn't go to prison, he probably fights and defeats Holyfield, and then who knows what would have happened? Several fights against Bowe? A fight against the other dominant heavyweight of the era, Lennox Lewis? A defense against Foreman? Lewis and Bowe square off? All those possibilities are tantalizing. As it was, to its eternal discredit, boxing allowed the era to pass without Tyson ever fighting Bowe, without Tyson ever fighting the resurrected Foreman, without Tyson fighting Lewis until 2002, when both were past their prime, without Lewis and Bowe fighting each other as pros. So many things never happened—largely because Buster Douglas decided to show up, and then some, that morning in Tokyo.

What actually happened after Douglas defeated Tyson? Douglas got millions to fight Holyfield—who crushed him, after Buster reverted to form by choosing not to care at all about his first title defense, putting on weight, lying down when he got hit.

Strangely enough, the most stunning outcome in the history of the fight game, arguably the most stunning outcome in the annals of sports, wasn't even the most consequential event to take place on February 11, 1990. For all the ways in which it altered the course of events, Tyson-Douglas is a distant second on that day. About eleven hours after Douglas knocked out Tyson in the tenth round, Nelson Mandela—the ultimate fighter—walked out of Victor Verster prison in Paarl, forty miles outside Cape Town, a free man for the first time in twenty-seven years.

19

What If? A Tour Through NBA Injury History

Neil Paine

Introductory Notes on the Topic "What if Bernard King hadn't been injured?"

by Mike Pesca

Kemper Area, Kansas City, March 23, 1985
New York Knicks vs. Kansas City Kings

> **Marv Albert:** And back the other way is Reggie Theus...Look out! King hurt himself as he gave the foul on Theus.
> **Butch Beard:** Turned an ankle...I think.

It wasn't an ankle. It was a knee, a blown-out knee, specifically a tear in the anterior cruciate ligament (ACL), which in 1985 meant there was a fair chance Bernard King would never play again and a near certainty that he would never dominate as he had. And *dominate* isn't hyperbole. The year prior to his injury, King placed second in MVP voting behind Larry Bird, and at the moment he went down King was averaging 32.9 points per game, which would lead the league that season.

As King was lifted off the floor by his teammates, the strains of Michael Sembello's "Maniac" playing in the background, Knicks fans had much to worry about. The season was lost already—the Knicks stood at 24-46 going into the game—and now it looked as if King was lost, too.

King was indeed done, at least as a Knick. He would miss an entire year rehabbing his knee, come back to play six more games in a Knicks uniform, and eventually sign with the Washington Bullets, where he played well if not spectacularly.

What Knicks fans couldn't have known then is that within two months the dominant question would transform from "Why him?" to "What if?"

On May 12, in a tense bit of pageantry televised live from the Waldorf-Astoria Hotel, NBA commissioner David Stern sprang on the world the very first NBA lottery. The winner would have the privilege of drafting seven-foot Georgetown center Patrick Ewing. Stern plucked the envelope from a clear plastic drum and revealed the Knicks logo for all to see. This moment has become the subject of endless conspiracy theorizing. How convenient for the NBA, that the team in its biggest market wound up with the biggest star in college basketball. Had the Knicks envelope perhaps been tampered with? Was Stern suppressing a wince while holding an envelope that had been frozen? Had he taken a course in advanced origami detection and developed an almost preternatural feel for minute irregularities in paper stock, such as the deliberately creased corner of an envelope? Or maybe the Knicks just won the damn draft pick; Lord knows they haven't won much else since.

Before we can assess the question of how the Knicks would've been improved with a Ewing/King tandem, it must be asked if they even would have been in a position to select Ewing had King played out the season. New York ended the season on a twelve-game losing streak, beginning with the game in which King went down. The loss of King devastated the Knicks. Could his presence have propelled them into the playoffs—which is to say, to miss the draft lottery?

The answer is the Knicks almost certainly would have been in the lottery even if King had stayed healthy. In fact, the Knicks could have won each of their final twelve games and still had a worse record than any team that made the playoffs. If you want to be really picky about things, it's true that a twelve-game winning streak would have included a victory over the Cleveland Cavaliers, who then would have slipped out of the playoffs in favor of the Knicks. So we can say that unless the Knicks had won every single game, their place in the lottery would've been assured.

And in 1985, the lottery's inaugural year, every eligible team had the same one-in-seven chance. This was pre–Ping-Pong balls. All seven nonplayoff teams had a single envelope in that big Lucite drum that David Stern drew from. Which is all for the better, since Ping-Pong balls tend to shatter upon freezing.

Over the next decade and a half, as Ewing turned into an excellent, albeit not singular, player, it was almost impossible for a Knicks fan not to ask, "What if he were playing with Bernard King?" The Knicks, perennially desperate for a second scoring option, found themselves not with one-time superstar Bernard King but with one-time supermarket checkout guy John Starks. (This isn't fair to Starks, a beloved Knick who in 1994, after King had retired, made the All-Star Game and led the league in three-pointers with 217, or what Steph Curry has tallied by early February.)

There is no way to avoid the conclusion that the Knicks would have been good, much better than they were, especially in the beginning of Ewing's career, which would have coincided with King's prime. This is the less than shocking effect of adding a thirty-three-points-per-game NBA scorer to a front court anchored by a guy whom people compared to Bill Russell in college.

Even so, there are caveats and complications in taking the solid premise that the Knicks would be improved and spinning that into NBA championships. There is the question of Patrick Ewing's style. He was not a creative passer or much of an offensive facilitator. (Upon reading that last sentence, a typical Knicks fan will think, "Yeah, and the bathroom in Penn Station isn't much of a day spa.") But who's to say how Ewing's game might have changed had he been paired with a reliable lethal option on his wing? It should also be noted that this was not a time of deficient basketball, especially in the Eastern Conference. In

Ewing's first couple of seasons, when the Knicks were terrible, perhaps too terrible for even a King / young Ewing combo to overcome, the Celtics were dominant. Boston gave way to Detroit's Bad Boy Pistons, who gave way to Chicago's Jordan Bulls, and then, by the mid-1990s, King's career would have been coming to an end, with or without an injury.

To me, the question of "What if Bernard King hadn't been injured?" isn't about the Knicks, or about what we can all imagine would have happened. It's a moot point. They might have won more but not won it all, who knows? Which seems an odd thing for the editor of a book of what-ifs to admit. To me, the interesting part of the question is that everyone who's ever rooted for a team with passion has such a question hanging over their fandom. Or around their necks. For Atlanta Falcons fans, it's the Brett Favre trade. For Buffalo Bills fans, it's "wide right." For more than twenty baseball teams, it's the guy they selected in the first round of the 2009 draft instead of Mike Trout.

But notice I did not mention Bo Jackson. That's because injuries are in a different category, especially the injury of a player who is in his prime and then is suddenly lost. "Untimely ripped" was the phrase in *Macbeth*. To a partisan who sees the future lying crumpled on the floor of a soon-to-be-disused NBA arena in an about-to-be-abandoned NBA city, it's hard to conjure the thought, "Yes, this is the way the universe was meant to unfold." It's so tempting to reach for an alternative, better explanation. It's also natural to think that the ill that befell your hero belongs on a list of all-time bad breaks. That part at least can be put to the test. Inspired by the ghosts of blown-out knees, degenerative hips, and ruptured discs, I asked Neil Paine, one of the best minds in sports analytics, to crunch the numbers. We cannot answer "What if?" but we can at least answer with some hard data the question "Who suffered the greatest blow?" The player you held on to for all these years as having been most unfairly sidelined may not wind up actually topping the list. Bernard King didn't. As a Knicks fan I don't know if that's comforting or yet another wound.

———————

Ten Worst NBA Injuries

Injuries are an unfortunate fact of sporting life, and nothing is more devastating to a franchise's long-term fortunes than a star player getting hurt. History is littered with examples of promising teams that crumbled before they could even scratch the surface of their potential, all because one bright young talent went down prematurely with a bum elbow or a blown-out knee.

NBA teams in particular are subject to the whims of the injury gods. With its combination of relatively few players on the court (only five a side at any given time, far less than football or soccer) and the ability to give one of them as many opportunities to dominate as possible—think of Michael Jordan taking over late in a game, determining what happens on practically all of his team's possessions—basketball is the most star driven of all the sports. So the same individual focus that makes the sport thrilling when a great player is healthy can also lead to ruin when a team plans its entire future around one brilliant-but-fragile superstar.

I'm going to dive into the tragic world of those broken stars, looking for the NBA players and teams that left us asking "What if?" I want to find the franchises whose fates were forever altered by one star player's absence, and reconstruct what could have happened if that player had been allowed to progress through the trajectory of a normal career. These are the all-time stories of what might have been but wasn't.

To pin down the best examples of teams whose hopes were dashed by a key injury, though, a few calculations were required.

How the numbers got crunched

First, I needed a way to determine a player's value for seasons going back to the 1960s. (Specifically, I began my data set in 1963, the earliest year we know how many minutes each player spent with each team, each season.) I combined two advanced metrics available historically at Basketball-Reference.com: Win Shares (WS) and Player Efficiency Rating (PER). Each has its own pros and cons—WS values efficiency highly and does a good job of capturing a player's defensive value, but doesn't quite know what to do with big-time scorers; PER does the opposite, giving plenty of credit to those scorers but shortchanging defenders and efficient shooters. So I've created a new measure that does a pretty good job of covering the flaws of WS and PER, and it can give us a sense of how important every player was to his team. I'm calling this metric Adjusted Wins, or AW, though you can think of it as a yelp of pain emanating from either the player or the player's fan base—"AW!"

Using Adjusted Wins, we also have to estimate each player's potential—and how far short of it our injured stars ended up falling. To do that, I ran a series of regressions predicting how much value a player had left in his career by age, based on how many AW he'd racked up in his career to date.

For instance, after Shaquille O'Neal recorded 8.7 AW for the Orlando Magic in the 1995–96 season, we'd have expected a player like him—with 55.8 career AW already by age twenty-three—to record about 156 more AW before retiring. Lo and behold, O'Neal produced (you guessed it) exactly 156 AW from 1996–97 through the end of his career in 2011. I swear I did not know the prediction would be perfect for Shaq, but I have to admit I used Shaq to illustrate my point for the very reason that the prediction was perfect.

That said, most predictions don't go anywhere near as well—in fact, this whole chapter is about cases where the predictions were wildly optimistic compared with reality—but this approach can give us a reasonable expectation for a player's career (and any subgroup of seasons within) if it followed the typical pattern of improvement and decline with age.

I also wanted to determine whether a team's fate was directly tied to a player's over- or (in this case) under-performance. To that end, I also ran a separate regression predicting how many games a team would win over the following five seasons, based on its track record over the previous two seasons and the average age of its roster (weighted by how many AW each player recorded). As we'll see in our honorable mentions, through great management and some good luck elsewhere, some teams were able to cover for the loss of a star player well enough to actually exceed expectations over the next handful of seasons. Those cases are rare, however. Most injuries to a promising talent ended up exacting a devastating cost on a franchise.

With all of those statistical tools in hand, we can compute the players (since 1963) who fell short of their Adjusted Wins projection the most due to injury (they had to miss at least half of scheduled team games) while also playing for a team that undershot expectations. My primary research focused on disappointment over a five-year period, since that's roughly as long as each team's current window of success/failure tends to last before the franchise heads in a different direction—and it also gives us enough of a sample to measure a few very recent, very notable cases of franchise-damaging injuries.

With all of that methodology out of the way, let's get to the players, the injuries that befell them, and the consequences for their teams.

Honorable mentions

Ironically, the injured player who sparked this entire conversation didn't make it onto the top ten list. Bernard King spent five seasons bouncing between the New Jersey Nets, Utah Jazz, and Golden State Warriors before seeming to find a home in New York as the Knicks' most dynamic scorer since the days of Richie Guerin and Willie Naulls. But at the tail end of a league-leading 32.9-PPG season in 1984–85, King suffered a terrible leg injury, and the Knicks wouldn't return to the playoffs for four seasons. So why isn't King higher on our list of franchise-altering injuries? He was too good afterward. King worked his way back and ended up producing a handful of solid seasons for the Washington Bullets late in his career. That meant other players on the list undershot their expected future value far more than King did, despite the heartbreak his absence caused New York hoop fans.

And remember when I mentioned that teams could potentially overcome bad injuries to stars with shrewd decisions and a little luck? That was the case with the Houston Rockets in the mid-to-late 2000s. A core of Tracy McGrady and Yao Ming had GM Daryl Morey dreaming of championships, but neither was able to stay healthy enough to fulfill their immense promise. Combined, Yao and T-Mac fell 81 AW shy of expected from the 2009–10 season onward, an enormous deficit that would destroy most teams. But Houston weathered the twin losses too well to end up on our list: Over the following five seasons, it ended up winning *more* games than we'd expect based on its track record and average age. Who knows how high the Rockets would have soared had their star duo stayed healthy, but it's also a little inaccurate to consider McGrady's and Yao's absences franchise crippling. (OK, so trading for James Harden several seasons later also helps.)

Speaking of teams who won games after losing promising talent... It's difficult to remember now, but back when Steve Kerr was running the Suns and Steph Curry was still a student at Davidson, much of the Golden State Warriors' future prospects still seemed tied up in the development of big man Andris Biedrins. Only fourteen players in NBA *history* had generated more AW through age twenty-one than Biedrins did, and he figured to have plenty more left to contribute after the Dubs gave him a six-year, $63 million contract in the summer of 2008. But after one more decent season, Biedrins was frequently injured and mostly terrible when he did play—he ended up falling nearly 100 AW (!) short of what might have been projected for his career after his best seasons. The Warriors' saving grace, however, was that Curry, Draymond Green, Klay Thompson, and company were on their way, and Golden State would survive Biedrins's flop so well that his injury is about as bemoaned by Warriors fans as the failure of the Articles of Confederation are lamented by American history scholars.

One player who would absolutely qualify if we consider his absence "injury related" is Magic Johnson. Johnson had already built a Hall of Fame career several times over by the 1991 off-season, when he made history of a different sort: He announced that he had HIV and retired from basketball. As a result, Johnson produced 27 fewer AW than expected over the following five seasons, and 38 fewer over the rest of his career. (The Lakers also fell into one of the rare down stretches in their history afterward, albeit briefly.) But because his ailment was an illness, not an injury sustained on the court, it doesn't feel *quite* the same to include Johnson's absence with the ailments suffered by the other players on this list.

Finally, I would be remiss if I didn't mention that my method can't include players like Greg Oden, Jay Williams, or even (to a lesser extent) Ralph Sampson, all of whom were drafted very highly but never actually played well enough—or just enough, *period*—in the NBA to project for a strong career based on their pro stats. (Yes, Sampson is a Hall of Famer, but his NBA numbers were average at best.) Nor can it pick up on the potential of someone like Len Bias, who never played in the NBA at all after dying of an overdose days after the 1986 draft. Perhaps a future iteration of this method can develop projections for those kinds of players as well, taking into account where they were drafted.

Now, on to the NBA's top ten most damaging injuries over a five-year period:

Willis Reed, 1971 Knicks

Expected 5-year AW: 27.0
Actual 5-year AW: 8.0 (–19.0)

Reed is best known by basketball fans for hobbling onto the court before Game 7 of the 1970 NBA Finals and inspiring the New York Knicks to win the franchise's first championship. Reed's career, however, should be defined by so much more than that one iconic moment: He was a regular-season MVP (1969–70), one of the most dominant rebounders in history, and the fourth-best player in the entire league over his first seven seasons according to AW (trailing only Wilt Chamberlain, Oscar Robertson, and Jerry West). But during the 1971–72 season, right in the middle of his prime, Reed developed knee tendonitis and was limited to eleven games. And although he played a role on the Knicks' 1972–73 championship squad, Reed was never really the same player from '72 onward, ultimately retiring in 1974. The Knicks were out of the playoffs within two seasons, and they wouldn't post another fifty-win season for nearly a decade. Reed's career was shaping up to be one of the best of any big man ever until he got injured, and although he was a Hall of Famer regardless, his premature departure played a huge role in New York's sharp decline as the 1970s dragged on.

Bill Walton, 1978 Blazers

Expected 5-year AW: 25.8
Actual 5-year AW: 3.5 (–22.3)

Few big men had a more diverse skill set than Walton, who could dominate games with his scoring, passing, rebounding, and defense. Walton had difficulty staying healthy early in his career—he played just eighty-six games in his first two NBA seasons—but when he took the court, his numbers could go toe-to-toe with those of the league's best. Which is saying something, since one of Walton's many foot ailments included a condition known as "interdigital neuroma."

But when healthy, particularly in the 1976–77 season, Walton was dominant, enjoying his best season by AW and leading the Cinderella Portland Trail Blazers to an NBA championship. Portland was looking even scarier in '78, but Walton injured his foot (interdigital neuroma) during the regular season and fractured it while attempting to play through the injury in the playoffs. Walton won league MVP that year, but it was the last truly great season of his career. Instead of producing 43 more career AW from 1978 onward, the injury-plagued Walton generated only 16, and the Blazers won twenty-five fewer games than expected over the following five seasons as their championship core was destroyed. It would be a decade before they'd muster another deep playoff run.

David Thompson, 1983 Sonics

Expected 5-year AW: 24.1
Actual 5-year AW: 1.1 (–23.0)

Thompson's career is one of the NBA's all-time what-if stories. He had a stellar college career at NC State, went No. 1 overall in both the 1975 NBA *and* ABA drafts, chose the latter (joining the Denver

Nuggets), and produced two tremendous seasons before the leagues merged. Then he was even better as an NBA rookie in 1977–78, averaging 27.2 PPG and generating 12.6 AW, third-most in the league. At this point, the twenty-three-year-old Thompson was on track for 137 lifetime AW—roughly as many as Scottie Pippen and Clyde Drexler had in their Hall of Fame careers. But after another solid season in '79, Thompson started losing his battles against injuries and addiction. He doesn't show up on this list as a Nugget—Denver managed to emerge from the Thompson era relatively unscathed thanks to Alex English, Dan Issel, Fat Lever, and company—but he still had some residual potential left as a twenty-eight-year-old after a good 1982–83 season with the Seattle SuperSonics. Instead of building on that for a second act to his career, however, Thompson was in and out of drug rehab and suffered a career-ending injury the following year, falling down a set of stairs while partying at Studio 54. He finished his career a whopping seventy-four wins shy of his peak AW projection, one of the biggest shortfalls in history.

Marques Johnson, 1986 Clippers

Expected 5-year AW: 25.0
Actual 5-year AW: 0.1 (–24.9)

A mega-talented six-foot-seven wing who could create for himself and his teammates, Marques Johnson was an early prototype for subsequent stars like Scottie Pippen and Grant Hill. The 73 AW he put up through his first seven NBA seasons represents one of the best starts to a career in league history, roughly equal to what Kevin Garnett, Steph Curry, and Rick Barry produced in their first seven years. Suffice it to say, by the time he turned twenty-eight in 1984, Johnson was easily on pace for a Hall of Fame career. But after Johnson was traded to his hometown Clippers later that year, his performance began to slip a bit, and then he severely injured his neck early in his third season with LA. The ruptured disc he suffered required surgery, and it effectively ended Johnson's career as an NBA player. The Clippers were not going to win, or even compete for championships, with Johnson, but they *completely* fell apart without him, going from a merely bad team to what was at the time the team with the second-worst record in NBA history.

Brad Daugherty, 1994 Cavaliers

Expected 5-year AW: 25.6
Actual 5-year AW: 0.0 (–25.6)

Perhaps because the No. 1 picks in the two years preceding him were Hakeem Olajuwon and Patrick Ewing, and the No. 1 pick in 1987 was David Robinson, Daugherty, the top pick in 1986, would go down as one of the most underrated players ever. In truth he steadily built a career as an All-Star pivot for the Cavs alongside point guard Mark Price in the late 1980s and early 1990s. Daugherty averaged 20 points and 10 rebounds per game for the three seasons from 1990–91 to 1992–93, ranking as the league's sixth-best big man by AW over that span (trailing only Robinson, Karl Malone, Charles Barkley, Olajuwon, and Ewing—all of whom are Hall of Famers). He also seemed to be hitting his stride in 1993 after producing a career-best 12.6 AW as a twenty-seven-year-old, but a herniated lumbar disc suffered midway through the '93–'94 campaign stopped Daugherty's career in its tracks. After logging fifty games for the '94 Cavs, Daugherty would never play in the NBA again, one of the most abrupt endings to a promising career in league history. Without his services in the second half of the '90s and beyond, Cleveland drifted progressively closer to the bottom of the league before bottoming out and drafting LeBron James in 2003.

Brandon Roy, 2010 Blazers

Expected 5-year AW: 30.0
Actual 5-year AW: 2.0 (–28.0)

If I were to tell you, in the first years of this decade, that a team from the West Coast would rise to take the NBA by storm behind the stellar play of a future Hall of Fame guard, it wouldn't have been incredibly surprising.

That it would be the Golden State Warriors, with Steph Curry, and not the Portland Trail Blazers under Brandon Roy? Maybe *that* was the shocking development. As a twenty-four-year-old in 2008–09, Roy had as many AW as defending MVP Kobe Bryant, and he was on the verge of challenging Dwyane Wade to be Bryant's successor as the league's best two-guard. But a year later, Roy was sidelined with a late-season knee injury and missed most of the playoffs. It was the beginning of the end: Over the next three seasons, Roy managed to play only fifty-two total games, with both of his knees deteriorating badly due to cartilage damage. After suiting up five times in a comeback attempt with the Minnesota Timberwolves in 2012–13, Roy officially retired from basketball. Instead of generating 86 career AW like our algorithm would have predicted at his peak (think Michael Finley or Glen Rice), Roy retired with only 37, and the Blazers have struggled to make a consistent playoff dent ever since.

Clark Kellogg, 1985 Pacers

Expected 5-year AW: 32.6
Actual 5-year AW: 1.3 (–31.3)

Most fans today know Clark Kellogg as an announcer for CBS's NCAA tournament coverage, but his career as a player deserves more attention. After going to the Indiana Pacers with the eighth pick in the 1982 draft, Kellogg immediately averaged 20.1 points and 10.6 rebounds per game as a rookie, and he generated more AW than all but two players aged twenty-three or younger during his first three NBA seasons. With the league's second-youngest roster and a rising star on their hands in Kellogg, the Pacers appeared ready to finally build in the NBA the kind of success they'd enjoyed in the ABA a decade earlier. But Kellogg's knees didn't cooperate with that plan—from 1985–86 onward, they allowed him to play only twenty-three total NBA games before he had to retire at the age of twenty-six. Instead of having a career like James Worthy, Kellogg fell short of expectations by sixty-two wins, and the Pacers' return to glory would have to wait several years for another savior, in the form of Reggie Miller. (Who also announces games nowadays. But less well.)

Gilbert Arenas, 2007 Wizards

Expected 5-year AW: 40.1
Actual 5-year AW: 4.3 (–35.8)

Gilbert Arenas still ranks as one of the most eccentric stars in NBA history—but in his prime, he was also one of the most dynamic. Despite going in the second round of the 2001 draft, Arenas quickly grabbed the starting point guard job as a rookie in Golden State, then officially announced his full-fledged stardom after signing with the Washington Wizards two years later. Between the 2004–05 and 2006–07 seasons, the last of which came when he was still just twenty-five years old, Arenas scored 27.7 points per game and produced the ninth-most AW of any player in the NBA, leading the Wizards to the playoffs in back-to-back seasons for the first time since the late 1980s. But during a game in April 2007 against the playoff-eliminated Charlotte Bobcats, Gerald Wallace rolled onto Arenas's knee, tearing his medial collateral ligament and keeping him out of the playoffs—and most of the following season as well. When he returned, Arenas was a shell of the player he'd been, though he was being paid one of the highest salaries in the league. Throw in a firearms scandal, and Arenas's days in the NBA were numbered. He retired in 2012 after a few failed comeback attempts, having produced sixty-five fewer wins than projected at his peak, and the Wizards spent the half decade after his injury out of the playoffs.

Derrick Rose, 2012 Bulls

Expected 5-year AW: 47.9
Actual 5-year AW: 5.8 (–42.0)

Derrick Rose was still a vaguely functional NBA player as of the 2016–17 season, so it's a little off to write about his game in the past tense. But even though he's still just twenty-nine years old, the Rose of today is light-years away from the pre-injury version that ascended to MVP status with the Chicago Bulls in the early 2010s. That Rose was one of the most productive young players in history—so much so that the league instituted a new contract–extension policy (often eponymously attached to Rose) rewarding players who performed at an incredibly high level during their rookie deals. According to AW, he was on pace for a career like those of Steve Nash or Dominique Wilkins, until disaster struck—a torn ACL for Rose in the Bulls' 2012 playoff debut. That sent Rose into a multiyear downward spiral of missed games, additional injuries, and poor play when he did eventually see the court. Rose's story isn't finished yet, but his chapter with the Bulls closed with Chicago winning far fewer games than we'd have expected before his first injury changed the franchise's trajectory.

Andrew Bynum, 2012 Lakers

Expected 5-year AW: 43.4
Actual 5-year AW: 0.6 (−42.7)

Throughout almost all of their history, the Lakers have been able to transition from the leadership of one Hall of Famer to the next with hardly any interruption: George Mikan preceded Elgin Baylor, who was later joined by Jerry West and Wilt Chamberlain, who in turn handed the reins to Kareem Abdul-Jabbar and then Magic Johnson, to be followed by Shaquille O'Neal and then Kobe Bryant and Pau Gasol. But when Bryant retired in 2016, there wasn't any obvious Hall of Fame talent to whom the baton could be passed—and Andrew Bynum's injury had a lot to do with that. Although Bynum was never the sturdiest player, he still managed to produce 40.6 AW through the age of twenty-four, a pace that our algorithm suggests carried the future potential of a Bob Lanier or Walt Bellamy (Hall of Famers, both). But Bynum's chronic knee troubles had the Lakers shipping him to the Philadelphia 76ers in the summer of 2012, after which time he played a grand total of only twenty-six NBA games. In an alternate universe where Bynum stayed healthy, it's unclear his presence alone would have been enough to reverse the Lakers' poor record since 2013–14—but LA never got the chance to find out. Their chain of Hall of Fame talent, which stretched back to the 1940s, finally had been broken by his injury woes.

This is, of course, far from the final word on franchise-altering NBA injuries. Beyond any set of numbers, a combination of fandom and nostalgia fuel our perceptions of how devastating the loss of a player was. But the metrics can also be illuminating. One fan's anger-inducing bust is another fan's heartbreaking crushed dream—the stats can find a middle ground. And maybe, for a certain type of fan, putting a number on "What if?" can help ease the pain of the question.

20

What If the Dodgers Had Left Brooklyn?

Robert Siegel

Wait. The Dodgers did *leave Brooklyn. The tears have not yet dried. Aha. This is a what-if of a what-if. It is written from a land and time when the Dodgers never left the borough of their birth, when Walter O'Malley remained as beloved a Brooklyn civic figure as egg creams, and where Dodger fans weren't known for leaving early to beat traffic, because the subway runs pretty regular.*
—Ed.

In the winter of '56, the City of Brooklyn (which was still something less than a city) stank with rumor and the fear of abandonment. It was just over a year since the Dodgers had won their first World Series, and already there was talk of the owner, Walter O'Malley, skipping out on the County of Kings and taking the ball club west to Los Angeles. It wasn't as if the Bums lacked for fan support. They had just finished yet another pennant-winning season and yet another seven-game World Series against the Yankees. OK, the '56 series is remembered for just one thing: Don Larsen's perfect game of which our Dodgers were the notorious hitless victims. Does anyone remember Game 2 of that series? Brooklyn won it 13–8, chasing the not-yet-immortal Larsen from the mound in the second inning. Duke Snider, Jackie Robinson, and Gil Hodges had combined for seven hits. OK, you couldn't call our team

World Champions again, but you couldn't call them anything less than a fine ball club, either.

When it came to putting butts in the ballpark, what was O'Malley complaining about? Attendance at Ebbets Field was second in the league and second only to Milwaukee, where a major league baseball team was still a novelty, the Braves having only arrived from Boston in '53. Hell, the Braves were such a big deal there, they were outdrawing the Yankees in those days. What else was there to do in Milwaukee, anyway? A city made famous by a beer? In Brooklyn it was the other way around; Walter O'Malley, after parting ways with the Methodist teetotaler Branch Rickey, accepted Schaefer beer advertising. That's right, Milwaukee: In Brooklyn we make the beer famous.

But in '56, that ugly whiff of rumor had the scent of betrayal about it. Could O'Malley really pack it in for California, when the Dodgers were playing the best baseball in their history, just because the city wouldn't build him a stadium with more parking? Would the National League really permit a rupture between the team that had fielded Jackie Robinson, arguably the only serious and positive thing the national pastime had ever accomplished, and the city that had welcomed modern Major League Baseball's first black player? Note: They did so in an era when the Dodgers' pinstriped rivals of so many subway series had flinched at signing the only true Bronx Bomber because Hank Greenberg, who had lived in the Bronx from age seven, might have been a little too Jewish for their posh clientele.

We Brooklynites have spent decades wondering, what if? What if O'Malley couldn't see reason? What if Robert Moses had not been made to concur with O'Malley's assessment that Ebbets Field was a rotting hulk? What if O'Malley & Co. had seen in their late fifties rosters only the ages of Snider, Robinson, and Reese, and failed to notice that youngsters Sandy Koufax and Don Drysdale had Hall of Fame stuff in the making?

In short, what if the Dodgers had actually left Brooklyn?

What if Robinson Stadium, a fitting ballpark for a majority-minority city, at Flatbush and Atlantic Avenues, right where O'Malley asked for it, had never been built (with a big financial boost from Jackie's political mentor, Governor Nelson Rockefeller)? What if the revival of construction, commerce, and culture in downtown Brooklyn had not taken off in the early 1960s? Would the still robust *Brooklyn Daily Eagle* have folded abjectly like all those old New York dailies across the river? Would Schaefer Beer have been gulped up by some out-of-town brewer and gone the way of Knickerbocker and Ballantine?

Would that hypothetical monstrosity, the "Los Angeles Dodgers" (what do Angelenos dodge, paparazzi?) have won six World Series in twelve appearances over the past fifty years the way the real Dodgers have? OK, the fictive LA bums couldn't have been any worse than the real-life Brooklyn Dodgers of the 1970s (when no one could beat Cincinnati, anyway). And what about the Mets? Would the National League have expanded into Queens with no NL rival next door? Could baseball have survived without the return of the subway series that became so common in the 1990s?

Would Brooklyn have fallen on permanent hard times, a place with its soul carved out of it and shipped someplace west, a place waiting for its real estate values to fall so low its prosperity would return only after the place was zeroed out, flattened, and gentrified like New York's Lower East Side and its nostalgically named "financial district"?

There are serious people, with serious academic credentials, who say that Brooklyn's brilliance in the late sixties and seventies, its coming-of-age as the East Coast's boom town, was kindled in October 1963, the great subway series in which the Bums swept the Yankees. Two wins for Sandy Koufax, pride of Brooklyn's own Lafayette High School. Six hits in just four games for outfielder Tommy Davis, pride of Brooklyn's Boys High. The serious people are seriously right: That moment of triumph (even if it wasn't followed by that many great seasons) gave Brooklyn the confidence to reclaim its municipal manhood.

While it's always hard to imagine history as it might have been, I'm convinced that if Brooklyn had limped through the sixties Dodger-less instead of prospering as it did, we would never have had the guts to dissolve the artifice that was the five-borough amalgamated City of New York—born January 1, 1898, deceased January 1, 1970—and become the country's fourth largest city, a metropolis in its own right just as it had been before financial realities had compelled consolidation seventy-two years before.

That New Year's Eve at the stroke of midnight, Brooklyn Borough Hall was restored to its past rank, City Hall. Down came the flag of New York City (a cartoonish tricolor with an Indian and a Dutchman—colonial swindler and his native mark—flanking a windmill) and up went the flag of Brooklyn (a young robed woman against a field of blue, the motto, translated from the Dutch: "Unity Makes Strength"). Playwright Arthur Miller read a tribute to the diversity of the Brooklyn of his youth. The fact that he shared an ex-wife, Marilyn Monroe, with Joe DiMaggio might have intensified his patriotism for the place, who knows? Brooklyn native Neil Sedaka made the crowd gathered on the steps of Borough/City Hall howl and shriek with a refashioned lyric to his most famous song. That night, it was "Breaking Up Is Great to Do."

At the very moment of Brooklyn's independence, John Lindsay was sworn in across the river to a second term as mayor of What Was Left of New York City and proceeded to bankrupt it. O'Malley was sworn in on our side and was regarded as the best mayor modern Brooklyn had until Koufax. At least he avoided running up deficits, taking on too much of the debt of the defunct consolidated city. Had we remained part of the City of New York, we would have shared in New York's financial crisis of the 1970s instead of thriving at bankrupt Gotham's expense as we did. Who knows, they might have built the World Trade Center in Manhattan instead of on our side of the East River.

How close had the Dodgers come to leaving? Turns out, back in '56 O'Malley was really intrigued by the prospect of going west. He and Phil Wrigley, of chewing gum and Cubs ownership fame, were close to swapping minor-league franchises, Brooklyn's Fort Worth club for Chicago's Los Angeles Angels of the Pacific Coast League. The deal would been the natural precursor to a move of the Dodgers, but Wrigley, also stuck in an antique ballpark and with attendance running next to last in the league, was mesmerized by O'Malley's view of a new future for baseball: sunshine and parking lots, stands full of new arrivals who missed the major-league games they grew up seeing someplace else. So infectious was O'Malley's imagery of California stadiums packed with eager (and, let's face it, white) fans that he converted the one man he needed *not* to believe him. Phil Wrigley pulled the plug on that potentially lethal minor-league swap. Brooklyn stayed put. The National League, unwilling to schedule for just one West Coast team, found Wrigley a fitting partner for the New York Giants, who eagerly moved to San Francisco.

It took baseball's pooh-bahs fifteen years to compensate the Second City with another National League franchise. Hence, the Chicago Wind—the source of one furious, successful pennant chase with Brooklyn in '75, many more indifferent seasons of flavorless, directionless baseball, and enough flatulence jokes to keep fifth-grade boys in Chicago giggling to this day. As for the Cubbies—who needs the reminder?—when the true heirs to the long hapless Cubbies finally won their World Series, it was as the National League champion Los Angeles Angels. And that's why the noted LA civic booster Ernie Banks said a thank-you to Chicago when he threw out the first pitch.

Me? I said: Thank you, Brooklyn.

21

What If a Blimp Full of Money Had Exploded over World Track Headquarters in 1952?

Paul Snyder

Before we get into it, I'm going to have to ask you to gather up your disbelief and wad it all up like you would if you had some trash you wanted to litter in a really showy way. Now take that balled-up disbelief and carve out any lingering shreds of it using a serving spoon like you might the goo from inside a jack-o'-lantern. OK, then toss it all into a grocery bag you might otherwise repurpose for scooping dog poop, and suspend that disbelief from a doorknob or whatever jutting object is available for suspensory purposes.

Now imagine, if you will, we are in the waning days of the year 1952.

Far too many things are happening globally to list here for complete immersive context, so we'll just touch upon a few happenings from the sporting world, because that's doable. And more relevant.

Baseball, in particular New York City baseball, is king as the Yankees defeat the still-Brooklyn Dodgers to win the World Series. Rocky Marciano is beginning his four-year undefeated streak, having no clue a young Sylvester Stallone is watching. College football's still bigger than the NFL, because television has yet to indoctrinate large swaths of the country into pro football fandom. The Lakers have a geographically sensible nickname and win an NBA title while playing in Minneapolis. And at the college ranks, the National Invitation Tournament still draws top teams, having not yet fallen to consolation status.

The average salary expenditure for an *entire NBA team* is under $80,000. Put down your calculator, because that works out to under $7,000 per player on a twelve-man roster, and closer to $5,000 if a team's carrying fifteen guys around. For some added perspective, U.S. census data from 1952 pins the average family's annual income right at $3,900. NBA players were still wealthy, but not the kind of incomprehensibly wealthy as is the case today.

It feels like a different era in 1952, largely because the economics of sports haven't quite met late capitalism. Big Money hasn't arrived on the scene—just checking to make sure your disbelief is still healthily suspended, because if it's not, please, suspend it now—but Big Money is on its way.

That's right: Having not learned our lesson fifteen years earlier, an enormous *Hindenburg*-esque airship has departed from the Bureau of Engraving and Printing in Washington, DC.

At the behest of lame-duck president Harry S. Truman (desperately seeking to rectify his tainted legacy and 22 percent end-of-term approval rating), $50 million in freshly pressed bills has been loaded aboard our aluminum airship, its pilot given concise directions to "take this bread straight to Basketball Headquarters in New York, New York!"

Basketball HQ is located smack dab in the middle of Times Square (where else would such an operation be housed?). The peep shows and low-grade smack dealers that will come to populate the Crossroads of the World are out of sight, lurking in shadowy alleys elsewhere; instead, the place teems with commerce.

And on the day of the cash-loaded airship's expected arrival, all eyes are to the sky. The president of basketball, J. P. Sportsfellow, stands atop the roof of Basketball HQ, staring expectantly at its mooring mast (installed just for this moment), alongside eager members of the press, waiting for the delivery. Sportsfellow grumbles something about socialism as he checks his watch.

Like any good airshipman, our pilot has a flair for the dramatic, and plots his course to include lavish, swooping circles around Philadelphia, the rough halfway point of his journey. Incited by the gathering crowds below him, the pilot continually lowers his altitude, until his left hand is visible from the ground, waving to the masses. It's a spectacular display of showmanship, until hubris rears its humbling head.

The blimp of cash snags itself on the cap of the William Penn statue atop Philadelphia's City Hall, and hydrogen begins whooshing out of the tear. It's not an immediate crash. Instead the mighty airship slowly descends, bills fluttering in its airy wake, until it plops into the Schuylkill River, and is submerged by the filthy flowing water. Some onlookers feign horror, but mostly they just scramble for the cash.

News reaches New York City by telegraph and radio. Soon newsmen who have raced up the just-finished New Jersey Turnpike deliver their canisters of film footage to all the big networks—CBS, NBC, and DuMont. Sportsfellow tone-deaf-ly decries this as the greatest disaster of Truman's presidency, and demands the NYPD send a battalion of its finest sleuths to track down the airship's contents.

But it's far too late. For the unscrupulous representatives of a far less prestigious sport have already dredged the river clean of all the money intended for Big Basketball: I'm talking of course about the shameless executives of the struggling Track & Field Corporation, who scuttle out of their subterranean office space, secretly hidden beneath the University of Pennsylvania's Franklin Field.

No press release is ever issued by T&F Corp, for obvious reasons, but word travels fast of the sport's newfound liquidity, especially around Philadelphia. The vague concept of amateurism goes out the window as we find ourselves in the Gilded Age of track.

Enter a spindly kid from the west side of town who is making a name for himself as a youth athletic phenom. Eventually that name will be Wilt the Stilt, but for now, he's just plain old Wilton Norman Chamberlain. Despite being nearly seven feet tall as a high school freshman, he dislikes basketball. (In *Wilt: Larger Than Life* by Robert Cherry, Chamberlain is quoted as calling it a "sport for sissies.") But Wilt loved track.

On the time line that actually manifested, by the time he gave up the sport to hone his chops in hoops, Chamberlain—per a 1955 Don Pierce article in the *Sporting News*—"high jumped 6 feet, 6 inches, ran the 440 in 49.0 seconds and the 880 in 1:58.3, put the shot 53 feet, 4 inches, broad jumped 22 feet," and was predicted by the University of Kansas track coach, Bill Easton, to clear over 7 feet in the high jump, if he chose to focus on it. For reference, the world record for that event in 1952 was 6 feet, 11⅛ inches, set by Lester Steers.

Well, on our current, blimp-aided trajectory, track and field is lousy with cash. There's suddenly greater financial incentive for Wilt to stick to track than there is for him to go all-in on a sport that, at this point, he doesn't even like.

And that changes everything.

From a strictly athletic performance standpoint, there's plenty of reason to be excited about Wilt's singular commitment to the sport. He was a once-in-a-generation athletic specimen, physically massive, but graceful; powerful, but gifted with incredible finesse. Basically, no matter what athletic pursuit Chamberlain had placed all his chips on, he was bound for greatness.

The modern high-jumping technique most commonly employed (the "Fosbury Flop") won't come into prominence until the 1960s, but Chamberlain will tighten up his own crappy form in his own unique way, being the innovative athlete he is, thanks to seven-days-a-week training. Now comical-looking 1950s plyometric exercises improve his vertical explosiveness at the cost of his overall strength and lateral quickness, which he no longer really needs. And through sheer repetition, he figures out the best method for clearing the bar that his gargantuan frame allows. With his form refined, improvements come fast, leading to serious discussion among high-jumping pundits (they are numerous and now highly paid) that he just might break a major milestone: the seven-foot barrier.

His fixation on stats and numbers may have occasionally hindered his basketball career and interpersonal relationships, but in high jump, individual numbers are all that matter. (Show me a man whose neuroticisms and ravenous libido drive him to keep a journal meticulously tallying his sexual conquests, and I'll show you a man whose obsessive tendencies can be effectively channeled toward accomplishing a feat rooted in numbers.) As soon as the notion of clearing seven feet buries itself into his brain, it takes root, and he becomes downright pathological in his pursuit of it.

Nearly every athlete who's held the world record in the event has stood between six foot three and six foot six. An argument could be made that that's the ideal stature for high jumping. But another high-profile athlete comes to mind who defies preconceived notions of what a particular event's platonic competitor should look like: Usain Bolt, who at six foot five towers over nearly every athlete on every starting line he's ever toed. Chamberlain and Bolt have in common uncommon physicalities that may hinder lesser athletes' explosiveness, but in their instances enhance it.

Driven by his fanatical desire to achieve something no man has before, his truly special corporeal form and now world-class mechanics buoy him to uncharted heights, giving track's ballooning fan base something to cheer about.

He makes track cool. And why shouldn't he? The physically huge man routinely wears a fur coat to meets, which he sheds dramatically just moments before he jumps. His sex-having tendencies and insomniac late-night exploits lend some erotic credibility to a sport previously lacking any. And the public goes wild over the iconic photo of him holding up a crude hand-drawn sign depicting the number seven following his historic shattering of the seven-foot mark. Rumors persist for years about who came to own the high bar that Wilt eventually cleared to set the record.

But what ultimately ensures track's continued commercial viability once the blimp money runs dry is the rivalry between Chamberlain and Bill Russell, who shocked and jilted the basketball world with his 1961 retirement. Following his Celtics' demolition of the Lakers in five games to secure yet another NBA title, the media-shy Russell grabbed the nearest *Boston Globe* reporter, bent down, and muttered in his ear: "I'm going after Wilt."

And thus, one of the greatest head-to-head rivalries in sports history rages on within our alternate reality, albeit in a different athletic realm.

As a collegiate high jumper at the University of San Francisco, Russell cleared 6 feet 9¼ inches, which was not only superior to Chamberlain's best as a Jayhawk, but was also the seventh-highest clearance in the world in 1956. Plus, Russell's stature (six foot nine) more closely resembles that of a traditionally great high-jump specialist. And even today in this alternate world, Russell is known for his sheer ability to win, which he manages to do on occasion over the bar against Chamberlain.

The spring-loaded giants make the rounds of the American track circuit, drawing crowds wherever they duel.

Though perhaps the more inherently skilled jumper of the two, Russell's late return to the event, as well as the two additional years he has on Chamberlain, work against him. But the sport and its fans are still treated to some supremely entertaining showdowns.

Who can forget the poorly named "How-High-Go in Chicago?" The two men put on an exhibition before a sold-out Soldier Field in late April 1962. It was unseasonably cold, and a mid-spring snowstorm reduced the bleachers' human contents to one undifferentiated mass of quivering, shapeless parka. Nonetheless, the new titans of track and field continued to raise the bar to a shade above seven feet, both jumping in full gray sweatsuits and track-spike-modified Chuck Taylors. No winner was declared, as they matched each other clearance for clearance, until the wind picked up to the point of knocking off the bar, forcing the match to be called in a draw. Piss-drunk, aging Chicagoans still reminisce about the battle, and pick sides as vehemently as they would in a Sox-Cubs argument.

Chamberlain bested Russell in the majority of their head-to-head battles, but it's clear Russell was at his best when duking it out with his rival. On the field (Track? Runway? Track may be popular in our dirigible-inflected reality, but it still lacks the catchy, shorthand vernacular of other sports) the two are bitter rivals with a clear respect for each other. But off the track they are extremely friendly, despite their vastly different public personas.

Philadelphia's showier son is just the right brand of flashy-with-a-touch-of-contemporary-conservatism to be palatable to mainstream white audiences. But for the average white American, Bill Russell's presence at the table of many a civil rights discussion is too much. Russell no longer benefits from having teammates like Bob Cousy, white athletes outwardly opposed to racism, but who racist sports fans can inherently accept. As such, Russell plays the villainous foil to Chamberlain's all-American, bravado-laden brand of heroism.

(Of everything predicted in this chapter, this is likely the least speculative, as evinced by the backlash against Colin Kaepernick's kneeling during the National Anthem. There has been, and sadly will be for the foreseeable future, a considerable swath of American couch dwellers who cry foul over an athlete taking a public stand to suggest maybe America isn't perfect.)

Russell does well for himself financially, but as endorsement deals creep into the equation, Chamberlain is the preferred superstar, given the public perception that he is the less socially agitated of the high-leaping giants. Indeed, Chamberlain becomes a very wealthy man over the course of a decorated career, as he establishes a lifetime best and new world record of 7 feet, 6½ inches after forgoing college entirely. His record stands until the mid-1960s, and while actively jumping, he secures a bronze medal in Helsinki and consecutive golds in Melbourne and Rome.

Would-be stars in other sports take note and follow the money, the glitz, and the glam over to the track. Participation numbers in track swell across the nation and drop in all other sports, as an activity with no real barriers to entry slowly assumes its place atop the national sports popularity hierarchy.

Chamberlain walks away from high jumping after his second gold medal in 1964 to focus on bolstering his statistics in other, more worldly pursuits, but leaves track in a good place and at a good time.

With the Vietnam War bubbling into ill-conceived existence, and the civil rights movement becoming unignorable to white America, Chamberlain's Nixon-apologizing, Republican-leaning public persona gives way to a new cadre of track and field superstars.

Not every talented athlete of the early 1960s is syphoned off by track, of course, but as the potential for fame and fortune increases in its sphere, several prominent football figures take notice, and you have guys like

O. J. Simpson (in real life a member of a one-time world-record-setting 4×110 relay) and Bob Hayes (in real life a double gold medalist at the 1964 Tokyo Olympics) gravitating toward the oval. Glenn Davis never enters the NFL Draft and never joins the Detroit Lions; instead he continues dominating the 400-meter hurdles and wins a third individual gold medal in the event at Tokyo (in real life he won it in 1956 and 1960). After setting a then–high school national record in the javelin, Terry Bradshaw shies away from the gridiron, while enjoying similar levels of fame and fortune without the nasty side effects of concussions.

Plus, would-be ABA (and to a lesser extent, NBA) stars are drawn to the high jump, given its now culturally mainstream legacy. And from the ashes of the ill-fated basketball league, additional theatrics and (alleged) cocaine use come to track.

Basketball and football bleed way more of their athletically freakish stars than baseball, naturally. And soccer, though still just a gleam in the collective eye of America's scarf-wearing dads, will never pick up any steam at all. Its most promising young stars start training for the marathon, perhaps even booting their old soccer balls into trash cans in a really obvious and symbolic gesture. It all works together to bloat track's talent pool while draining that of all other sports.

And this is where the hypothetical money blimp and its long-term repercussions on the world of track become even more vague, and generally speculative.

In real life (and I suppose in this fake one, too), Jamaica is an island with under three million people living on it. Yet it's notoriously dominant in the short sprints on both the men's and women's sides. That's just what happens when all the potentially great athletes in a population are basically relegated to focusing on one sport. In Jamaica, sprinting is wildly popular, and the culture surrounding it is celebratory to the point of discouraging other sports from ever gaining traction.

We see something similar in the East African nations of Ethiopia and Kenya, where distance running is not just a popular activity, it's a way of life. You run for fun. You run to commute. You run because you're good at it, because you've been running your whole life, and so by the time you compete in an organized race for the first time, you've already amassed thousands of lifetime miles and absolutely smoke the rest of the world's top adolescents, who were reared on *Halo 2* and Bagel Bites.

Well now, in 1960s America, as track's popularity has soared, we are a nation of nearly two hundred million people, where the best athletes eschew ball sports for the national pastimes of these much smaller, track-focused nations.

In all likelihood, every American record gets rewritten at a staggering rate, and the world records and Olympic medals come flying in. But just in terms of numbers and probabilities, the people becoming track's brightest stars aren't the athletes we celebrate in our current reality. It'll be the kids who would have otherwise settled on "the wrong sport" as high school freshmen, driven by pushy parents and ill-conceived notions of what prospective mates find attractive: the girl who was a mediocre volleyball player, who possessed the talent necessary to eventually be the first woman to ever break 29 minutes for the 10,000-meter run, the boy who rode the bench as a JV wide receiver with an undiscovered aptitude for the triple jump, even the kid who burns out after quitting baseball to become a silly high school weed dealer.

The landscape of American sporting heroes starts to look drastically different, with less charming athletic figures forcing themselves into the public consciousness. But some of our most beloved athletes still manage to steal the show. One can imagine Lisa Leslie (high jump) or Allen Iverson (1,500-meter run) defecting to track and still achieving a status as hugely successful stars. Maybe not world beaters or even Olympians, but their elusive combination of charisma and talent still proves captivating.

Over in the other, deeper pages of the sports sections we'd still have tales of athletes like Wayne Gretzky, Mia Hamm, or Serena Williams. Though athletic, their skills do not suit them for the dominant sport, track, so they're stuck excelling in pursuits further down the food chain. This is also the case with basketball's Michael Jordan, who can hang aloft for quite some time, but whose true gifts veer toward the intangible. Competitiveness and clutch performances matter less in a sport where the list of requisite skills per event lies in the single digits.

And because of track's near total reliance on physical gifts, rather than nuanced skills, doping becomes even more of an issue for the sport now that it's the biggest show in town. In real life, it's undeniable that track has had a doping problem for decades. But with the stakes now raised even higher (television deals, endorsements, massive prizes awarded for world records), the incentive to skirt around antidoping protocols becomes too great to ignore. But in our hypothetical, track fans don't seem to mind the dark, seedy, and performance-enhanced undercurrent running through the sport. Fast times are fun to watch, and they make for more exciting television broadcasts and in-person experiences. Eventually, track's governing body shrugs and shortens its list of banned substances to chemical compounds that have been scientifically proven to result in sudden death. (At the end of the day, athletes dropping dead mid-contest from catastrophic and drug-induced heart failure is bad publicity, no matter how captivating the performance was up until that point.)

Doping culture slowly permeates all ranks of track and field, all the way down to the youth level. But as performance-enhancing drugs become a mainstream factor in the sport, the PED manufacturers are held more accountable. Kiddie PEDs that minimally improve red blood cell count and that are ingested orally are reviewed by *Consumer Reports*, and track parents banter at meets about the trials and tribulations of finding the right, safe doping system for their special little track star.

If that last part lost you, think of how many parents in the United States encourage their young kids to play tackle football, well aware of the long-lasting repercussions of concussions. And think of the mental bargain football fans have made with themselves with regard to doping in their sport. There is almost never an outcry or a backlash when an NFL player is suspended for using performance enhancers. Football is culturally pervasive in real life in the way that track becomes culturally pervasive in this scenario.

In this blimp-based reality, we tune in to watch the *Monday Night Meet* instead of *Monday Night Football*. Schoolyard disputes are settled with a footrace instead of a fistfight. Sneakerheads line up around the block to get their hands not on Jordans, but on the latest Asics training shoe, bringing the norm-core movement into the spotlight of style. Suburban driveway basketball hoops are a rarity, and in their place sit massive foam high jump pits. Instead of "striking out" conversationally at the bar on a Friday night, you "drop the baton." Company softball games are eschewed in favor of company relay races. The Boston Marathon overtakes the Super Bowl as the premier hangover-inducing sporting holiday all across the nation. *Chariots of Fire* (not *Rudy*) serves as the default film shown to bored middle school students by their history teachers who happen to also be coaches, on days they don't feel like teaching. Bruce Springsteen's "Glory Days" reminisces over his "friend who was a big shot put thrower / Back in high school / He could toss that steel orb farther / Than twenty-four meters as a rule."

I do have to say, that as a diehard fan of track, I don't think having historically canonized high jump battles between Chamberlain and Russell would be worth the sacrifice. Our current transcendent stars, like Jordan or Williams, have served us well, especially as purveyors of crafts that require a wide variety of athletic abilities as opposed to track, which favors a brand of single-minded, highly specialized, vaguely masochistic weirdos.

Those runners, jumpers, and throwers are my people, but I like following their exploits as a niche passion. And that wouldn't be possible if that blimp had rained riches, and change, on the broke sport I love. Besides, American culture is too big and brash for track to lead the charge. Track is apologetic. Track lacks the mechanisms to truly disrespect your competitors. Watching track requires some patience. The American experience would be fundamentally altered without the slam dunk or hard-hitting tackle. Would we be kinder and gentler as a nation? Perhaps. From a humanistic or utilitarian perspective, would that be for the best? More than likely. But would we—as individual Americans—be as blissfully happy and entertained to the point of removal from our problems when we watch sports? Probably not.

22

What If Baseball Teams Only Played Once a Week?

Will Leitch

The 2017 World Baseball Classic was the most electrifying baseball event since...OK, well, since the Chicago Cubs won the World Series just five months earlier. But *before* that it had been a few years. The World Baseball Classic brought an excitement, an urgency, to baseball that isn't typically native to the sport. Every game, every pitch, and every second of the World Baseball Classic felt apocalyptic; players and fans partied like each game of the World Baseball Classic would be the last baseball game ever played.

In an elimination game Puerto Rican second baseman Javier Báez got so excited by the throw from teammate Yadier Molina that he tagged the runner with his left hand, without looking at him, while pumping his fist and pointing at Molina with his right. Every home run was celebrated by players streaming out of the dugout and leaping around as if the turf were electric. Pop-ups to second were pimped and strutted; even a couple of American players smiled a few times. It was a blast. Crowds howled and players screamed like every game was the seventh game of the World Series. The games were held in mid–March. It was like nothing baseball had ever seen before.

Some of this was attributed to the players' patriotism, especially in the case of teams from the Dominican Republic and Puerto Rico, where the highest echelon of sport cannot be pursued at home. There's also the freedom of not having to adhere to a stringent set of unwritten rules of baseball etiquette, rules your culture had little say in crafting. And there's inherently more emotion when you're playing for where you are *from* rather than where you are *now*. (People don't get tattoos of their adopted town's area code.) Another reason the World Baseball Classic was so compelling was that every player cared so much and, more important, *showed* that they care. Baseball is not a private game. It exists because fans want to watch it. Emotion lets us all in. The World Baseball Classic was the ultimate inclusive sporting event.

But I'd argue it wasn't just geography, or a player's roots, that made them care so much about each individual game. It was that each individual game meant so much, not in the heart, but in the *standings*. The way the WBC was structured, a win or a loss in any particular game could mean the difference between advancing to the next round or going home. It was playoff-level intensity—even more so; at least in the playoffs you get a best of five or seven—right there in the middle of March. One game had the power of thirty, maybe forty regular-season baseball games. The joy of baseball's regular season is that it is a constant in our lives, every day, a backdrop in our daily routines. The downside to that is that, deep down, not every game matters, not really. There isn't that emotion because there isn't much to be emotional about: If you lose, hey, we play again tomorrow.

Which makes me wonder: What would it be like if baseball, from the beginning, just played one game a week? What if baseball *wasn't* a daily activity? What if it were like football? What if every game meant so much?

It is not known, or at least widely reported, why baseball decided to play every day. The 1876 season, considered the first baseball season on record, featured two teams that played fewer than sixty games (the New York Mutuals, the Philadelphia Athletics), five teams that played fewer than seventy games, and the Boston Red Stockings, who adhered to a schedule of exactly seventy games. By 1898, though, the twelve National League teams were playing fourteen games against every opponent, totaling 154 games. Since 1920, they've never played fewer than 154, and since 1962, no fewer than 162. Once a money-making enterprise proves that it can generate revenue on a daily basis, it is hard for the owners of that enterprise to accept anything less than just that.

This has made us take baseball games for granted. We devalue each one as simple, small drops of paint in a much larger picture that only makes sense when seen in total. But in a world of instant gratification and immediacy, the slow build has hurt baseball. This shows up in an empirical way in the Nielsen ratings, and less tangibly in the feel of baseball; there's less active urgency, and therefore it holds a smaller place in the public consciousness. No baseball game is an event, and we are an event culture now. So what if, like the NFL that so rules our sporting landscape, baseball was played only once a week?

Twenty-six games. (That way you still play half the calendar year like you do now.) Six playoff teams from each league. One-off playoff games, off to a Super Series one-game playoff at the end of the year. We are not talking about what it would be like if baseball switched to this now, because we know what would happen then: mass fury and rebellion among the sports' most devoted fans. (Myself included.) We are talking about what would happen if the game would have *always* been like this. If they had finished that 1876 season and thought, "The game's great, we love it, but...let's pare the season down. Too many games. Let's play once a week. The coal mines need us the other six days anyway," this is what the game would look like.

Let's take a look at our imaginary world where baseball is a weekly game from two different, but equally important, angles: *Gameplay*, and *Pastime*.

Gameplay

First off, having baseball as a weekly game would instantly alter basic roster construction. You wouldn't need twenty-five players on a roster anymore: Not once since rosters expanded to twenty-five players in

1968 has a team used all twenty-five players in one game. Teams would need, at most, twenty, and probably not even that many. But let's promote employment expansion and say twenty. Eight starting fielders—and there would be no need for a designated hitter in a game where rest is rarely required and pinch hitting is a constant—plus a starting pitcher, plus say, five backup hitters and six men in the bullpen (this would allow Tony La Russa to have a place in the reimagined game as well).

Basic lineup construction, one would think, might stay mostly the same: Position players already play six games out of the week anyway. Maybe there would be more of an emphasis on putting your best hitters 1-2-3 rather than worrying about a cleanup man; you would, after all, be facing the other team's ace every single game, and thus you would be less likely to put together a ton of hits in a row or score a bunch of runs. Just get your best hitters up as often as possible.

Of course, a large part of baseball, one of the reasons it's such a difficult game to play, is the constant churn of games. In Barry Svrluga's *The Grind*, a book chronicling the toll a 162-game Major League Baseball season takes on everyone who's a part of it, most players say that the hard part of baseball isn't *baseball*; it's that there is *always* baseball. This is why baseball is sneakily as physically taxing as any other sport, if not more so. Sure, in one individual baseball game, players move less than in the other sports. But over a season, one game almost every day for six months is *grueling*. It is an endurance test in a way no other sport is. The baseball season today begins at the beginning of March for Spring Training and extends into October—late October if you're lucky. NFL teams play sixteen games a year; the NBA and NHL play eighty-two. Baseball doubles that and occasionally throws in two games in one day. It leads to a numbing, often disorienting march that affects the lives of everyone connected to the game.

But that is eliminated in this scenario. Now players are at their freshest every game: as healthy and rested as they can possibly be. This works out perfectly for an oft-injured slugger like Giancarlo Stanton (assuming Giancarlo Stanton is still born and not eliminated from the face of the planet years before in a chaos theory sort of deal resulting from our blatant disregard for the ramifications of altering history).

Now every slugger susceptible to soft-tissue injury has to be ready only one day a week and can just lift weights and nap the other six days. In fact, let's look how it helps or hurts individual types of players:

- **Power hitters.** By far the most helped in this scenario. In a one-game-a-week scenario, the effect of the One Big Smash is multiplied. A power hitter could conceivably go one-for-fifteen with one homer over a three-week span and still be personally responsible for winning 33 percent of his team's games. Plus, you can rest those bulging muscles more.
- **Speedsters.** On one hand, the stolen base is extra-important in a one-game scenario: It, like the big homer, could be the difference between a good month and a bad one. That pinch runner who can't do anything else comes in quite a bit handy if he can win you one-twenty-sixth of your season by himself.
- **Defensive specialists.** If anything, with one game meaning so much, you'd almost expect great defensive players to come into the game late if your team is winning, sort of like a line change in hockey. Get up by two and then let them take over. It's pulling out all the stops, every game.
- **Backup catchers.** There would be no more backup catchers. Teach your third baseman to do it if you absolutely have to. Sorry, Sal Fasano. The sport is poorer without you.

Of course, we're burying the lede here: No position in baseball is altered more by the one-game-a-week change than the pitcher. Essentially, teams would need only one ace. You think the Dodgers are good now? Imagine if Clayton Kershaw gets to pitch *every* game. There is no longer any need for your innings eaters like Bronson Arroyo or Lance Lynn. Every pitcher is a flamethrower who can go all out, at all times. Need 125 pitches from your ace? Want him to floor it from the first inning on? Go ahead and do it: There are no more games for another week. Leave it all out there.

Doesn't this tell you *more* about a team, not less? Having one pitcher pitch every game may seem strange; we're conditioned to think that depth and flexibility in a pitching staff matters. But why? We don't think that about position players. This, more than anything, turns pitchers into the regular position players they were likely envisioned to be in the first place. Pitchers were initially seen mostly as ball-delivery devices. As they learned to move the ball around, though, we turned them into special unique snowflakes. Doesn't this split the difference? Doesn't this make them important but not coddled?

You would basically just need that ace, two lefties in the bullpen, two righties, and a closer. In this new world, ironically, the closer would gain even more mystical powers than they have right now. Think of them not as closers, really. Think of them as clutch field goal kickers, the Mariano-Rivera-as-Adam-Vinatieri principle.

And, speaking of football, changing baseball to a football-esque schedule would also echo another aspect of football culture. The starting pitcher would take the importance of a quarterback in football. Every MLB Draft would be obsessed with finding the next Franchise Pitcher, the guy who can take the ball every day for the next ten years. Clayton Kershaw is Tom Brady, Felix Hernandez is Brett Favre. The pitcher becomes the showcase player on every team. It's not the New York Yankees vs. the Boston Red Sox. It's C. C. Sabathia vs. Chris Sale, every game, until they both retire. You think teams fetishize pitchers now? Imagine what happens when they pitch every game.

In this way, the game reverts to its roots, its *original* roots, in which Cy Young can win 511 games because he pitches all of them. One man can get hot and win you everything. The starting pitcher becomes the quarterback, the point guard, and the goalie all wrapped up in one package. All you need is one. You can figure the rest out later.

Pastime

There are two major factors cited when people try to argue that baseball is no longer America's national pastime, in spite of the fact that the sport sets record profit numbers every year and is currently being watched by more people than at any other time in human history:

Television ratings. Before the Cubs' historic run in 2017 led to a massive ratings uptick, World Series ratings had been at all-time lows; the 2012 World Series between the San Francisco Giants and Detroit Tigers, a four-game sweep, notched only a 7.6 rating, which was actually lower than the Pro Bowl, the NFL's infamously dull and pointless all-star game.

Performance-enhancing drugs. Even though your average football player is jacked up with more medication than your average dinner-plate-destined steer, it is baseball that has been tattooed with the scarlet *S* of steroids. When Starling Marte, a Pittsburgh Pirates star center fielder, tested positive for a banned substance in April 2017, you read countless media reports about the Stain of PEDs on baseball, even though a star player being busted is a sign that the testing program is *working*, not that it isn't. But baseball always has to wear the PED cloak of dishonor in a way that other team sports don't.

But under our scenario, both these problems are quite easily solved.

The problem with baseball's ratings, I'd argue, is not that the game is too slow, or that it doesn't translate well to television. The problem is that there are so *many* baseball games. One of the primary appeals of baseball—that it is always on, that it is always there for you when you want it, and also always there when you don't—is exactly what causes it so much trouble in television ratings: There is no scarcity. Television thrives on event programming, particularly in an age of DVRs and streaming services. But baseball, by design, is not meant to be an event. It's local programming writ large, thirty regional channels with a dedicated audience every day throughout the year. It's hard then, come October, when the World Series is asked to transcend the very nature of the sport. Baseball is like an old-school soap opera that rewards devoted viewing. But there's a reason soap operas are—or were—on during low-risk, low-stakes time periods: In prime time, you need the big hits. Baseball floods the market with its games. Remember when *Who Wants to Be a Millionaire?* was a massive hit for ABC before they ruined it by putting it on every night, thus diluting the market and causing the ratings to plummet? That's baseball.

Overabundance isn't an issue if you play one game a week. One game a week essentially turns the sport into, well, football, the sport that dominates the ratings in the United States. No one gathers at a friend's place to watch a full day of baseball on a random Sunday in July. But they might if the game were responsible for one-sixteenth of a whole season like it is in football. Fantasy baseball would be easier to follow, like fantasy football; gambling would be more concentrated. You would, basically, have to pay attention to baseball only one day a week, which would surely bring in more (extremely casual) fans and increase television ratings dramatically. If every baseball game were this Big Event, it would change the way we talk about the sport entirely. Because we have become so lazy and headline oriented about media news, the perception would be that baseball is thriving because it gets such incredible ratings. *Even though fewer people would be watching baseball.* And there would be less baseball. The MLB Game of the Week would just be The Game. This actually even turns one day of the week into Baseball's Day. College football owns Saturdays. The NFL owns Sundays. What day does baseball own? Take your pick.

And despite the public's belief that PED usage among baseball players is motivated by a desire to increase power, the primary reasons players use PEDs are to recover from injury and to stay strong during the long, grinding season. This problem is lessened considerably in a weekly schedule. Sure, there might be some PED users here or there, but more to the point, you can expect far less outrage in a world where baseball records are presumably less fetishized than they are now. For that matter: In this world, are we so obsessed with baseball statistics in the first place? Is sabermetrics ever even invented? Or would it all just be Small Sample Size?

Either way, baseball gets a boost in surface-level ubiquity and becomes less urgent to the obsessives who have made the game an obsession.

Once-a-week-baseball does up the hype, the excitement, and the drama. It imbues the once pastoral sport with a football-esque insistence. It strips away nuances that can be observed only after repeated viewing. It accelerates the sport's resting heart rate and obviates the languorous tobacco spitting and sunflower seed expectoration that characterizes optimal dugout bonding. I wonder if the words *clubhouse* or *ballpark* would be applied to a pursuit with such crisis-level stakes. I cannot see an organist leading a swaying crowd in a sing-along of a song written in 1908 in a sport with so much on the line; there is nothing *languid* when baseball is played at this pace. I cannot see the administration of a hot foot being countenanced given the seriousness of every moment. I cannot see a chicken becoming a beloved team mascot. In short, though I am the author of this alternative supposition, I have to say I believe it would be horrible and would ruin everything I love about baseball. Which means, of course, it would be incredibly popular and remunerative.

23

What If Bobby Fischer Had Received Proper Psychiatric Help?

Dylan Loeb McClain

The day after Bobby Fischer won the world chess championship in September 1972, he lay in his hotel room in Reykjavík, Iceland, his arm draped over his face. In his hand, he clutched a check for more than $78,000, part of his share of the prize fund. It should have been his moment of greatest triumph, the culmination of everything that he had worked so hard to achieve. But as he later told Johnny Carson on *The Tonight Show,* he felt terrible. "I woke up the day after the thing was over and I felt different, like something had been taken out of me."

Shelby Lyman, who provided move-by-move commentary of the championship for PBS—the highest-rated broadcast in public television history—said years later, the problem was, "He didn't really, after he won, know what he wanted to do with his life. He reached an end point when he was twenty-nine."

Into the vacuum of that lack of purpose rushed the paranoid demons that he had long struggled to keep at bay. Dr. Anthony Saidy, a childhood friend and an international master, said, "It was as if he was at war with himself."

Fischer single-handedly toppled the Soviet chess empire when he won the world championship by beating Boris Spassky. Today, he is still considered among the most dominant chess players who ever lived. Jeff Sonas, who created a widely followed and well-respected ranking system called Chessmetrics, has calculated that Fischer had the single greatest year ever for a chess player in 1972, followed by Garry Kasparov in 1990 (when Kasparov defeated Anatoly Karpov to defend his title). In rankings of the best players, Fischer often shows up at No. 1 or at No. 2, just behind Kasparov, who held the title from 1985 to 2000.

Fischer's reign spanned only one-fifth of Kasparov's: It began dramatically in 1972 and ended in a pique in 1975 over negotiations with the World Chess Federation for the terms of his title defense. After that, he became a recluse, only to reemerge briefly in 1992 to play a rematch against Spassky—a match that violated United States sanctions and made Fischer a pariah and a fugitive.

He died in January 2008 in Iceland, at sixty-four, a political refugee from his home country and a broken and lonely man.

Most everyone who knew him through the years agrees that he had psychiatric problems—problems that worsened as he grew older and as he fermented in a self-imposed state of isolation. His mother, Regina, had been worried enough when he was young to seek psychiatric treatment for her son, but she had been unsuccessful.

What would have happened if he had received treatment for whatever ailed him? Perhaps it would have unburdened him to some degree, but part of what makes a great chess player is the ability to anticipate the opponents' plans and thwart them. A master develops a sense of danger, almost paranoia, and everyone agrees that was a pronounced quality in Fischer. Might treatment have diminished his sublime ability at the chessboard?

Dr. Frank Brady, who wrote two biographies of Fischer, does not believe so. "[Chess] was his muse, that was his art," Dr. Brady said.

Dr. Brady said that while Fischer was obsessive about chess—he really focused on nothing else—anyone who becomes great at something must be obsessive, and he did not see that as part of Fischer's psychiatric problems.

Dr. Brady said, "I mean, to hear people say he was obsessed with chess and he couldn't do anything else, well, would you say that of Vladimir Horowitz?"

While Fischer's psychiatric demons noticeably worsened as he grew older, he had always been erratic.

Largely self-taught, he had risen from a poor, dysfunctional family in Brooklyn to win the United States Championship before his fifteenth birthday. Within another year, he had earned the grandmaster title, becoming far and away the youngest to ever do so. (The record would stand for thirty-three years.) A few months later, he dropped out of Erasmus Hall High School, noting, "You don't learn anything in school. It's just a waste of time."

By nineteen, Fischer was already considered by many to be the best player in the world, and it seemed clear that his destiny was to become world champion.

That achievement would take another decade, however, partly because of the obstacles put in his way by the Soviet authorities, who could plainly see the threat he posed to their hegemony over the chess world. But quite often, the obstacles were his own unpredictable and often outrageous behavior.

In a *Sports Illustrated* article in 1962 titled "The Russians Have Fixed World Chess," he accused the Soviets of colluding against him during the previous candidates tournament to select a challenger for the world championship.

Fischer's paranoia was based on both fact—declassified documents after the fall of the Soviet Union showed that there had been some collusion by the Soviets—and also his childhood experiences.

His mother, Regina, was a brilliant woman who spoke six languages and eventually became a doctor. She also held subversive views, had lived in Moscow for several years, and had a disparate group of friends and associates who held left-wing views. For these reasons, for years she was persecuted by the FBI—the file compiled on her eventually ran to 750 pages—and she lost many jobs after agents from the Bureau unexpectedly turned up at her places of employment asking questions about her. Mindful of this, she instructed her son for years that, should any agents with the Bureau try to stop and question him, he was to reply,

"I have nothing to say to you." Though Fischer was never stopped, Regina's fears doubtless planted seeds of paranoia in his mind.

Feeling that his path to the world championship had been unjustly blocked in 1962 (winning the candidates tournament would have qualified him to play a match for the title in 1963), Fischer refused to participate in the next interzonal tournament in Amsterdam, which was the qualifier to become a candidate. Fischer's refusal was paradoxical, as by then the World Chess Federation, in response to Fischer's charges and demands, had switched from having a candidates tournament to a series of matches to select a challenger.

Fischer initially decided to play in the next cycle, and was winning the 1967 interzonal tournament in Sousse, Tunisia, when he quit because the organizers would not agree to his demands to change the playing schedule. As Dr. Brady wrote in *Endgame*, the biography he published after Fischer died, "He, not the organizers, would decide when he'd play and when he wouldn't."

Indeed, he had long displayed such an attitude. In 1961, a match had been organized between Fischer and Samuel Reshevsky, who had been the top American player for two decades before Fischer emerged in the late 1950s. The match was tied at 5.5 points apiece when Game 12 was rescheduled because one of the principal benefactors of the match, Jacqueline Piatigorsky, had a conflict with a recital given by her husband, the cellist Gregor Piatigorsky.

Fischer refused to play the rescheduled game and forfeited. He then forfeited the subsequent game and the match.

Two years later, when the Piatigorskys sponsored a major international tournament in the United States, which included Tigran Petrosian, the Soviet World Champion, Fischer refused an invitation after they would not meet his financial demands.

"If they don't give me what I want, I'll just punish them and not play," he told Dr. Brady. Reflecting on it years later, Dr. Brady said, "That sounds almost like God speaking, doesn't it? 'If you don't behave yourself, I will strike you down, I will punish you.' He was just twenty. I've never heard anyone speak and use those words."

Even when he finally qualified to play for the world championship in 1972 against Boris Spassky, Fischer still kept the chess world on tenterhooks.

The match was supposed to start on July 4 in Reykjavík, Iceland, but when the day arrived, Fischer was still in the United States protesting the playing conditions, in particular the prize fund of $125,000 (almost three-quarters of a million dollars, when adjusted for inflation), which was eighty times more than the prize fund for the previous match. Only when a British investment banker named Jim Slater stepped in and doubled the prize fund, while also subtly suggesting that perhaps Fischer was afraid to lose, did Fischer actually fly to Iceland.

Once there, he continued with his antics. The match was to last up to twenty-four games, with wins worth one point and draws worth a half point. After Fischer made a simple blunder in Game 1 and lost, he forfeited Game 2 over a dispute about the filming of the match. This led Game 3 to be played in a room reserved for Ping-Pong rather than the large theater where the match was supposed to be staged. After Fischer won that game, he finally calmed down and the match proceeded more or less smoothly until Fischer won, 12.5–8.5.

That success did not mellow Fischer. Instead, he stopped playing, and when it was time for him to defend his crown three years later against Anatoly Karpov, the challenger who had won the candidates matches of 1973–74, Fischer drew up a huge list of conditions for the match. After protracted negotiations with the World Chess Federation, which acquiesced to many, but not all, of Fischer's demands, Fischer abruptly resigned the title.

In the years that followed, he became a recluse, exhibiting increasingly bizarre behavior that alienated his dwindling circle of friends and associates.

He briefly came out of retirement in 1992 to play a match for $5 million against Spassky in Serbia, which was then under United States sanctions for its genocidal war against Croatia and Slovenia. (The money came from Jezdimir Vasiljević, a Serbian businessman.) The United States government wrote him a letter ordering him not to play as he could face fines and/or imprisonment. In a memorable press conference, Fischer held up the Treasury order and spit on it. After Fischer won the match, the United States issued a warrant for his arrest.

Unable to return to the United States, Fischer lived fairly anonymously for years in Japan and the Philippines. But on the day of the attacks against the United States in September 2001, Fischer, who had become increasingly anti-Semitic (frequently citing as proof of his world view the vile and wholly discredited *Protocols of the Elders of Zion*), went on a Philippines radio show to exult.

"This is wonderful news. It's time for the fucking U.S. to get their heads kicked in," Fischer said. Later, in the same interview, he added, "I'm hoping [the U.S. military will] close down all the synagogues, arrest all the Jews, execute hundreds of thousands of Jewish ringleaders."

Fischer's rant drew the American government's attention. Three years later, while passing through an airport in Japan, he was arrested as his passport had been revoked. Imprisoned for close to a year for traveling on an invalid passport, he was eventually offered asylum in Iceland—the site of his greatest triumph.

He lived a lonely existence there, supported and humored by a small circle of friends, until he died in January 2008 of a curable kidney disease that went untreated because he did not trust doctors.

Fischer's behavior was noticeably odd even when he was very young. After he began playing chess obsessively when he was in elementary school, Regina took him to psychiatrists and psychologists when he was about ten to see if he was normal or if something could be done to get him to play less chess.

One psychiatrist, Ariel Mengarini, who was himself a master-level player, was not worried. "Leave the boy alone," he said. "He could be doing much worse things."

Still not satisfied, she took Fischer to Reuben Fine, a noted Freudian psychoanalyst who had once been among the two or three best players in the world. He tried to gain the boy's confidence by playing some chess with him. Fischer was intrigued, but when, after a couple of sessions of chess, Fine began asking non-chess-related questions of him, Fischer stormed out. "You've tricked me," he shouted.

That was the end of Regina's attempts to get psychological counseling for her son.

Dr. Joseph Ponterotto, a professor of psychology at Fordham University, wrote a book about Fischer after he died titled *A Psychobiography of Bobby Fischer*. Dr. Ponterotto tried, based on publicly available information, including documents and interviews with Dr. Brady and other people who knew him, to figure out what was wrong with Fischer psychologically. His conclusion was that Fischer suffered from neurosis and paranoia brought on by attachment disorders stemming from the absence of a father and the fact that his mother, Regina, as the sole breadwinner, worked long hours and was rarely present during Fischer's upbringing.

The story of Bobby's father was a key element in Fischer's formation, according to Ponterotto.

Hans-Gerhardt Fischer was listed as Fischer's father on his birth certificate, but most people believe that it was really Paul Nemenyi, a Hungarian physicist and refugee from the war. Regina had met Nemenyi while studying at a college in Denver. The FBI, which was already surveilling Regina because of her pro-Communist sympathies, also believed that Nemenyi was Fischer's father, according to files subsequently obtained by Dr. Brady when he wrote his book.

After Bobby was born in March 1943, Nemenyi sent Regina some money whenever he could and came to visit them occasionally when they eventually settled in Brooklyn. Nemenyi kept up the practice of occasionally funding the family until the time of his death, just before Bobby's ninth birthday. Fischer grew up never knowing for sure who his father was.

Dr. Ponterotto believes that if Fischer had gotten counseling at a young age, and if his mother and his older sister, Joan, who was frequently thrust into the role of chaperone and caretaker in the absence of their mother, had gotten assistance, Fischer could have been helped and been less disruptive and more stable as he grew up.

Many counseling techniques taken for granted now did not exist then.

"Given the services that we have now, which are multifaceted and interdisciplinary, he would be targeted early on for early intervention, he would be supported at school in group counseling, in family counseling. His mother and sister would have gotten help," Dr. Ponterotto said. "Back then, just from my knowledge of the mental health system, when he was at an elementary school and when he was at Erasmus in high school, there probably wasn't much mental health services."

Dr. Ponterotto thinks that the most likely solution for Fischer would have been behavioral therapy.

"They would have given him behavioral therapy, behavioral modification, a rewards system that if he studies for an hour then he can play chess for an hour," said Dr. Ponterotto. "The reason that a patient is reluctant to change his behavior is because he is afraid of a bad outcome. But if the patient changes the behavior and nothing catastrophic happens, he realizes, 'Oh, maybe I can be by myself, maybe my mom does love me even though she is going to Washington to march.'"

(Regina became increasingly politically active in Fischer's later years and finally left him alone when he was seventeen to go on the 1961 San Francisco to Moscow peace march. Along the way, she met an Englishman whom she married and eventually lived with in England.)

Though Fischer did not seem to have any delusions or overtly psychotic behavior, he might have still been put on one of the medications that existed at the time.

Dr. Ponterotto said, "I think in the late 1940s and early 1950s, we did have antianxiety agents like Valium or Librium. We didn't have Ativan or Xanax, some of the newer classes of benzodiazepines which work well for anxiety. But maybe with a good assessment of his psychiatric needs, maybe a low dose of medication may have helped him be less anxious, be more focused."

If the behavioral therapy had worked, if Fischer had been taking some mild forms of medication, would it have sapped him of his competitive spirit or perhaps led him to give up chess or not take it up at all?

Dr. Ponterotto and Dr. Brady admit that is one possibility, but neither believes that would have happened. Indeed, both think it would have helped him become champion sooner and remain champion longer.

Dr. Ponterotto said, "Another possibility is that there was something about him and he just had a natural gift for chess, and even with distractions that may have been healthy; he would always come back to chess." He continued, "If he is healthier and does not quit chess, he may have won earlier because, remember, he quit tournaments and he lost his right to play."

Dr. Brady conceded that it's unknowable how treatment would have affected the quality of Fischer's game, but guesses that any change would have been for the better.

A more psychiatrically stable version of Fischer also would have attempted to defend his title in 1975—and many, including the man he was to play, Anatoly Karpov, believe he would have won. The consequences for chess in the United States would have been profound.

A chess boom brought on by Fischer's success would have flourished even more than it did, and many more children would have taken up chess. "Every school would have a soccer club and a chess team," Dr. Ponterotto said.

And Fischer, who was always concerned about his legacy, might have married and had children—perhaps a child who was also a champion like his father. All that was not possible because the undue importance that Fischer placed on succeeding at the game ultimately drove him away from it.

Dr. Ponterotto said, "I think his whole life, his search for his father, his search for his identity, was found through chess. And when he beat Spassky, his chess identity and his personal identity merged as one. Now he had found himself, he had found his father figure, so to speak, through chess."

Fischer himself was cognizant of how connected he was to chess. Just before the world championship match, he said in an interview, "Chess and me, it is hard to take them apart. Chess is like my alter ego, you know?"

But with his identity forged, it could also be lost. Dr. Ponterotto believes that the aborted match in 1975 against Karpov represented to Fischer more than a tough opponent and a set of challenges on the chessboard. A defeat would have been devastating. Dr. Ponterotto said,

"It isn't just losing a chess match and getting ready for a rematch, it is losing a sense of identity."

Though it is impossible to know what would have happened if Fischer had received treatment and counseling when he was young or had access to more modern medicines that might have calmed his nerves while preserving his exceptional ability, almost a decade after his death, Bobby Fischer's legacy is interwoven with the strangeness, frustrations, and mystery of his mind, and not just the masterpieces that he created at the board.

24

——

What If Basketball Rims Were Smaller Than Basketballs?

Jon Bois

Kevin Harlan: Curry for three! No. Rebound Draymond, kicks it back out to Curry, fires again. Off the back of the rim. Klay with the tip-in, no. Portland with the rebound. You know, it's like the rim has had a lid on it all quarter for Golden State. The Warriors are a combined oh–for–seventeen in the second.

Reggie Miller: And you know, Kevin, they might just have to shoot through it. If you go through a dry spell, you can hopefully depend on your teammates to pick up the slack. But sometimes, when the whole team isn't shooting well, it can be a little tough to shake out the cobwebs and get going. It's kind of a snowball effect.

Harlan: The silver lining for Golden State, of course, Reggie, is that Portland can't seem to get it going in the first half, either. Four minutes before halftime, both the Blazers and Warriors have put up a goose egg, a combined zero-for-sixty-eight! Have you ever seen anything like it?

Miller: Many times, yes.

Harlan: Lillard will try his luck from three, that misses the mark, he seems to think he caught some contact on that one. No whistle, though. We're still locked at Warriors 2, Blazers 0.

Miller: I went through a lot of these stretches, Kevin—

Harlan: Pardon me, Reggie. Check that, the score is 0–0.

Miller: I went through a lot of stretches like this one in my career. Dame is just having one of those nights. It seems like you're gonna have those games no matter how good you are. Basketball's just a cruel game sometimes.

Harlan: You know, I'm reminded of something the great John Wooden once said: "It is impossible to score. It is important to practice for no reason."

Miller: (*laughing*) And it's so true, Kevin. So true. So said the great Wizard of, uh...

Harlan: Wizard of Westwood!

Miller: Wizard of Westwood, yes! It's impossible to score.

Harlan: Steal by Harkless inside! Up to Lillard on the break, Portland has numbers. Puts it up for Aminu—*ohhhh!* Rejected by the rim!

Miller: Well... (*laughing*)... if you wanna get on a poster, young man, you've got to finish! You've got to finish! You have to put both hands on the ball and play a sport in which scoring is feasible if you wanna get all those oohs and ahhs.

There's a lesson for all the kids out there watching. When you're on the court, you don't need to showboat. No funny business. No anything, actually. Please do not play basketball.

Harlan: The uh, the boo birds are coming out here in the Moda Center. Fans clearly not happy with the effort they're seeing out of this Portland team.

Miller: And... and Kevin, see, I don't think the booing is fair. You spend your hard-earned money to take your family to an NBA game, of course you want to see a good showing out of your team. Believe me, I get that. Before I ever set foot on an NBA court, I was a fan first, and I remember being a Lakers fan as a kid. It seemed sometimes like they could never hit a bucket to save their lives.

Harlan: They couldn't! No one could. No one ever can!

Miller: Exactly! Exactly. And so when I was drafted, you know, my first thought was, "I'm gonna drain every shot I shoot." You know, when you're twenty-two years old, you think you're king of the world.

Harlan: (*laughing*) Sure, sure.

Miller: Needless to say, it didn't work out that way. Every single game, no matter who you are, your shot is just not gonna be there for you. And I think too many fans these days don't get that. They think that just because you're an NBA player, you should hit every big shot, every dunk. It's just not realistic. I'm sorry! You've got me going on a rant!

Harlan: (*laughing*) Well, Reggie, as a Hall of Famer, I think you've earned a minute or two on the soapbox...Thompson again missing, Lillard takes it upcourt. Lillard driving in, *rejected* by Durant! That's three blocks already for Kevin Durant, and the war of words between those two figures escalates after that little exchange. Kerr calls time out.

This all started after Game 1 of the series, when Durant tweeted at Lillard, quote, "You can't even score any of the points when you are playing in the basketball game." Shortly after, Lillard fired back with a statement:

"I'm not concerned with what anyone in the other locker room has to say about my play. My goal as a Trail Blazer is, and has always been, to try to hit a bucket and bring a field goal back to Portland. Everything else is just noise."

Miller: I like his attitude.

Harlan: And, folks, don't forget that at halftime, our guys in the studio will be talking to NBA commissioner Adam Silver, so stay tuned for that.

Klay to inbound. Let's go to David Aldridge on the sideline. David?

David Aldridge: Well, Kevin, I overheard what Portland coach Terry Stotts was going over with his guys. He was saying, "We have to retire. We all have to retire right now and try to get a job in a factory or something." Evan Turner asked what kind of factory. Stotts shot back, "Apples or cars or whatever. Anything. There's a reason the court is made of wood. We are rattling about the floor of a casket. We are as forgotten cigars and coins and baubles rolled out from the suit pockets of a dead tycoon." Kevin?

Harlan: Some harsh words from Stotts, who has seen a lot of cold shooting from his starting shooting guard as of late. Monday night at Oracle Arena, Turner was oh-for-eleven from the floor, and worse yet, he suffered an o-fer at the charity stripe, hitting none of his six free throw shots.

Harkless with a *long* three! Misses badly.

Miller: That's just not his shot at all, Kevin. You know, there's an emerging school of thought in the NBA that says, well, if you shoot from far away, the basketball appears smaller as it moves away from you. If you hold a basketball in your hand, it seems pretty big. But if you shoot it a long ways, it looks smaller. So maybe it's shrinking small enough to be able to fit inside the rim. But in reality, the basketball is the same size the whole time. It's just that it appears smaller because it's farther away.

Harlan: Curry drives in, puts it up, and—

Miller: Is that a goaltend?

Harlan: *That's a goaltend! The officials call goaltending! Ride 'em cowboy! What a play!*

...And a loud orchestra of boos from the Portland faithful.

Miller: Yep, if you look at it...see, the ball's not on the way down. Jusuf Nurkic clearly got his hand on it before it came down.

What an unbelievable error on Nurkic's part. Unbelievable. That's the one thing they teach you at every level: Never, ever give the refs any reason to call a goaltend on you. The basketball is bigger than the rim! It's not going to go in! Just let the shot happen, and then grab the rebound. Just an absolutely thoughtless error.

Harlan: And we're getting word from the truck. Those are the first points of Steph Curry's career. It's all smiles on the Golden State bench as Curry takes a seat.

And look at that, the Blazers have actually put Curry's achievement on the scoreboard.

Miller: That's just class. Curry has earned this. He's earned the respect of the entire league over the years. Amazing handle on the ball, always finds an open look for his teammates...he's one of the greatest players of his era, no doubt. And now that he has these points? He's still a young man, I know, and it's probably too early to say it. But he's a Hall of Famer. Steph Curry is a Hall of Famer.

Harlan: With the first half just about over, the Warriors now lead 2–0, a lead that at this point certainly seems insurmountable.

Miller: Well, there's a half still left to play, Kevin, but I have to agree with you. That right there was the dagger. There's no other way to score than to hope your opponent has a bonehead moment and commits goaltending.

Harlan: Final seconds of the half, Lillard puts one up from half-court...and it *almost* went in! It would have counted, there was about a second left on the clock, but unfortunately, the basketball is too large to fit through the rim. We'll go again now to David Aldridge, who is with Steve Kerr. David?

Aldridge: Steve, with those two points coming just before the half, your guys have enormous momentum going into the locker room. Any adjustments you're going to make before the second half?

Steve Kerr: We're just gonna go home.

Aldridge: An awfully conservative strategy, Coach.

Kerr: Well, yeah. I mean, we know they won't be able to score even if they have an empty floor. Rather than risk goaltending ourselves, we're just gonna let them run out the clock.

Aldridge: Safe travels, then. And from here I'll send it right up to the studio. To Ernie, Kenny, Charles, and Shaq.

Kerr: Hey, what if we made the ball so that it could actually fit insi—

(*Cut to studio.*)

Ernie Johnson: Thanks for joining us, everybody. You've been watching Game 2 of the first-round series between the Blazers and Warriors, and it sure looks like Golden State has this one wrapped up, Kenny.

Kenny Smith: Yeah, although I gotta say, Ernie. You know what I'm about to say.

Johnson: (*laughing*) Ohh, I know.

Smith: I don't like the Warriors leaving at halftime. I understand they've got the game in the bag and that logically, it makes sense. It's just a trend I've seen more and more over the years, and it's a trend I don't like. I think it's a poor display of sportsmanship.

Shaquille O'Neal: I don't mind it. I don't want to see any more of them. I don't want to see any more of this game. Neither team can score.

Charles Barkley: None of the teams can shoot a basket in any of the basketball games.

Smith: Well see, I gotta say, Charles, there's where you're wrong. You can shoot all the baskets you want in the basketball games.

Barkley: Yeah, but the problem comes in where, look. If I'm a player, I can shoot all the baskets I want, you're right. But I won't be able to make any of them. You know I hate to get into semantics. But if you've got a ball that's this big, and a rim that's only *this* big, it's just not going to work for you. Even if you shoot the ball perfectly accurately, the sides of the ball will hit against the rim and it'll just bounce out, because the ball is just too—

O'Neal: It's too large. The ball is too large and the rim isn't big enough.

Barkley: Right. The ball is too large and the rim is too small, exactly right.

Smith: That's the thing, though! You'll never know for sure unless you try to shoot it! Why not just try to shoot it?

Barkley: All of the basketball players have been trying to shoot it for more than one hundred years, including you and me, and none of us have made a basket.

Smith: That's true, but maybe if you shoot it really hard, like as hard as you can, and if you're superaccurate and you really try to do it, you could do it.

Barkley: Absolutely not. Absolutely not.

Johnson: Tell you what, guys, I know we've had this debate before, and we'll have it again. But for right now, I want to bring in

Commissioner Adam Silver, joining us live from NBA headquarters in New York. Mr. Silver, great to have you with us.

Adam Silver: Ernie, it's great to be with you guys.

Johnson: So you know, Commissioner, you just heard our guys having the same debate that's raged among NBA fans for as long as I can remember. It's always coming down to scoring. In your view, is it too hard to score in this league?

Silver: Well you know, Ernie, it's important for us to preserve the traditions that have made the game what it is today. But it's also important to make sure we're keeping the game fun and exciting, and of course, scoring is a big part of that. We've certainly been discussing some rule changes that we believe might result in some more scoring.

Johnson: One such rumored change is that the league might perhaps make the ball smaller, or make the rim larger.

Silver: Absolutely, that's one of many options that's certainly been discussed. As the rules currently stand, the rim is eighteen inches wide, and the ball is twenty-four inches wide. We think that by tweaking those dimensions a little, we can encourage more scoring. And in so doing, we can give our fans more scoring and encourage younger would-be fans to take an interest in the game.

O'Neal: Commissioner, what are the new dimensions you're thinking about?

Silver: Well, we want to keep the rim at eighteen inches while shrinking the basketball to twenty-two, even twenty-one inches.

Barkley: That might work.

O'Neal: (*inaudible*)

Johnson: Now, Commissioner, is that proposal a result of what's been experimented with in the NBA's developmental league?

Silver: Very much so, Ernie, yes. The D-league has served as an invaluable testing ground. Last season, we played a number of exhibition games with hundred-foot rims and one-inch basketballs. And you know, the problem we ran into was that as a shooter, you couldn't get far away enough to shoot it, put it in, and still remain inbounds. The fans didn't like it, the players didn't like it, nobody liked it. We also tried an eighteen-inch rim and a nine-inch basketball, but the ball kept falling through the rim and landing on the floor. So we tried another few games with four-inch rims and three-feet basketballs. (*laughing*) And as you can imagine, that didn't exactly work out.

Johnson: (*laughing*) Oh, without a doubt! How would the ball even fit through the basket?

(*inaudible*)

Barkley: Ha! Brick city!

O'Neal: I am going to walk into the forest and live there for the rest of my life.

Johnson: Commissioner, it certainly sounds like some necessary changes are being considered, and kudos to you for approaching this issue head-on. Thanks for talking with us.

Silver: Of course, Ernie. Any time.

Johnson: After the break, we'll show you highlights of the best passes and shot clock violations from around the league. And after that, we'll get you right back to Portland for the second half of Game 2 of the 1998 Western Conference Semifinals, which of course is being played in 2017 as a consequence of Game 1 requiring nineteen years and 55,478 overtimes to complete. The winner will face the eventual winner of the Spurs-Rockets series, which has been locked in Game 4 since 1977.

25

What If the AFL-NFL Merger Had Been Complicated by the Jets' Loss in Super Bowl III?

Michael MacCambridge

Joe Willie in his white shoes, dabs of eye-black under his piercing gaze. The palm trees swaying in the Miami breeze as an increasingly startled sellout crowd witnesses the New York Jets taking an early lead. John Unitas sitting stoically—the only way, really, he ever sat—on a metal folding chair, watching his team-mate Earl Morrall having the worst game of his career. Colts turnover after Colts turnover. Gerry Philbin and the rest of the Jets defense frustrating Baltimore at every turn. A look of disbelief in the eyes of NFL followers. And then at the end, in the symphony of flashbulbs that lit the gathering twilight of the Orange Bowl, Namath trotting off the field and into the tunnel with that one passing iconic gesture—the raised index finger—before disappearing into the bedlam of the Jets dressing room. On the biggest stage in sports, the biggest star from the biggest city had engineered the biggest upset in pro football history.

Jets 16, Colts 7. It remains one of those rare moments in sports history when the unthinkable actually happened, in this case pretty much exactly the way the quarterback in white shoes had said it was going to happen.

The effects were profound and long-lasting. In the short term, it vaulted Namath into a kind of American pop-cultural superstardom that transcended sports. In the same stroke, it jolted and humiliated the perennially powerful Baltimore Colts.

The win came in the midst of seismic change in the structure of pro football. Just months later, in the spring of 1969, the NFL confirmed that following the coming season, the fully merged leagues would encompass two thirteen-team conferences, the National Football Conference (comprising thirteen established NFL teams) and the American Football Conference (consisting of the ten existing AFL teams, plus three of the sixteen NFL franchises that would move over to join the new loop). The first team to agree to make the move was the Colts, in part because they could be in the same division as the Jets, offering owner Carroll Rosenbloom two chances a year to avenge Baltimore's Super Bowl III defeat.

That summer, reminders of the shocking loss were all around. In the book *One More July*, coauthored by Colts center Bill Curry and the writer George Plimpton, Curry recalled the horrific off-season following the game, Baltimore cloaked not merely in disappointment but embarrassment, while the Jets became the toast of pro sports. Curry would remember being "subjected to the Jets on television, in commercials, on the printed page, smiling at us, singing, washing, shaving, eating soup, standing alongside cars, wearing sports clothes. The most obnoxious by far was the one in which Gerry Philbin was shown eating Manhandler soup, whatever *that* was, just stuffing his face like he was never going to have another meal in his life."

It wasn't just Curry who felt tormented. The blast radius was extensive, in both distance and time. It pierced the façade of invincibility the NFL had possessed and caused a major fissure in the relationship between owner Carroll Rosenbloom and Colts coach Don Shula. When future Super Bowl–winning GM Ernie Accorsi began work as the public relations man with the Colts in the spring of 1970—nearly a year and a half after Super Bowl III—the damage was still clear.

"I've never seen an organization of qualified individuals so paralyzed," said Accorsi. "They were *still* in shock. I don't care what anyone says, Carroll Rosenbloom never forgave Shula."

Some players never recovered from the cognitive dissonance. Nearly fifty years later, Colts linebacker Dennis Gaubatz remained adamant: "The only way they could beat us is if that game was rigged; and it was rigged."

It wasn't, of course. But the outcome was so shocking, so significant, and so pervasive that it altered the future of the sport. In retrospect, with the benefit of a half century of accumulated lore, the outcome now seems necessary, inevitable even.

But in the weeks and months after the game, Colts supporters and NFL loyalists remained fixated on the hypotheticals: What if Morrall's pass in the end zone to Tom Mitchell hadn't been tipped by Al Atkinson? What if Morrall didn't also miss a wide-open Jimmy Orr on a flea-flicker? What if Tom Matte didn't fumble on the second play of the second half? They were convinced that if a few of those bounces had gone differently, the Colts would have won easily.

Whether that's the case is debatable. But if one *were* to change the outcome of that single game, the dominos fall far and fast. A few obvious (and not-so-obvious) differences to consider, in an alternate universe in which the Colts were crowned as champions of Super Bowl III:

The Dolphins Don't Become a Dynasty

With a victory in Super Bowl III, Shula would likely have received a bonus and a new contract, and he would have remained in Baltimore for years to come. Instead, the loss left Rosenbloom so stunned and inconsolable that he spent much of the Colts' post–Super Bowl "victory party" seated alone behind a large potted plant. He couldn't comprehend it, and he came to blame his bright young coach.

Had the Colts won the game Shula certainly wouldn't have left for Miami just one season later, in 1970, after a protracted falling-out with Rosenbloom. That means Shula wouldn't have elevated that franchise overnight, and led the Dolphins to a 27–24 overtime upset of Kansas City in the Longest Game Ever Played on Christmas Day 1971. The Dolphins wouldn't have marched to their perfect 17-0 season a year later, behind the "No–Name Defense" and quarterback Bob Griese (backed up by aging vet Morrall, acquired from Baltimore). There would be no Jim Kiick and Larry Csonka on the cover of *Sports Illustrated*, with the latter flipping off the camera.

The absence of Shula in Miami would also mean the absence of one of pro football's best-known annual traditions, with Mercury Morris and Nick Buoniconti, Paul Warfield and Larry Little, and all their '72 Dolphins teammates popping champagne corks each year when the last NFL team falls from the ranks of the unbeaten.

The Colts Stay in Baltimore

Those who knew him say Super Bowl III changed more about Rosen-bloom than just his relationship with Shula. But Shula might have seen it most clearly. "During that off-season, [Rosenbloom] started to, in my mind, take a lot of heat from his golfing buddies about the loss. He became known as the first owner to lose to a team in the new league... He wasn't used to losing at anything."

If the Colts had won, the city of Baltimore would have been more likely to give Rosenbloom the upgraded stadium facilities he was seeking, and he would have been far less likely to consider moving or trading his franchise, as he did with Bob Irsay, new owner of the Los Angeles Rams, in 1972.

The implications of that are numerous and far-reaching: no Irsay-owned Colts team fleeing Baltimore for Indianapolis under cover of darkness, and thus no Cleveland Browns moving to Baltimore in 1995 to become the Ravens. There's more: no Los Angeles Rams moving to Anaheim (as they did when Rosenbloom controlled the team), and subsequently no moving of the Rams out of Anaheim to St. Louis (as Rosenbloom's widow, Georgia Frontiere, later did). And if the Rams had never left Los Angeles for Anaheim, it's likely that Al Davis never would have tried to move the Raiders to LA, setting up a showdown with the league that scarred the NFL for decades, and emboldened other franchises to move.

Joe Namath Doesn't End Up in Canton

The advanced metric used by Pro Football Reference called Approximate Value attempts to place players on a uniform scale, comparing performances across leagues and eras. Namath, during his thirteen-season career, compiled an Approximate Value of 115. The other quarterbacks with the same AV were Norm Snead and Craig Morton. Both were good quarterbacks, neither great. Namath's numbers—173 touchdowns, 220 interceptions over thirteen seasons, in four of which he played in less than half his team's games due to injury—fit in comfortably with Snead's and Morton's career numbers.

Of course, Namath was a huge signing for the AFL, and the first pro quarterback to pass for 4,000 yards in a season. His cultural significance went beyond his passing stats. Even without the Super Bowl win, he is still Broadway Joe, with the llama-skin rug and the Fu Manchu, the most controversial player—and most eligible bachelor—of his era in pro football.

But without the Super Bowl III accomplishment, and all that surrounded it, his résumé doesn't get him elected to the Hall of Fame.

The Biggest Upset in Pro Football Is Postponed a Year

If the Colts had won Super Bowl III, the myth of NFL superiority would have been even more pronounced heading into Super Bowl IV; and the point spread, which had the Vikings favored by two touchdowns, would have been even greater. "They're doing it again," mused the Oakland Raiders' George Blanda in the week before that game. "They haven't learned a thing since last year. They're underestimating the AFL all over again."

When the Kansas City Chiefs—bigger, faster, better coached, better trained—came out and dispatched the Minnesota Vikings, 23–7, it served as a final reckoning, the deciding argument for the AFL's ultimate worth and accomplishment.

"Most people in the NFL thought that the Jets' win in Super Bowl III was a once-in-a-lifetime upset," said Steve Sabol of NFL Films. "It didn't really cause people to change their opinion. Everyone said, 'If they played the game ten times, the Colts would win either eight or nine times.' But after Super Bowl IV, nobody was saying that. After that, there was no doubt anymore—you had to grant that the AFL had reached parity. At the least."

But if the Colts had won Super Bowl III, the Chiefs' win would have been even more shocking. It would have stood alone as the lone Super Bowl victory for the AFL before it ceased to exist. If so, that game would likely be remembered in the same way as Super Bowl III is today, as one of the biggest upsets—and greatest acts of revenge—in sports history.

Realignment—and Everything Else—Is Irrevocably Different

On January 10, 1969, two days before Super Bowl III, National Football League commissioner Pete Rozelle walked confidently to the podium at the Hilton Plaza Hotel in Miami Beach to light a cigarette and field questions, in what was becoming known as his "state of the league" address.

Rozelle's facility at this task was so assured, his mastery of details and nuance so complete, that the sportswriters and broadcasters covering him were almost uniformly disarmed and dazzled. A few years later, when Dan Jenkins wrote the novel *Semi-Tough*, which imagined a parallel future world of pro football, he had Rozelle leaving the NFL to become a U.S. senator. This did not seem particularly far-fetched.

On the Friday before Super Bowl III, though, Rozelle was dealing with the possibility that the third straight Super Bowl—the offspring of the NFL and AFL's merger in 1966—would be a mismatch. After a close first half in Super Bowl I, the Packers had dominated the Chiefs, 35–10, in front of 61,946 fans (and about 32,000 empty seats). The next year, with the game selling out only hours before kickoff, the Packers trounced the Raiders by a similar score, 33–14. The NFL entry had never trailed, winning two games by a total of forty-four points. Now, as the 15–1 Colts were preparing to take the field as nineteen-point favorites over Joe Namath and the Jets, Rozelle was faced with doubts about the competitiveness of the league's ultimate game.

He responded by floating a trial balloon suggesting that, with the full merger coming following the end of the 1969 season, perhaps the structure that had led to two straight mismatches, with a third one seemingly imminent, might change.

ROZELLE INDICATES TOMORROW'S SUPER BOWL CONTEST COULD BE NEXT TO LAST was how the *New York Times* headline described it the next morning. Noting that the two separate leagues would come together after the 1969 season, *Times* writer William Wallace mentioned that the league's merger and realignment committee was exploring two plans, one of which called for a complete mixture of teams in the two leagues, with realignment "based on such considerations as geography, established rivalries, and stadium capacities."

The other one, favored by AFL founder and Chiefs owner Lamar Hunt, would have kept the old AFL-NFL distinction. There were obvious reasons for this, but there was also a downside. By virtue of being the older league, the NFL owned a vast majority of the top ten media markets. After two straight mismatches, few NFL teams wanted to cross the line to join a less prestigious league. And the conventional wisdom of the time held that it might be a decade before the AFL truly "caught up" with the NFL.

If the Colts had won Super Bowl III then, the pressure would have been even greater for a full blending of teams irrespective of NFL and AFL affiliations. At the very least, you would likely have had a different group of teams heading over to the AFC. And with that, the rest of the history of the league changes.

If the Steelers don't move to the AFC, you don't get the Immaculate Reception, because you don't have the Steelers and Raiders playing in the divisional round in 1972, the first in a string of five consecutive years of playoff battles in the defining rivalry of the 1970s. If Cleveland didn't move, you don't have the Browns' and the Broncos' epic championship games from the late 1980s. And if the Colts hadn't gone to the AFC, you wouldn't have had the Colts' and Patriots' marquee playoff pairings of Brady and Manning for much of the 2000s. In fact, to take a step further back, if the Browns don't move you may not have Bill

Belichick winding up in New England at all, but instead building a Browns renaissance in Cleveland.

All because of the outcome of one football game.

Imagine instead: The Colts completing a dream season. Tom Matte's fifty-eight-yard-run becoming part of Super Bowl lore. Jimmy Orr catching a flea-flicker for a touchdown in one of the most dazzling plays in the game's history. Don Shula carried off on the shoulders of Colts players. Rick Volk becoming a household name. Earl Morrall bringing back the crewcut to late sixties American culture, and later going on to model L'eggs pantyhose . . .

Well, OK. Maybe not *all* of that.

That's the problem with "What if?" Like so much in life, the changing of one outcome wouldn't just change that one thing. It might have changed everything.

In the end, only one thing seems irrefutable: If the Colts had won Super Bowl III, Bill Curry surely wouldn't have had to spend the next year watching Gerry Philbin eat soup.

26

What If the National League Had the DH?

Rob Neyer

Everything seems inevitable. You know. Once it's actually happened. The American League adopted the designated hitter in 1973—officially, merely on a three-year trial basis—because hitting in the league was down and (coincidentally or not) so was attendance, especially relative to the National League. Unimpressed, the NL continued to let its pitchers flail away, to little effect as usual.

And that's where we stand today, nearly half a century later.

But this hardly had to be the Official History of the Designated Hitter. In the 1890s, for God's sake, a proposal to eliminate the pitcher from the batting order nearly passed in the National League (this was roughly a decade before the American League even existed). In the 1920s, National League president John Heydler supported the institution of the "ten-man rule" (they weren't calling it a designated hitter yet, but the idea was the same). It's been written that the National League actually approved the change, but the American League nixed it (although it's not clear that the matter actually got quite so far).

And so the matter essentially lay until 1973, when the American League voted for the designated hitter, the National League demurred, and Ron Blomberg started thinking about a catchy title for his memoir (*Designated Hebrew*, 2006).

Well, the first two of those, anyway.

And it worked! Well, it sorta worked. Considering that most of the full-time DHs were old broken-down hulks like Orlando Cepeda and Tony Oliva, perhaps nobody should have been surprised when those early DHs failed to threaten any hitting records. But the American League's OPS (on-base percentage plus slugging percentage) still jumped nearly 10 percent in one season, from .649 to .710.

More to the point—for the owners, at least—there was a corresponding increase in attendance. A strike in 1972 depressed attendance, so we'll use 1971 as our baseline. In 1971, the American League drew only 69 percent as many fans as the National League. But in '73, with hitting up—and it should be said, the Kansas City Royals moving into a gleaming new stadium—the Americans' attendance increased by 13 percent (to 13.4 million), which in turn was 81 percent as high as the National League's.

So, progress. And proof, of a sort, that fans weren't all that thrilled by pitchers hitting. In 1977, the American League actually drew more fans than the National League. Yes, thanks largely to a couple of new American League teams, in Toronto and Seattle. But for any number of reasons, the AL *was* closing the gap. And one of those reasons was *probably* the DH.

In 1980, the St. Louis Cardinals' general manager was John Claiborne, and Claiborne wanted the DH in his league, too. All he needed was a majority: a yes vote from seven of the NL's twelve clubs. At a league meeting on the thirteenth of August, the matter came up for consideration once more.

At the time, executive vice president (and de facto general manager) Bill Giles was running the Philadelphia Phillies; his boss was owner Ruly Carpenter. In Giles's memoir, *Pouring Six Beers at a Time*, published in 2007, he places this meeting in 1977, but the details suggest that he almost certainly was remembering events of 1980. Giles:

> There were six teams in favor and four against when the vote came around to Philadelphia and Pittsburgh. Harding Peterson, the GM of Pittsburgh, was told by owner John Galbraith to vote the same

way as the Phillies because the teams were big rivals at the time. I tried to reach Ruly by phone but was told he was out on the ocean fishing. I did not know how to vote because of the year delay in adopting the rule [pushing the change from 1981 to 1982], so I abstained and the Pirates abstained. An abstention is the same as a "no" vote, and as a result of my inability to reach Mr. Carpenter that fateful day, there is no DH in the National League.

Again, it seems that time has blurred Giles's memory. Just a couple of months after the meeting, Bill Conlin quoted Giles citing a different reason for his abstention: The proposal was for full ratification, instead of a presumed one-year trial period. And Conlin has the vote going five in favor, four opposed, and three abstentions: the Phillies, the Pirates, *and* the Houston Astros.

Late in 2016, I spoke to the men who represented the Pirates and the Astros at that meeting: respectively, Harding "Pete" Peterson and Tal Smith. Peterson doesn't recall the meeting, but Smith told me that his boss, Astros owner John McMullen, had just recently purchased the franchise and wanted to avoid making a controversial decision. So Smith's instruction was to abstain, which he did.

Given the temporal proximity of Conlin's recounting—and assuming that Giles and Conlin both accurately reported the details—the story remains essentially the same: The National League didn't begin using the DH in 1981 (or '82) because Giles couldn't get Carpenter on the phone.

With victory seemingly so close, Claiborne said he would keep bringing up the DH until he got the votes.

Five days later, the Cardinals fired him.

But what if Giles had been able to reach Carpenter? Or what if he'd simply taken some initiative? Which he might have done, had he not been personally opposed to the DH. *What if?*

When wondering what might have happened if Ruly Carpenter hadn't been on that fishing trip—and, presumably, had given Giles the thumbs-up, with the Pirates coming along for the ride—we might start with the Phillies. If only because we know the most about their plans.

As the story goes, Ruly Carpenter favored the designated hitter for two reasons: veteran slugger Greg Luzinski and rookie slugger Keith Moreland, both of whom were born designated hitters. At the time, Luzinski was playing left field (poorly) and Moreland was catching (poorly). If you believe Giles, the plan was to install at least one of those big fellas in the newly created DH slot.

In fact, the Phillies would dispatch both of their prospective DHs to Chicago after the 1980 season: Moreland to the Cubs, where he became an adventuresome outfielder, and Luzinski to the White Sox, where he did become a full-time designated hitter.

My *guess*—and yes, we're just a few months past our historical hypothetical and I'm already guessing—is that the Phillies would still have traded (or sold) Luzinski, as he would have been restricted to left field and DH, while Moreland still had some nominal value as an occasional catcher. Plus, Luzinski had *not* hit particularly well in 1979 or '80, while Moreland was still young and (theoretically) improving. The Phillies also had Lonnie Smith, *another* born DH, on hand.

Point being, the Phillies wouldn't have needed Luzinski even with the DH. That said, he did enjoy a fine 1981 with the White Sox, and might well have done the same with the Phillies. As it happened, the Phillies qualified for the postseason by "winning" the first half of the strike-bifurcated regular season. They lost their League Division Series against the Expos, and all three losses were reasonably close: 3–1 in Games 1 and 2, and 3–0 in the decisive fifth game. And it's impossible to say who would have DH'd for the Expos in that series, as they opened the regular season without a single good candidate for the role. This actually placed them in the minority, as seven or eight National League teams (including the Phillies) closed 1980 or opened '81 with multiple fine DH types.

In 1982, the Phillies finished three games behind the first-place Cardinals. Moreland didn't hit all that well with the Cubs, while Luzinski did some serious damage with the White Sox. So whether or not the DH would have helped the Phillies depends on which hypothetical DH the Phillies had kept. Of course, one would have to project a DH onto the rival Cardinals' roster, and in backup catcher Gene Tenace they had an excellent candidate. It just goes to prove that the game of designated hitter counterfactuals is not an exercise for the faint of heart.

In 1983, the Phillies finished six games ahead of the second-place Pirates, topped the Dodgers in the National League Championship Series, then lost to the Orioles in the World Series, four games to one. There wasn't a DH in that World Series—they were still alternating in those years, odd years with no DH—but of course there would have been one if both leagues were using the rule. Hardly an edge for the Phillies, though, as the O's featured one of the best DHs, Ken Singleton.

And…yes! You're right! We've already pulled this thread far enough! Maybe too far. Getting one year out from the fateful meeting in 1980…well, OK. But two years out? Three? We're not talking here about a butterfly flapping its wings a few thousand feet above Mongolia, more like the explosion of Krakatoa.

We tried, though. We looked at *one team* and were faced with ever-increasing waves of uncertainty. What if we look at individual players?

As it's turned out, there have not been many tremendous designated hitters. Ever.

One fairly reliable metric for hitting production is Adjusted Batting Runs. From 1981 through 2016, there were nineteen player-seasons in which a designated hitter finished with at least forty-five Adjusted Batting Runs…and those nineteen player-seasons were turned in by only seven players: Edgar Martinez (seven seasons), David Ortiz (four), Travis Hafner (three), Frank Thomas (two), Manny Ramirez, Rafael Palmeiro, and Victor Martinez.

What a universal DH would have done is create a larger market for these players, along with other fielding-challenged sluggers like Gary Sheffield, Adam Dunn, Paul Molitor, Aramis Ramirez, and even Matt Stairs. Does Stairs spend his age twenty-six season in Japan if his National League team (Montreal) has an open DH slot? Maybe not.

But the old saw remains *almost* entirely true: If you can hit, they'll find a place for you. Even in the National League. With the exception of Stairs and perhaps a few others, the guys who should have been DHs *did* play regularly, somewhere. (You might argue that Rusty Staub would have spent his last few years with the Mets as a DH, instead of mostly pinch-hitting, which might well have gotten him to 3,000 hits—he finished 284 short—which in turn would likely have gotten him into the Hall of Fame.)

What might a DH have meant for National League pitchers? Well, more complete games for sure. In the first four seasons after the AL got the DH, its pitchers tossed 40 percent more complete games than National Leaguers; a decade later, it was still 35 percent more (of course, today almost nobody throws complete games at all, so there's no real difference between the leagues). But if pitching *with* a DH meant more innings for American Leaguers, it was also somewhat *easier* for them, because there's some (granted, small) evidence that when a pitcher does well as a hitter, his pitching suffers (slightly). Most of the other differences people talk about—more hit batters in the American League because the pitchers don't have to worry about retaliation, more injuries to National League pitchers because they have to stand up there and hit—aren't borne out by the numbers. The most *noticeable* difference would have been the absence of a tiny number of good-hitting pitchers in the National League; instead, fans in the eighties were treated to the legendary feats of Tim Lollar, Don Robinson, and Dan Schatzeder.

So we can do a fairly good job of guessing what would have happened to the players. The teams, though? It seems likely to me that if the DH had been universalized in 1982, many or even *most* of the World Series since then would have been won by different teams. If only because the composition of the National League contenders' lineups would have been significantly different, from Opening Day through the last game of the Series.

From 1982 through 1993, for example, seven of the twenty division titles were decided by three or fewer games in the standings.

Wait a minute. Only seven? Yes, only seven. And most of those seven were decided by *exactly* three games. Turns out maybe the pennant races we nostalgize weren't as close as we remember. But of course there have been dozens and dozens of races since 1993, for division titles and for wild cards, and many of those were close-run things. And the further you get from 1982, the less sense it makes to draw a distinction between the leagues. Because at some point all those players are in the same pool, competing for jobs and attention. And figuring out where all of them would have gone and how much they would have played—as opposed to how *well* they'd have played—is almost impossible. Practically speaking, that is.

Those three World Series the Red Sox won? They probably don't win them without David Ortiz. They might not win *one* without Ortiz. And if twice as many teams were looking for a DH in 2003, when the Red Sox signed Ortiz, does another team make him a better offer? It's not like the Sox were in love with him; he started roughly half their games in the first two months of that season, having opened the season behind Jeremy Giambi on the depth chart.

That's just one example. You simply can't radically change the lineup for *most* of the teams in the major leagues for thirty-odd years without creating a seismic change in the final outcome of each season. Even if we can fairly estimate the amount of talent in those spots, we cannot estimate exactly how and when that talent would have manifested itself. You might, like the Little Engine, think we can. But we cannot.

The three things we do know? For sure?

If the designated hitter had been added to the National League all those years ago, there would now be literally no difference between the two leagues. Same umpires, same rules, same managerial tactics. If the leagues were functionally the same we would all have one fewer thing to argue about. And if the leagues were the same, we wouldn't be treated to the spectacle, however occasional, of Madison Bumgarner and Bartolo Colón hitting home runs. This remains one of the small joys of baseball, defying the societal trend toward maximizing spectacle and profits.

Would any one of these things serve as a convincing argument against *finally* standardizing the rule and bringing the designated hitter to the National League? Not in these parts, no. All three of them, though? Hell yes. If you want to take the bats from the Senior Circuit hurlers, you'll have to pry them from our cold, dead hands.

It is therefore not implausible to conclude that had Ruly Carpenter delayed his fishing trip by one week, he wouldn't have had fish for those days, but Matt Stairs would have had enough fish for a lifetime.

27

What If Nixon Had Been Good at Football?

Julian E. Zelizer

When he was young, Richard Milhous Nixon loved to play football. He adored the game, mastering the minutiae of the playbook and savoring the thrill of gladiator-like competition. For a young man who was always trying to prove himself, football seemed like the ultimate arena in which to show what kind of man he was.

The problem was that Nixon was not very good at the sport.

This didn't stop him from trying. Although he had played soccer while in grade school, he turned to football—as well as basketball and track—once he reached high school, first at Fullerton Union and then at Whittier High School in California. Nixon was a meager 140–160 pounds (estimates of his weight have varied), perhaps better suited physically to the debate team—where he excelled—than to football.

To compensate for his stature Nixon became one of the hardest-working players on the junior varsity football team—during practice, at least. Even on the JV, young Dick Nixon, as his friends called him, almost never got much playing time. The methods that he liked to use in debate, like trying to bait an opponent into the wrong answer, were not very effective on the gridiron. Nixon lacked the basic physical tools required by football. Nobody who saw him play expected him to go far in the sport. "Dick just didn't seem to have the feel for it," one teammate said.[1]

Nixon did so well academically in high school that he earned admission into Harvard University. His family didn't have enough money to send him there; what money they did have went to the treatment of Richard's brother Harold, who'd fallen ill with tuberculosis, and they needed Richard to work at the family store. So instead of Harvard, Nixon attended Whittier College, a small, private Quaker school founded in 1887 and named after the poet John Greenleaf Whittier. Not being able to attend Harvard devastated Nixon, who would spend much of his life feeling that the Cambridge crowd didn't respect him.

Nixon would have to make a name for himself at Whittier. Based on his mediocre record in high school, Nixon didn't think that he could make the football team, which was quite good despite the school's size. The team's coach, Wallace "Chief" Newman, had been an all-American player at USC, and by most accounts was overqualified for the job. The Poets, as the team was called, played in the Southern California Intercollegiate Athletic Conference (a minor association of college teams in the Los Angeles area). The students called Newman "the Chief" because of his Native American heritage. He ran a pretty good team, and in Nixon's freshman year in 1930 Newman found himself short on players.[2] The coach invited Nixon to join the team to serve as a backup tackle. Nixon accepted.

While Nixon did slightly better at basketball and track, success in the game he loved eluded him in college as it had in high school. "We used Nixon as a punching bag," the coach recalled. "If he'd had the physical ability he'd have been a terror."[3] One of Nixon's teammates recalled that "he wasn't cut out to play the sport," while the team's water boy said that Nixon had "two left feet."[4] He was inspirational to his teammates only because he was so motivated despite being manifestly ill equipped for the game. Nixon "was undersized for a tackle, but he was too uncoordinated and slow-footed to play in the backfield," wrote his biographer Evan Thomas. "Mostly he was used as cannon fodder for the first team at practice and sat on the bench during games."[5] His teammates understood that when he came into the game an offsides penalty was soon to follow. Young Nixon was so enthusiastic he usually bolted over the line of scrimmage before the quarterback yelled "Hike!"[6] "Anyone who could take the beating he had to take, the physical beating, was brave," said another of his teammates.[7] Newman knew how to rouse Nixon. "He inspired in us the idea that if we worked hard enough, we could beat anyone," Nixon later recalled. That wasn't really true, but those words still motivated Nixon.

Nixon was called on to play in a game only if Whittier was so far in the lead there was no chance of losing. He weighed about twenty pounds less than any of his teammates, and he was painfully aware of his shortcomings. At one rally that was held on the field, he joked: "You know, it took me eighteen years to do it, but I've finally made it. I've got off the bench and onto the playing field."[8] The fans loved him. Toward the end of the games in which the Poets were losing badly, the fans would chant: "We want Nixon! Put Nixon in!"[9] Some of his outlook came from Newman, a leader he deeply admired, who liked to say, "Show me a good loser, and I'll show you a loser."[10] He had another aphorism: "You must never be satisfied with losing. You must get angry, terribly angry, about losing."[11] It was a refrain that Nixon would hang on to throughout his life.

By the time that Nixon attended Duke Law School in 1934, any dreams about a future in sports were long gone. Although he attended Duke football games with a religious passion, classmates called him "gloomy Gus," and he was known as something of a "slightly paranoid... oddball" during his years in North Carolina.

What if Nixon had been better at football? What if his physical talents had matched his aspirations, his enthusiasm, his savvy, his mind for the game? We can imagine a successful career at high school would have been followed up by a prime spot in the starting lineup in college. Playing at Whittier, which drew approximately six thousand people a game, might have been thrilling to an awkward young man wanting to be embraced by his peers.

Picture the young Nixon taking the field as the Poets' starting guard. Picture him leveraging his small frame and pancaking the defensive linemen trying to get to his quarterback. Or maybe picture him as an offensive weapon—a tight end, maybe, getting crunched over the middle and still coming down with his quarterback's passes. Picture him as a hero at Whittier, a big man on a little campus.

A change in Nixon's football fortunes might have set American political history on a different trajectory. At the most obvious level, a robust football career might have pushed Nixon away from an interest in politics, a combative arena in which he very much hoped to demonstrate the manful prowess he lacked on the football field.

But let's assume he went into politics anyway. Perhaps his football years might've yielded a different, more confident sort of politician. Historians of the Watergate scandal stress three different psychological dimensions to Nixon:

1. He was incredibly shy and socially awkward.
2. He saw himself as an outcast who was hated by all the popular and influential figures.
3. Though professionally and personally functional, he suffered from a persecution complex, believing that most people who knew him wanted to bring him down.

"You won't have Nixon to kick around anymore," he said after his defeat in the 1962 California gubernatorial race. It was a statement that defined so much of his political career.

He made his bones in Congress as a vicious anticommunist partisan who was constantly slashing his opponents. Later as president, he displayed strategic brilliance and an impressive command of public policy, but the darker qualities were always front and center. Nixon felt isolated from many of the major power brokers in Washington, operating from a defensive posture and nursing paranoid thoughts about the different players out to get him. Despite his own accomplishments, such as the opening of relations with China, he always believed that the Washington elite and many voters didn't appreciate what he was doing. He also spent much of his presidential life convinced that his enemies were relentless and unscrupulous. He didn't trust anyone, even his closest advisers, and he was prepared to ruin any person or damage any institution that gave a hint of wanting him defeated.

Evan Thomas reminds us that when Nixon was not in a formal setting, he exhibited an intense shyness that allowed strong and malevolent voices in the White House to push his presidency in bad directions. Nixon's infamous "enemies list" was the ultimate manifestation of this dynamic. Even at the height of his power, in 1972, Nixon created a culture in his reelection campaign whereby his underlings felt compelled to do whatever was necessary to cut down the Democratic opposition. The Watergate scandal and the aggressive, resentful presidency it ended had many causes. But it is clear that Nixon's shy, paranoid, and insecure personality was a central factor in bending the White House toward his skewed view of reality.

Now let's substitute for this Nixon our counterfactual conquering jock of Whittier—a winner still basking in the praise and perquisites that accrue to such athletes. Would this Nixon have been more of an extrovert? A schmoozer eager to bring as many people as possible into his circle? We are familiar with these kinds of politicians—congressmen such as Jack Kemp, who won an AFL MVP while quarterbacking the Buffalo Bills; or Mo Udall, a basketball star at Arizona; or Ronald Reagan, a starting guard at Eureka College—and it's tempting to draw a line between the success they enjoyed in sports during their formative years and the sunny-jock ease with which they approached public life. Even Fidel Castro, who ruled Cuba during the tenures of all those aforementioned American names, was a skilled baseball player. For all Castro's brutality and abuses, insecurity was not among his flaws; perhaps his sports-based confidence played a small part in his ability to hold power for fifty years.

It is also interesting to note that the man who would serve out Nixon's term was a skilled center and linebacker at the University of Michigan. And while Gerald Ford cannot be said to have had a successful presidency, he did lead a happier life, marked by geniality and a sense of being confident in his own skin.

Is it possible that a stellar college football career might have made Nixon a different man? He might have felt more certain of himself, less concerned that everyone was trying to tear him down. The historian Robert Dallek wrote that Nixon was "a secretive, devious, thoughtful, energetic, erratic, and painfully insecure man who struggled against inner demons and sometimes uncontrollable circumstances to reach for greatness."[12] But what if he'd already achieved greatness in a different arena? Rather than being focused on continually proving himself to a political culture that didn't think much of him, a more secure man might not have surrounded himself with the kinds of shady operators who bugged the Democratic National Committee headquarters in an unnecessary effort to win an election that was already all but won.

Nixon did remain a huge fan of football throughout his life. He often thought of football when he was president, frequently using the metaphor of the sport to support some of his most aggressive political actions. "His use of football analogies was so revealing," said cabinet member Elliot Richardson. "Anything was OK, except what the referee sees and blows the whistle on."[13] Nixon even once explained to his seasoned national security adviser Henry Kissinger that fighting wars was like playing football: "You give ground in the middle of the field, hold the line at the goal line, and then score a touchdown."[14]

Failing at football seemed to teach Nixon the grim lesson that he had to be ruthless to get by and that he had to give triple the effort of everyone else to succeed. Lacking what he saw as the natural skills of his peers, Nixon schemed, connived, and did everything he thought was necessary to achieve victory. Divorced from the knowledge that Nixon oversaw one of the darkest chapters in presidential history, a simple assessment of his skills as a politician and an aspiring football player read as virtues. Determination, grit, resilience, refusing to succumb to limitations, a kind of courage: These are all traits most of us would like to see in our children. Of course, they all can turn into vices, and that's precisely what we saw in Nixon.

Still, it is captivating to ponder the possibility that success in the game he loved most could have kept those character traits from curdling. The actual Nixon was ever the wounded animal, so lacking in social and personal confidence that it led him down the rathole of a scandal that shattered the public's trust in American politics. But imagine a Nixon who was driven but not deranged. Strategic but not constantly scheming. Ever prepared but never paranoid. This Nixon, imbued with a self-worth derived from bona fide achievements on the fields of play in his youth, might still have had the drive to become president, but he would also have had the good sense never to have emboldened the criminals who broke into the Watergate Hotel, or at least the character to immediately own up to the misdeed. That Nixon might have finished his second term as a stunning success, as the president who remade relations with China and the Soviet Union and enjoyed a massive reelection victory. Maybe, just maybe, that Nixon would not have helped create a public so disenchanted with American politics that they would be willing to elect a game-show host to the White House.

The Nixon we got was never the star, never even the starter. He was the tackling dummy. He was cannon fodder, the victim of constant beatings and humiliations. And for that we all paid the price.

28

What If Bill Walton Had Healthy Knees?

Bob Ryan

The 1976–77 Portland Trail Blazers went into the NBA Finals as distinct underdogs versus the star-laden Philadelphia 76ers, who featured Julius "Doctor J" Erving, George McGinnis, Doug Collins, Darryl Dawkins, and Lloyd Free. They dropped the first two games in Philadelphia. But once back in the raucous Memorial Coliseum, they were a different team. They won Games 3 and 4 by a combined total of fifty-four points, defeated Philly by a 110–104 score in Game 5, and brought home the championship with a 109–107 triumph in Game 6. Bill Walton was the Finals MVP, and with a starting lineup including no one over thirty, the future was extraordinarily bright.

Indeed, for three-quarters of the 1977–78 NBA season, the Portland Trail Blazers had completely dominated the league, going 50-10 in the first sixty games. If the Blazers could finish the season at the same rate they had played the first five months, they'd finish with the third-best regular-season record in NBA history up to that point. But Walton came down with a foot injury, and he was soon joined on the sideline by more starters. A depleted Trail Blazers team finished the regular season at 8-14 and then was sent home in the first round of the playoffs by the Seattle SuperSonics in six games. The great promise was never fulfilled.

I spoke with Walton about that team and I did some research. And so I have concocted a scenario in which the devastating injuries that wrecked their team never occurred and nature had taken its proper course instead. I believe they would have beaten the Washington Bullets in 1978, Philadelphia in 1979, and anyone who was put before them for several more years. I believe we would have seen one of the great title runs in NBA history—and, of course, Bill Walton agrees.

PORTLAND THREE-PEATS AS CHAMPS

by Bob Ryan, Globe Staff, June 2, 1979

PORTLAND—It was nothing we haven't seen before. Here, yet again, were the Portland Trail Blazers elevating the sport of professional basketball to a true art form. They executed exquisite half-court patterns. They ran textbook fast breaks. They played exceptional team defense. They simply imposed their will on the Philadelphia 76ers, wrapping up a third straight NBA title with a 118–99 destruction that was really not that close.

"The ball never stops," crowed Bill Walton, the obvious Finals MVP. "*We* never stop."

"We're not a dribbling team," Walton continued.

No, they're not. And another thing they are not is aged. Here they are, winners of three consecutive NBA titles, and with no starter yet to reach the age of thirty. The NBA is going to be confronted with the reality of the Portland Trail Blazers for a long, long time.

The Trail Blazers do have their occasional hiccup. They undoubtedly didn't expect to be returning home for a Game 5 after that 125–94 joyride in Game 3 had given them a 3–0 series lead. But credit Philly and the noble Julius Erving for showing some pride and class with that overtime win in Game 4. Dr. J reminded everyone just who he was with his forty-point effort.

But the reward for all that was a trip to the Memorial Coliseum, where the 12,666 sound like 126,666, and where, as Walton put it, "the fans never let us quit. They lift us up to make us better than we could ever be on our own."

The game began with Walton backward-bounce-passing a feed to a cutting Bobby Gross, and that was the beginning of what could only be described as a hoop clinic. We have known for some time the combination of these particular players and this particular coach has placed the Trail Blazers on an aesthetic level that has been matched in league history only by the Russell-era Celtics and the Knicks of the late sixties to early seventies.

But the coach is Jack Ramsay, who has written a book titled *The Coach's Art*, in which he describes his sport of choice as "a ballet, a graceful sweep and flow of patterned movement counterpointed by daring and imaginative flights of solitary brilliance." God love Red Auerbach, but he never talked like *that*.

The Trail Blazers are all that and more. Finesse is fine, but finesse sometimes needs to be augmented with a little muscle, which is where Maurice Lucas comes in.

Now it would be foolish to deny that Mr. Walton is the best player on this team. About the only one who won't concede that point is Bill Walton. That said, the Trail Blazers would be a far different proposition were it not for the oft-menacing presence of Lucas, whose official nickname is "the Enforcer." Recall the '77 Finals, when he stood up physically to the hulking Darryl Dawkins. Many say that was the turning point in the series.

Walton is president of the Maurice Lucas Fan Club. "Maurice does what others can't or won't do," Walton explains. "He is the greatest teammate I've ever had. He has a saying: 'I'll take care of it.' It could be a basket, a rebound, a pass, or, if necessary, knocking someone on his butt."

It might even be a handshake. People seem to have forgotten that just prior to Game 3 of the '77 Finals, Lucas broke away from his team's huddle. He ran down to the 76er huddle and held his hand out to Dawkins, with whom he had engaged in a titanic tussle the game before. "No hard feelings," he said as he shook Dawkins's hand. A befuddled Dawkins wasn't sure how to take it. "We didn't have to worry about him after that." Lucas chuckles.

Among the great attributes of this great team is its versatility. There is no question their first preference is to run. Ramsay emphasizes this by writing, as Walton says, "in big, bold letters," the words RUN-RUN-RUN on the blackboard in the dressing room. "Then," Walton continues on about his coach, "he looks at Gross and says, 'This means *you*, Bobby.'"

The small forward out of Long Beach State is the true unsung hero of this team. His only individual accolade thus far in his career has been a second-team All-Defense nod this past season. What he is for this team is sort of a poor man's John Havlicek, which is not a bad thing to be.

"Bobby Gross is the key to our flow," says Walton. "The ball never stops with Bobby."

In a league loaded with glamour small forwards, Gross's name is seldom mentioned as being among the elite. This will happen when you play with the likes of Walton and Lucas. "He gets matched up against the big names and they will usually have better stats," Walton explains. But at the end of the game Bobby has played a better game of basketball.

"He's a brilliant post feeder," Walton adds. "He moves so well without the ball. He goes back door. He leaves the opponent dizzying with possibilities." (Yes, Bill Walton actually does speak this way.) "He's just a great athlete. Golf. Tennis. Doesn't matter."

Starting with that opening backdoor layup, Gross put on a typically understated Bobby Gross show with twelve points, six rebounds, and five assists.

The champs are not limited to one gear when they run. Here they were, cruising along nicely in the first quarter with a 28–17 lead. That was when Ramsay went to the bench, inserting Johnny Davis for starter Lionel "Train" Hollins, and then things really got interesting. The Trail Blazers were about to go from 45 rpm to 78.

The way the ever-enthusiastic Walton tells it, there's Fast, Faster, and Johnny Davis.

"The fastest guy in the history of basketball," gushes the Big Redhead.

That may be a tad hyperbolic—remember that Walton has never had gray in his Crayola box—but the fact is that with Davis zooming up and down the floor the Trail Blazers expanded that 28–17 lead to an impregnable 57–32 lead before Ramsay gave him a blow.

Interspersed with all that running were some beautiful half-court maneuvers, some initiated by the guards and some by Walton, who has entered the discussion as to who just might be the best passing center of all time.

By the way, it may very well be that to refer to him solely as a great "passing" center is to damn with faint praise. For upon closer examination Bill Walton might be the best center we've ever seen. Period.

This thought would qualify as utter heresy to fans of such great post players as Bill Russell, Wilt Chamberlain, and Kareem Abdul-Jabbar. And, yes, it's way too early in Walton's career for him to have accumulated the numbers or acquired the hardware that august trio has amassed. But simply based on what each man could do to help his team win any specific basketball game, Bill Walton is absolutely their equal.

He is the control tower through which any coach would run both his offense and defense. He is not out there specifically to score, but like his idol Russell he scores when it is available and/or necessary, as Memphis State can tell you. He averages eighteen a night, but he can get you thirty. He is a superb rebounder, with flawless technique. He ranks with Russell and Wes Unseld as an outlet passer. Quite frankly, he is a better team defender than either Wilt or Kareem, and he is a better offensive player than Russell, and that's while recognizing Russell's vastly underrated passing skills. No center has ever brought more to the table that could be translated into winning a single basketball game than Bill Walton.

This game was a typical Bill Walton outing: nineteen points, twenty-one rebounds, seven assists, three blocks, and complete control of the game at both ends.

He would be the first to tell you he couldn't have found a better coach. Jack Ramsay is not just a good X-and-O man; he has a higher vision. He also has a passion and focus second to none. When it was announced that he was leaving Buffalo to take the Portland job prior to the 1976–77 season, he was asked how he was going to deal with all that rain in Portland.

"During the season," Ramsay replied, "I don't have time for weather."

The incessant Portland winter rain does not keep the adoring fans from coming out to see this magnificent team. You know what? It wouldn't matter if they *did* play outdoors. It would be worth getting a little wet to watch this team play.

Bill Walton never healed, at least not in Portland. He missed all of the 1978–79 season. He went to San Diego for an unfulfilling six-year run, during which he missed two more full seasons and was only able to play in 179 of 492 games. He went to Boston, where he was the Sixth Man of the Year on the championship 1985–86 Celtics. He was injured again the following season, playing in just ten games. He retired in 1987. The Trail Blazers got back to the Finals once in 1992, losing to the Chicago Bulls. Their only championship was in 1977. Says Walton of the '77 champs, "Not winning with that group again has left a stain on my soul."

P.S. His son Luke was named after Maurice Lucas.

29

What If Roger Bannister Trained Today?

Liam Boylan-Pett

It's June 21, 2017. Runners all around the world—high schoolers and professionals alike—are posting the same image on Instagram. It's a grainy black-and-white photo of John Landy from sixty-three years ago. He's in white short shorts, a dark tank top, and a race bib numbered 2. The captions are different but the same, paying homage to the man who, on that June day in 1954, became the first human being to run a sub-four-minute mile.

One man isn't posting a photo, though. Roger Bannister isn't joining the celebration. About two months before Landy's historic feat, Bannister was in the best shape of his life. He figured he was going to be the first person to dip under that magical 4:00 barrier. Life is weird, though. Two months before the race that would make John Landy a name synonymous with speed and the limits of human achievement, Roger Bannister marked a milestone of a different sort. He became the first human to be cryogenically frozen. He was unfrozen in May 2017, and, after urinating for, you guessed it, three minutes and fifty-nine seconds, he was told to join a professional running group. These scientists wanted to see how fast he could be. Bannister, too, was invested in gauging his land speed. He was far less interested in commenting on a photo of his one-time rival John Landy on some palm-sized computer that doubled as a phone.

We should now admit, for the two readers who were unsure of the nature of this enterprise, or of science, that no, Roger Bannister was never actually frozen. In fact, on May 6, 1954, Roger Bannister ran 3:59.4 to become the first man under four. But suppose he hadn't. What if an in-his-prime Roger Bannister *was* transported to the present day? How fast could he go?

Sure, had Bannister been cryogenically frozen, a few interesting occurrences would have transpired. The Oceania region for a time would have taken over the world of athleticism thanks to Sir Edmund Hillary of New Zealand summiting Everest *and* the Australian Landy conquering the mile. But for our purposes there is the more fundamental question: How fast would Bannister be today? With sponsorship money for pro athletes and technological advancements in training, tracks, and racing shoes, would he still be one of the best in the world? Or would a thawed-out Bannister have looked at the current world record in the mile—3:43.13—and said, "I have no chance"?

Physically, Bannister had the tools, then and now—prefrozen and unfrozen—to be one of the world's best. But while many of today's best milers run upward of eighty miles per week, Bannister found time to work out while getting his medical degree. In fact, before he broke four for the first time, Bannister took the previous five days off from running—which would be a laughable scenario given today's training standards. Even so, Bannister was the best miler in the world in 1954, and some think he could be one of the world's best in the 2010s, too.

Dr. Michael Joyner certainly believes in him. "Bannister would be at least 3 percent better today than he was in 1954," Joyner, an expert in human performance at the Mayo Clinic, says confidently. For Bannister, a 3 percent improvement would equal 7.16 seconds. With a personal record of 3:58.8—a race in which he beat Landy head-to-head in August 1954—Bannister would, Joyner believes, at the very least be a 3:51-miler in today's track and field landscape.

"The 3 percent puts him at 3:51 or so," Joyner says. "Then I'd give him a second or two thanks to more competitive races. That puts him under 3:50. Then give him a second or two for training past the age of twenty-five and having a longer competitive career. Would he have run 3:45 in a real world? We don't know. But is it reasonable to think he could dip under 3:50? Yes."

Joyner published a 1991 paper in the *Journal of Applied Physiology* predicting that a human could run a marathon in 1:57:58. In 1991 that prediction seemed crazy, but after Kenya's Eliud Kipchoge ran 2:00:25 in a controlled Nike-sponsored race with the help of multiple pacers and ideal conditions, Joyner is looking more and more like a seer. Joyner believes that VO_2 max (an athlete's aerobic capacity, or how well oxygen is transported through the body), lactate threshold (the point at which the burning occurs in your legs while running), and running economy (stride efficiency) are the three most important aspects to distance running. While we have learned more and more about these areas in recent years, Joyner has seen test results that show runners from the 1950s reaching similar levels of VO_2 max and lactate threshold to the athletes of today. Athletes have been training hard enough to build up VO_2 for a while now, he says. "This idea that current athletes are substantially better in sports like running," Joyner says, "it's just not there."

Joyner isn't saying that Bannister would be the best miler in the world today, but he does believe Bannister had the tools to mix it up with the top athletes—especially when considering the advancements in technology in 2017 compared to 1954.

First off, tracks and racing shoes were terrible in comparison to the speedy surfaces and lightweight shoes available today.

In Bannister's heyday, tracks were made of packed cinders, crushed rocks that have a similar firmness to pumice. Cinder tracks weren't exactly slow—especially the new one at the Iffley Road Track in Oxford, where Bannister broke four in 1954—but compared to the all-weather synthetic tracks of today, cinder tracks are akin to running in grass instead of running on cement. Cinder tracks are much softer than synthetic tracks—meaning that a runner uses much more energy to push off against the ground than he or she would against the hard surface of a track, which is much bouncier. Many estimates say a cinder track is good to slow a runner down about one to two seconds per lap.

In a TED Talk from 2014, David Epstein researched cinder tracks, and, with the help of biomechanics experts, discovered that cinder tracks are about 1.5 percent slower than the synthetic tracks athletes race on today. Epstein is the best-selling author of *The Sports Gene*, a book on the science of extraordinary athletic performance. A runner himself, he's very intrigued by how fast Bannister would run today—and Epstein thinks Bannister could have been a great. "Having looked at his training logs and having talked to him," Epstein says, "I think he'd potentially be a sub-3:50 guy."

Getting to sub-3:50 would be possible not only because of a newer track—state-of-the-art shoes would help, too. Not as much as you'd think, however.

Spencer White is the vice president of the Saucony Human Performance & Innovation Lab in Waltham, Massachusetts. There, Saucony uses high-tech equipment and high-speed cameras to measure how shoes affect an athlete's foot strike and body movement. White says that racing spikes haven't advanced as much as we might think they have.

Bannister broke four minutes in a custom pair of track spikes that weighed a reported 4.5 ounces. Saucony's lightest distance spike weighs 2.8 ounces (Nike's Zoom Victory weighs 4.1 ounces). White calculates that every three ounces in spike weight translates to an improvement of 1 percent in speed, meaning Bannister's spikes weren't holding him back much based on weight.

In terms of construction, Bannister's spikes were made from thin leather and had permanent half-inch spikes jutting out of the leather soles to cut through the cinders. With each step, those spikes sliced into the cinders and then skidded back out. "Pushing the spikes in and then pulling them out adds a tiny bit of time," White says, "but the tiny things add up."

White says that spike and track technology have purposefully advanced in tandem. The give of the track interacts with the firmness of the shoe, which affects the amount of spring a runner has in each step. Newer spikes are made with more cushioning thanks to lightweight foam and plastic spike plates. The biggest advantage in today's spikes, according to White, is that extra bit of cushioning that doesn't compromise the weight of the shoe—and more cushioning makes for a more comfortable shoe. And while it is very hard to put a number on it, a less pained runner is, in general, a swifter runner.

The next major area to consider is Bannister's training, which, compared to a modern runner, might be considered not training.

Kyle Merber is a 3:52 miler in the United States. His sponsorships and race winnings allow him to run full-time. Merber runs eighty to ninety miles per week mixing in workouts (something like 3 × 800 meters at 1:55), tempo runs (ten miles at 5:05 per mile pace), and long runs of sixteen to twenty miles. Plus, he's in the gym lifting weights and receiving treatment from physical therapists and sports masseuses to stay healthy.

Merber's training mixes endurance and speed—Bannister's was mostly what is called speed endurance. In *The Four-Minute Mile*, which Bannister wrote the year after he achieved the feat, Bannister published some of his training logs. While he did run a staple workout that milers still do today (10 × 440 yards at 59-second pace), Bannister's training was much different in that it consisted mostly of interval training. The longest distance he ran in the month leading up to his 3:59 was nine miles. Plus, two weeks before his May 6 race, he took a weekend off to go rock climbing in Scotland to relax. A coach would lambast an athlete for such an act today.

"To run under four minutes in the way that he did shows that he was clearly a specimen," Merber says. "With fifty years of elite track athletes experimenting with optimal ways to train, he'd be at the level of top runners today, too." Merber predicts Bannister would run 3:49, especially when you add in the level of competition he would face.

Bannister had two incredible pacers in Chris Chataway and Chris Brasher to lead him through three-quarters of the race when he broke four, but, depending on the conditions of a modern race, he could have had a warren of rabbits in front of him. In 2015, running on the historically fast track at Monaco, Matthew Centrowitz—who in 2016 became the first American to win Olympic gold in the 1,500 meters since

1908—ran 3:30.40 for 1,500 meters (the equivalent of a 3:47.17 mile). Centrowitz placed tenth. If Bannister found himself running on the back of a train of racers, it's hard to imagine that his competitive nature wouldn't kick in and he finish at least within the pack.

Or he might have faltered with so many competitors in front of him. Running is more than the spikes and cinders of gear and the ability of the human body. There's a mental aspect to the sport, too. Mental strength set Bannister apart in the 1950s, but it's what might have ruined him in the 2010s.

Everything written above has supposed that Bannister would be all-in on training full-time—but what if he wanted to go to medical school? It may sound foolish, but if someone had already broken four, would Bannister be as interested in setting a record at all? Bannister retired shortly after breaking the barrier—he was only twenty-five—and was much more interested in his medical studies than in racing. In fact, he's *Sir* Roger Bannister not because of his running, but because of his work as the chairman of the British Sports Council.

David Epstein thinks Bannister would be capable of running sub-3:50, but he also has his doubts that Bannister would want to. "I think the most likely scenario is that he probably would have been a less competitive runner in some ways," Epstein says. "The fact that he was able to go cold turkey on running at the age of twenty-five suggests it wasn't something he *had* to do."

According to Epstein, doing something significant was what drove Bannister: "He told me when he got fourth in the 1952 Olympics, if he had gotten the bronze, he would have stopped there. There was something patriotic about it to him. Breaking four was what drove him."

In January 2009, I ran a mile in 3:59.40 to become the 315th American under the mark. (I would eventually run 3:57.75, which, according to Dr. Joyner and his Bannister Three Percent Rule, would be worth a 4:04.88 in 1954. Damn.) For me, four minutes was a milestone, but not an unprecedented one. It's the difference between circumnavigating the globe in a modern sailboat versus being Magellan—but it was still a life-changing moment. It was a day filled with all those cliché emotions of working your ass off to accomplish something and actually doing it, and it still is something I talk about whenever running comes up. When someone finds out you're a runner, they first ask if you've run a marathon. Then, once you tell them that you ran at the Olympic Trials, they ask you your mile time. Most would be impressed if you told them you had run 4:59—saying 3:57 blows their mind. Because of Bannister, the general population knows what four minutes and the mile means. At least six thousand sub-4:00 miles have been run, according to alltime-athletics.com. The large number has rendered the mark less significant, but it's still a milestone—one that people get behind. My phone exploded with text messages when I did it for the first time in 2009, and that was before I could even post a photo on Instagram celebrating my feat.

It would therefore make sense that as a driven and talented runner, even a med-school-crazy Bannister would want to dip under four just once, establishing himself as a great, if not the greatest, runner. Most of today's professional runners spend all day as athletes—Bannister would scoff at these runners napping and playing video games in their free time—but others have succeeded while pursuing other careers. Daniel Lincoln set the American record in the 3,000-meter steeplechase while in medical school. Annie Bersagel ran a 2:28 marathon while working as a full-time lawyer. Wesley Korir finished fifth in the Boston Marathon while serving as an elected member of Kenya's parliament.

Plus, Bannister might have jumped at the chance to experiment with new technologies and training methods like going to altitude. The question is: How much of his life would Bannister want to put into running? According to the man himself—not that much.

In 2014, Bannister told *Sports Illustrated* he wouldn't have been a world beater. "I accept the fact that were I running today, I wouldn't be breaking world records," he said. "I just happened to be there at a crucial time." He admitted he wouldn't have put off medicine to pursue a professional running career, saying, "It's not really life as a whole, is it?"

Imagining Bannister had been cryogenically frozen and then thawed in 2017, though, it's hard to fathom he'd just ignore all the hard work he had already put in and simply walk away from his sport—especially with Landy getting all that credit. Bannister would have to give it at least some semblance of a try.

So, we shall stipulate that a 2017 Bannister was sufficiently motivated, properly equipped, modernly trained, running on faster tracks, and adequately defrosted. He also would be better remunerated, although Bannister was never driven by riches.

The only thing not in Bannister's favor is that he wouldn't have been a history maker. Even if he somehow beat Hicham El Guerrouj's world record, it's not the same as leading humanity under four (Bannister's name is much more recognizable to the public than El Guerrouj's).

Each expert I spoke with said Bannister had the tools to challenge sub-3:50, but Epstein's warnings about Bannister's psyche stood out the most to me. Bannister was a special athlete, and he had a special mental skill set. It really does seem that he wouldn't have been singularly dedicated to becoming the best runner in the world today. He likely would have run 3:53 or 3:54 and been a phenomenal runner—perhaps making the Olympic team for Great Britain—but his pull toward medicine never would have abated.

Bannister would break four at least once. He would make sure to run faster than Landy ever did. Then he would post a photo of himself on Instagram, similar to that image of him on the Iffley Road Track from 1954, his face full of pain and exhaustion, but this time in new spikes and on a synthetic track. His caption would read: "Got you, John."

Satisfied, he would then retire and head to the office to study.

30

What If Nat "Sweetwater" Clifton's Pass Hadn't Gone Awry?

Claude Johnson

The NBA was founded in 1949 with seventeen franchises, an awkward number that created an unbalanced schedule. Why was there no eighteenth team, and why did the league omit the New York Renaissance, a highly successful, all-black professional barnstorming squad, as one of its charter franchises? A closer look reveals that history might have turned on a single possession in an over-looked game. What if the play had gone differently?

It was the evening of Saturday, April 10, 1948, and Robert Louis "Bob" Douglas was at the Hotel Grand, a "Negro hotel" on South Parkway and East Fifty-First Street on the South Side of Chicago. His basketball team, the all-black professional New York Renaissance Big Five, was staying there. They were perfectly fine with not using the Morrison Hotel on Madison Street in the downtown Loop district, where most of the white teams entered in the Tenth Annual World's Championship of Professional Basketball were housed.

Though the Morrison was much closer to Chicago Stadium where they would play in the tournament's title game the following night, the "Rens," as they were known, preferred to lodge in the part of town where they were welcomed and embraced as heroes: Bronzeville.

Besides, the Grand was one of black Chicago's most fashionable hotels. Quiet yet ritzy, overlooking the bronze statue of George Washington at the entrance to Washington Park, it was the hostelry of choice for the country's topmost African–American entertainers, athletes, and business owners. It was where the Rens always stayed, ever since 1939 when they won the Chicago-based tournament's inaugural championship.

Sponsored by the *Chicago Herald-American* newspaper, the event had become a yearly classic that was always "the greatest parade of basketball stars ever seen in one meet."[1] Douglas felt confident. The Rens had amassed a record of 110-10, or about twenty wins a month in a season that included a twenty-two-game winning streak.[2]

It had not been easy, though. As an independent team, they did not have the luxury of a regular league schedule, which meant the Rens had to travel near and far to generate income. Their barnstorming schedule took them to Connecticut, New Jersey, Pennsylvania, Ohio, and Illinois, as well as to West Virginia, Kentucky, Missouri, Tennessee, and Georgia, where Jim Crow laws and customs severely restricted their access to basic travel resources like lodging, restaurants, and gas stations. Getting back to the South Side and the Hotel Grand for the annual championship was an incentive and a reward in and of itself.

Earlier in the day, news had arrived from Germany that the Nuremberg war crimes trial was over and that fourteen Nazi SS officers were sentenced to hang for the murder of millions of Jews. Wire service reports said they were guilty of leading special brigades of "triggermen" ordered by Hitler to "wipe out Jews, gypsies and others tagged by the Nazis as *racial undesirables.*"[3]

For many African Americans, this news seemed hypocritical because those war criminals sounded very similar to Jim Crow lynch mobs. Black folks were asking, "What about us?"

Bob Douglas was asking and answering this question in his own way, through basketball, and he had every reason to be proud. Since founding the team in Harlem in 1923, the diminutive and charming St. Kitts native had achieved more success than anyone ever could have dreamed. The Rens had utterly dominated basketball, winning 2,588 of 3,116 games for a staggering winning percentage of 83 percent over twenty-five years, which averaged to about 103 victories per season. Despite the travails of the times, Douglas achieved these successes with unwavering honesty, charm, and cheerfulness, which earned him the nickname "Smilin' Bob."

However, something was gnawing at the man. For him, the next day's title matchup against the top-seeded Minneapolis Lakers, the leading team in the National Basketball League, had far-reaching implications that made it more than just a must-win championship game.

Yes, winning this tournament signified basketball supremacy; it would bring praise and would certainly be an honor. Additionally, the champion would get the event's $5,600 prize, a relatively large sum considering that in New York City the rent for a three-room apartment with a Frigidaire in a quiet neighborhood was $26 a week.[4] That would definitely help.

But there was an even bigger prize. He wanted equality. Douglas was tired of the "Colored Champions" label. He wanted the New York Renaissance to belong to a top professional league so they could be called simply "Champions." This would also provide the financial stability for which he yearned.

Douglas believed he had an angle. The best pro clubs played in the NBL and in the younger, less established Basketball Association of America. Less than a year earlier, the BAA had voted to deny Douglas's effort to join, despite advocacy from Joe Lapchick, the star coach of that league's most important team, the New York Knicks. Yet both the NBL and the BAA were struggling with gate receipts. They had begun scheduling doubleheaders that used the Rens and the Harlem Globetrotters, another powerful African-American basketball squad, for the front-end games to entice more ticket buyers for the main event. However, this caused a backlash. "The lily-white BAA will gladly use the Globetrotters or the Rens to draw in the crowds, but draws a rigid line on Negro players or Negro teams playing in the league," one African-American publication voiced.[5] Still, though these were whites-only leagues, Douglas felt that now, economic necessity might make them overlook race.

He was encouraged in this way of thinking when the less prominent though more established American Basketball League, a small-town circuit, began employing black players, including Cleveland Indians baseball star Larry Doby, who was signed by the Paterson Crescents.[6] The ABL was even reportedly courting Smilin' Bob himself.

However, Douglas was holding out in hopes of first winning another outright World Professional Championship title, which he could then leverage for a greater negotiating position with the leagues.

Of the eight professional teams invited to compete in the Chicago tournament, five belonged to the NBL—the Anderson Packers, Fort Wayne Zollner Pistons, Tri-Cities Blackhawks, Indianapolis Kautskys, and Minneapolis Lakers. Another team, the Wilkes-Barre Barons, belonged to the ABL. The two African-American teams—the Rens and the Globetrotters—were independent barnstorming clubs. Teams from the BAA did not participate.

To win the championship, Douglas went whole hog to stack his team. That meant padding his existing roster with any new ringers he could sign. This was common practice, year after year, but this time the ambitious owner got the season's biggest coup, a player who gave the Rens a clear shot at upsetting the favored Lakers.

Minneapolis had been almost unstoppable that season. Their high-powered offense featured two future Hall of Fame players in six-foot-ten center George Mikan of DePaul University, the game's first true big man, and six-foot-four small forward Jim Pollard of Stanford.

The Rens had seven players on their official tournament roster. At point guard was future New York City Basketball Hall of Fame member Eddie "the Rabbit" Younger. Roscoe "Duke" Cumberland, an all-time great former Globetrotters player, played shooting guard. So did Sonny Woods, a veteran of the all-black Washington Bears team that had won this tournament in 1943. The frontcourt had Jim Usry, a former Lincoln University star, at small forward; William "Dolly" King, a future member of the Long Island University Sports Hall of Fame, at power forward; and team captain and future Basketball Hall of Fame member William "Pop" Gates at center. George Crowe, who was Indiana's first "Mr. Basketball" and is enshrined in the Indiana State Basketball Hall of Fame, was a versatile utility player. In 1946, Crowe had played alongside Jackie Robinson with the Los Angeles Red Devils, a pro squad that split a two-game series with the Chicago American Gears, an earlier NBL team that featured Mikan as a rookie, by keeping the towering goaltender in check.

In the past, this would have been more than enough talent to win. But that was before Mikan. No one on the Rens roster was taller than six foot four. They still needed a true big man, and that was where Douglas made his shrewd move. He signed a highly talented six-foot-seven, 220-pound center named Nathaniel "Sweetwater" Clifton as his eighth player.

This was a coup. Everybody wanted Sweetwater, who was "conceded to be one of the best pivot men in the business."[7] Clifton was a fine rebounder at both ends who could handle the ball and run as well as defend in the pivot. "He is one of the greatest *bucket men* we have seen in some time," wrote the *Woodstock Daily Sentinel*, an Illinois newspaper.[8] Some sportswriters felt he was as good as Mikan. Yet there was nothing flashy about him. "He is the stolid, silent, Joe Louis type of athlete," reported the *New York Age*, a leading African-American newspaper, referring to the notion, which many people believed regardless of their race, that the more physically dominating a black athlete, the more docile, friendly, funny, or even subservient he ought to appear.[9]

Born and raised on Chicago's South Side, Clifton had been a highly publicized star at DuSable High School, located just five blocks from the Hotel Grand. He averaged nearly thirty points a game during four years as a starter and even scored twelve points in an AAU game against the DePaul University freshmen, a squad led by George Mikan.[10] "Sweetwater Clifton will enroll at DePaul in the fall," wrote a local columnist after the senior's last official high school game in 1942, a loss to Mt. Carmel despite twenty-eight points from the center. "He hopes to be a doctor."[11]

Instead of DePaul, Clifton turned up at Xavier University of Louisiana, where in one 1943 game against Benedict College he scored forty-two points before setting a new scoring record in the Southern Intercollegiate Athletic Conference postseason championship tournament.

After serving nearly three years as a United States Army staff sergeant in Europe, he returned to basketball and reportedly signed a contract with the Harlem Globetrotters in 1946, appearing in a press release for their season-opening tour of Montana. Trotters' owner Abe Saperstein was thrilled about acquiring Clifton and would later say, "He can do more tricks with a basketball than a monkey can do with a peanut."[12] That same week, though, Saperstein's excitement turned to fury when Clifton never showed up.

The center went to New York City instead and signed a contract with the Rens! His professional basketball debut was on November 5, 1946, in a home game with the Bridgeport Bullets at the Renaissance Ballroom in Harlem.

Saperstein was so upset that he filed a lawsuit charging that Clifton was "rightfully his property." But even while that case was in court, Clifton no-showed again, this time ditching the Rens and reappearing with the Dayton Metropolitans of the National Professional Basketball League, a small-town loop in the Midwest.

He played a few games with the Mets until, one day in January 1947, a newly created franchise, the Detroit Gems of the National Basketball League, announced they had signed Clifton to a two-year contract reportedly worth a then-unimaginable $1,700 per month. However, the big man played just *one game* for the Gems, only to vanish again.

He resurfaced with the Dayton Metropolitans, whose owner, a local businessman named Elwood Parsons who ran the Metropolitan Clothing Stores chain, insisted, "He's my property." Simultaneously, Rens owner Douglas roared, "Clifton is my player!" Meanwhile, Globetrotters owner Saperstein staked his claim to the superstar by stating for the record, "I'll take the case to the Supreme Court of the United States if necessary." Not to be forgotten, Detroit Gems owner C. King Boring chimed in. "We brought him here from Dayton and signed him to a two-year contract," the entrepreneur insisted. "We'll go to court if he isn't returned."

Renowned *Pittsburgh Courier* sportswriter Wendell Smith called it "the 'Strange Case' of Sweetwater Clifton."[13] At this point, Clifton's pro career was barely three months old.

With the 1947 World Pro Tournament approaching, Douglas declared that the Rens, a top draw at the box office, would withdraw from the event unless the rangy center played for his team. This settled the matter of Clifton's allegiance, for the time being. He wore the navy-and-gold uniform of the Rens, who lost in the first round.

Despite his contract jumping, Sweetwater's game was beyond reproach as he began the 1947–48 season. Rens manager Eric Illidge marveled that Clifton "can shoot like blazes and handles the ball like it's a golf ball."[14] He remained "the people's choice."[15]

Douglas saw the 1948 World Championship as a showdown between his Rens and the seemingly unstoppable Lakers. He knew they could be defeated. Sure enough, before a mid-February sellout crowd of 17,823 fans at Chicago Stadium, Mikan and his team suffered a dramatic loss to the Harlem Globetrotters on Ermer Robinson's long-distance swish that just beat the timekeeper's gun. The contest had been billed as the "Game of the Year."[16]

Now the Rens took note of how the Trotters had pulled off that win, by double-teaming Mikan to the point of frustration. Using the same strategy, Douglas would employ Clifton and William "Dolly" King, both powerful and physical players who were solid defenders, to cover Mikan.

After defeating the Bridgeport Newfields and the Tri-Cities Black-hawks in the preliminary rounds behind twenty-eight and then nine-teen points from Clifton, the Rens were ready, and the stage was set for the Sunday night championship showdown with the Lakers at Chicago Stadium.

The game got underway with a 9:30 p.m. tip-off in front of 16,892 fans, but the Rens' double-teaming strategy quickly backfired when both Clifton and King drew three fouls apiece just a few minutes into the first quarter and had to be benched. That left George Crowe, an all-around athlete with a reputation for outstanding defensive skills, to guard Mikan. He got help from Duke Cumberland. The plan worked well. Even though Mikan had fourteen points, the first quarter ended with the Rens down just 18–17.

The Lakers ran their offense through Mikan, but they had many scoring options, so he responded by looking for assists. This forced

Clifton and Cumberland to back off, which allowed Mikan to attack. Out-of-position defenders had to foul him or allow easy buckets, so the Lakers' center began racking up free throws, ten altogether in the second quarter. Minneapolis surged ahead, and Mikan had twenty-eight points as the Lakers went into halftime leading 43–35.

To start the second half, the Rens fought and scrapped on every possession, holding Mikan to just five points in the third quarter, until they were down by just one basket, 57–55, at the end of the period.

Then it was Clifton's turn to take over the game. He led a rally early in the fourth quarter, pushing the Rens ahead, 58–57. The Lakers answered. Four straight field goals by Jim Pollard and a basket from Paul Napolitano led to another Rens comeback and a tremendous see-saw battle, until, with one minute to play, the Rens were down 73–71.

The Lakers had possession in a half-court set, attempting to milk the clock while the Rens frantically pressured on defense. Time was running out when suddenly Sonny Woods stole the ball. Turning, he spotted Clifton, who had been guarding the pivot spot and was now racing up the middle of the court. Woods hit Clifton with a pass in stride, and instantly the big Rens center was in the middle of a three-on-one fast break with two teammates streaking up ahead to his left and to his right in perfect position to tie the game. This was textbook basketball, as basic as a two-handed chest pass taught to six-year-olds first learning the game.

But what happened next stunned everyone in the stadium. Clifton, the sure-handed, fundamentally sound, undemonstrative center, threw a *behind-the-back* pass...straight out of bounds. *Behind his back? What?!*

Now it was the Lakers' ball with only seconds left in the game. They inbounded to Mikan, who iced it with another field goal for the win. Final score Minneapolis 75, New York 71. The Lakers were world champions.

"Clifton threw the game," Crowe told me point-blank, when I asked him about that play during a personal interview in 2009, more than sixty years after the fact. By then, having suffered a stroke, Crowe was living in a nursing home, the last surviving New York Rens player. Sitting on his bed in a sparsely decorated room wearing pj's, he literally had little to protect or hide. Those comments echoed what he had shared in 1991 with Ron Thomas, author of *They Cleared the Lane: The NBA's Black Pioneers*. "He threw that ball away and that cost us the World Championship," the fiery former Rens guard said then. Though his speech had slowed down, Crowe was sharp, witty, and conversational. It was clear that he was still bitter about that incident and was not mixing up the facts. After all, no one in Chicago Stadium watching the game that night had had a better view of what happened than Crowe—he was on the court trailing that fatal, final fast break, directly behind Clifton.[17]

The pass was shocking not only because it was such a bad breach of fundamental basketball—the kind of needless antic that would get any modern-day AAU player benched—but also because it was completely out of character for the Harlem-based team. Douglas, their owner, did not like showmanship.

In addition, the Rens missed twelve free throws that game. This was curious, since two nights earlier, they had hit their first 17 attempts from the charity stripe, and 21 out of 24 total. Six of the free throw misses were by Clifton, who finished with 28 total points, while Mikan alone accounted for a dozen of the Lakers' 15 total free throws and 40 points in all. This was the difference, as both teams had made 28 field goals each. RENS BLOW FREE THROWS AND NATIONAL PRO CAGE TITLE, read that week's *Chicago Defender* headline. "The New Yorkers also *blowed* away a lot of admirers," the newspaper continued, adding insult to injury while hinting at the seemingly obvious suspiciousness involved.[18]

Rens owner Bob Douglas was devastated.

Afterward, no one could tell whether Clifton had merely blown or outright *thrown* the game. Though a poll by newsmen voting him to the All-Tournament team put Clifton in the clear, circumstantial evidence seemed to point to another conclusion.

There was no doubt the DuSable High School graduate was in basketball for the money; in fact, for all it was worth, and then some. Perhaps this was because Clifton was a newlywed, having been married in February as the World Pro Tournament was approaching, and was in need of a financial cushion.[19] Maybe that mercenary approach was informed by Clifton's hardworking parents—his father was a shelfer and his mother a machinist. Or by his grandparents, tenant farmers in Indian Bayou Township outside Little Rock, Arkansas, who, by definition, went where the crop money was. They could make a living but within limits, especially in Arkansas, where "white landowners understood that their continued prosperity depended on the exploitation of black sharecroppers and laborers."[20]

As if to confirm suspicions that cash ruled him, on July 31, 1948, newspapers reported that Clifton "became one of the highest paid Negro athletes in history yesterday when he signed with the Harlem Globetrotters for a reported more than $1,000 a month."[21] Abe Saperstein and the Globetrotters would begin their 1948–49 season "fortified with a new star, Nathan 'Sweetwater' Clifton."[22]

These reports may have revealed just who had had the most to gain by the Rens' loss that night. It may have been Saperstein. The entrepreneurial Globetrotters owner had not only financial ties to the NBL and the BAA, forged behind the scenes in unwritten backroom agreements, but also a strategic stake. Remember, the leagues were struggling with gate receipts while his Trotters were rolling in profits. Saperstein wanted to keep it that way. So he agreed to help the circuits boost attendance using his Trotters in their doubleheaders, but only if they agreed never to sign any black players.

It was an unwritten rule. "There might have been an understanding, but nobody would ever dare put it in writing," longtime Philadelphia Warriors employee Harvey Pollack remembered.[23] Saperstein wanted an exclusive lock on African-American basketball talent. BAA and NBL owners were so afraid to lose their sure-fire draw that they allowed themselves to be bullied into complying with Saperstein's wishes.[24] "They were afraid that Abe Saperstein, if they took one of his players, he would tell them to jump in the lake, which would cost them hundreds of thousands of dollars," recalled Carl Bennett, then general manager of the Fort Wayne Pistons.[25] But the Globetrotters owner got a double financial benefit. He not only got a cut of the gate receipts but also, since he controlled the supply of African-American hoopsters, he could negotiate lower salaries with them.

Why were the Globetrotters so profitable? They played first-rate hoops *and* entertained fans by adding comedy to the game. They *clowned*. This was something that Douglas refused ever to do. It was not in his DNA, mainly because Smilin' Bob was in it "for the betterment of the race," as the old Colored YMCA branch fund-raising posters of the 1910s used to say. But this refusal cost him. The Rens couldn't compete with the salaries Saperstein offered, even when he kept contracts artificially depressed. In addition, Saperstein's backroom understanding with NBL and BAA owners obliged them to block Douglas from booking large-capacity arenas they controlled, like Madison Square Garden, which seated 18,000; Minneapolis Auditorium, with capacity for 10,000; or Philadelphia Arena, which could hold 8,000.

The 1948 tournament was the last edition of the annual World Championship of Professional Basketball, which had enjoyed a decade-long ride. The basketball landscape was changing. The BAA and the NBL, despite being the leading professional hoops circuits, were unsure which franchises would remain in their respective leagues. This uncertainty was the result of continual fighting between the leagues over the rights to top college recruits, and the player salary bidding wars that followed. This animosity had started when the BAA was formed in 1946 and promptly began raiding NBL franchises for their best players and venues.

For the vulture-like BAA as well as the reeling NBL, which would face difficult choices during the 1948 off-season, the outcomes of the upcoming World Pro Championship and subsequent NBL Finals pitting Minneapolis against Rochester were pivotal.

NBL owners were scheduled to meet in early May, but even before they could convene, the Minneapolis, Indianapolis, Fort Wayne, and Rochester franchises bolted from the league to join the BAA. The BAA now had twelve teams while the NBL was reduced to seven, with only three franchises in its Eastern Division. With the 1948–49 season approaching fast, the frantic NBL hastily added a team called the Detroit Vagabond Kings, a new creation of former Detroit Gems owner C. King Boring.

The league had its eight teams to start the season, but soon realized that the Vagabond Kings were bankrupt. Now more desperate than ever, they invited the New York Rens to replace Detroit. Rens owner Douglas would have been better off had the invitation been made before the season began. Instead, being out of options, he settled for adopting a losing franchise several weeks into its abysmal season. This meant the Rens had to move to Dayton, change their name to the Dayton Rens, and, worst of all, assume the Vagabond Kings' record of 2-17, last place in the league standings.

Nevertheless, on December 19, 1948, at the Dayton Coliseum, the Rens made history by debuting in the National Basketball League. "This is the first time a Negro quintet has ever played in the NBL and is considered a forward step by those who have followed the pro basketball situation over the years," wrote the *New York Age* on Christmas Day. "Now, the unpublicized bar is completely removed," the *Syracuse (New York) Post-Standard* exclaimed, "not by admitting individual Negro players, but by taking in a complete Negro team!"[26]

However, it may have been a Faustian bargain, because the Rens were out of playoff contention before they ever even suited up. Making the postseason would have meant winning every single remaining game, forty contests in a row.

In addition, Dayton's basketball fans didn't support their new all-black home team with ticket sales. Attempting to maintain revenues, Douglas was forced to split his squad so that a version of the "old" New York Rens could keep touring, despite a half roster, while the other half played on as the Dayton Rens. This strategy was admirable but had regrettable results, with the Dayton version of the team posting only a 14-26 record in their remaining games.

Furthermore, as the 1948–49 season ended, the NBL and the BAA began discussing a merger to form a new league called the National Basketball Association, which was to be in place for the 1949–50 season. Representatives of the leagues and teams met on July 1, 1949, in separate conference rooms at the Morrison Hotel in Chicago to plot out the details. "All nine teams in the NBL were represented at the meeting and appeared ready and able to field teams," initial reports said. "It was indicated that all teams in both leagues desiring to continue in pro basketball would operate any merged organization," newspapers further reported. "It would mean at least a 21-team circuit."[27]

The first casualties were three financially struggling BAA clubs, the Indianapolis Jets, Providence Steamrollers, and Washington Capitols. Four NBL teams were also rumored to have withdrawn due to lowly business results.

"The Dayton team of the NBL had a poor financial season last year and finished the campaign as a road team," it was reported, as the alleged reason they opted out.[28] Obviously. They were not even welcomed in their own city, Dayton, as a replacement for a bankrupt Detroit organization. Yet every pro franchise was struggling. "The majority of the teams of both leagues reportedly lost money in their last campaigns," it was said.[29] Besides, Douglas was no stranger to lean years, having kept the Rens afloat even during World War II, with all of its cutbacks and rations. Despite these rumors, Dayton still appeared to be in the running for inclusion in the forthcoming NBA. Douglas was on the doorstep of triumph.

The NBL had not ruled Dayton, its own franchise, out of consideration for what was to be a nineteen-team league. However, when this proposal reached BAA president Maurice Podoloff, he rejected it. "We turned this down because our owners felt such a group would be too unwieldy for schedule purposes," he said.[30]

But was that the real reason? If he had wanted fewer teams, couldn't Podoloff merely have encouraged Providence, the one other franchise rumored ready to withdraw, to just go ahead? This would have resulted in eighteen clubs, a balanced number for scheduling, since it would allow for three divisions of six teams each.

The real motive seemed to become evident on the second day of the NBL-BAA merger discussions. NBL president Ike Duffey took the BAA's rejection at face value, walked away from the negotiating table, and announced, "The NBL will operate again this winter as a nine-team league, with the Indianapolis Olympians replacing Dayton, which has dropped from the league."

However, something did not add up. It was later learned that the NBL had pulled a fast one.[31] In its scramble to acquire college stars, the

NBL made a disingenuous play for four seniors on the prior season's NCAA national champion University of Kentucky team. Instead of bidding against the BAA for the players' contract rights, the NBL simply created the Olympians as a new franchise with the former Kentuckians on its roster, to snatch them off the would-be free agent market all at once.

But that wasn't all. It was soon revealed that the Olympians were so assured of their inclusion in the NBL that they had already leased the Butler Fieldhouse for their games.[32] This assured that the facility's former occupants, the Indianapolis Jets of the BAA, would cease to exist.

Clearly, the talks were not officially over, as there seemed to be a lot of face-saving behind-the-scenes negotiation still in progress.

To recap, the Olympians of the NBL were in, while the Jets of the BAA were out. The fledgling NBA now stood at eighteen teams without needing to "replace" the Dayton franchise. So, was it true that the Rens voluntarily "dropped from the league"? Or was this a premeditated ouster designed to provide cover for the "sure-fire" Olympians?[33]

Waiting for the other Chuck Taylor to drop did not take long.

PRO BASKETBALL LEAGUES UNITED, read the astonishing headlines by month's end, without advance notice. *What?* "Big time professional basketball now is just one huge happy family of 18 members," wire services reported.[34] All along, the leagues had been holding secret meetings in Indianapolis, where they finally reached agreement. Official statements coming out of this conclave did not mention the Dayton Rens.

The newly organized National Basketball Association would include ten out of the twelve original former BAA teams, all but the Indianapolis Jets and Providence Steamrollers, and seven out of the nine original NBL teams, all but the Hammond Calumet Buccaneers and Dayton, plus a new franchise, the Indianapolis Olympians.

By now it was exceedingly clear that the leagues' intention was to get rid of Douglas and the Rens. They wanted not only an eighteen-team circuit but also the removal of the African-American team. This was no supposition, as evidenced by a shift in the way the Dayton omission was characterized once the merger became final in early August 1949.

Whereas previously "they dropped out," implying it was by choice, reports began stating the franchise was affirmatively "dropped" and "eliminated" and "wiped out."[35]

Moreover, the vaunted eighteen-team arrangement never actually materialized, because the Oshkosh All-Stars were also summarily "dropped from the NBA," just weeks before its season opener, because, as news accounts explained, "no one in Oshkosh offered payment of the league dues before last Saturday's deadline."[36]

This is how the NBA began with just seventeen franchises when its 1949–50 season began in October. It was an awkward number, with the league now forced to reshuffle into three uneven divisions, the East, Central, and West. The three-card monte was completed when NBA commissioner Maurice Podoloff told the Philadelphia Basketball Writers Association, "the present setup of 17 teams divided into three divisions is unwieldy," and that he was considering applications for new franchises from Grand Rapids, Cincinnati, and Cleveland for the 1950–51 season.[37]

It certainly would have been an opportune moment to invite the Dayton franchise back into the equation, thus rounding the number back to eighteen. But that didn't happen. For the NBA, the Rens card was never even in the deck.

At that moment, Bob Douglas was, in effect, ruined. The New York Rens organization folded, its players disbanded, and Douglas walked away from his life's work. Meanwhile, Abe Saperstein re-signed Clifton to another $10,000 contract with the Harlem Globetrotters for the 1949–50 season.

Looking back, what might have happened if Sweetwater Clifton's pass in the 1948 World Championship of Pro Basketball had been accurate?

The Rens would have scored on that fast break to tie the game, with momentum in their favor. They could have pulled out a win either in regulation or, had the tie stood up, in overtime.

That win would have meant African-American teams had captured four of the ten world championship titles, including the first and the last. Douglas would have had the advantage negotiating with the BAA and the NBL.

He might not have joined the NBL nor felt compelled to do that so deep into the 1948–49 season. Instead, the league would have invited the Rens as its first choice from the outset. Douglas might have passed on the NBL's invite completely and waited for an offer from the BAA. Why would the 1948 world champions stoop to rescue the desperate, weakened, and inferior NBL?

Had the Rens joined the NBL then it would have been on Douglas's terms, from the beginning of the season, with a clean slate, in a city and arena of their choice. Douglas would have secured Clifton under contract rather than lose him to the Globetrotters. With reliable gate receipts, the Rens owner would have kept his squad intact and they easily could have made the 1948–49 NBL playoffs as a likely two-seed in the Eastern Division. After defeating Hammond in the opening round, the Rens would have reached the Finals with a win over Anderson, to face the Oshkosh All-Stars, who they had defeated routinely over the years, and who in actuality were swept by Anderson.

As champions of the NBL, the Rens could not have been ignored in the NBL–BAA merger discussions.

Instead, rather than having the Rens be *replaced* by the Indianapolis Olympians, the NBL and BAA would have kept the Rens and *added* the Olympians, to make nineteen total teams in the merged league. If the owners did not object to the awkwardness of seventeen teams, then nineteen teams would have been just fine. When the NBA subsequently dropped Oshkosh, the number of franchises would have been reduced back to eighteen charter members, including the Rens, to create the balanced divisions and schedules that Podoloff and the league so desired.

In the first NBA Finals, the Minneapolis Lakers defeated the Syracuse Nationals in six games. Had the Rens been involved, there is a strong likelihood they would have reached the Finals instead of Syracuse, and faced Minneapolis with every possibility of winning in that best-of-seven series.

The NBA consolidated down to eleven teams before its second season, an awkward number. But with the Rens, there would have been twelve franchises in total, resulting in a nicely balanced schedule with six clubs in each division.

With the Rens in the league, the Lakers likely would not have won four out of the first five NBA Finals.

Meanwhile, the NBA's color barrier would have already been broken by the 1950–51 season. From the start, its owners would have been moved to stock their rosters with as many African-American players as possible. For that matter, what would have kept Douglas from trading his black players to other teams in return for white talent, and vice versa?

In all likelihood, Nat Clifton would not have been available for the Knicks to sign in 1950, as Douglas would have secured his contract with the Rens, assuming that the big center stayed put there. That makes it doubtful the Knicks would have made the NBA Finals, perhaps even at all, during those early NBA years.

The fates of the two men who along with Clifton broke the NBA color barrier would have been affected as well. The Celtics might not have waited so long—until the second round of the 1950 draft—to select Chuck Cooper. It's doubtful he would have even still been available by the time Celts owner Walter Brown got the fourteenth overall pick. Could the Capitols have afforded to wait until the ninth round to select Earl Lloyd as the one hundredth overall pick?

The 1950 NBA draft class featured four future Hall-of-Famers but after that only one other player who made at least one All-Star Game or a single All-NBA Team. What if the more than one hundred players drafted had included African-American collegians or independent free agents? Who else was out there?

Would there have been any hesitation about signing Harold Hunter, Chuck Harmon, or Isaac "Rabbit" Walthour? Would they still have been available by the 1950–51 season? What about former Olympian and UCLA star Don Barksdale, or his Oakland Bittners teammate Davage Minor?

Less known African-American stars like Benny McNeil, Henry

Singleton, and Clarence "Hank" Forbes of the New York State Basketball League would have gotten a shot. What about former New York
University star Jim Coward, also with the NYSBL, or phenomenal
Rutgers player William "Bucky" Hatchett? Not to mention the number
of outstanding players from historically black colleges and universities,
who were too many to count.

Moreover, how many Harlem Globetrotters stars would have aban-
doned the organization and jumped to the NBA, as did Chuck Cooper?
Abe Saperstein was pulling out the stops to keep his players secure...
tours of Mexico and Europe, lead roles in his motion picture deal, and
bigger salaries. Yet those temptations did not stop Cooper from quitting his Trotters contract to join the Celtics, so it stands to reason others would have followed suit.

In addition, it is possible to imagine that the league-wide pressure on
African-American players to conform to certain patronizingly imposed
character traits might have been lessened. "In those days you weren't
picked on your ability," said Henry "Hank" DeZonie, who was in
actuality the fourth black player signed by the NBA. "You had to be
the Pope, you had to be a saint."[38]

No doubt, the path would not have been easy, but had the Rens not
been shut out of the NBA, then the league's racial integration would
have unfolded at a quicker and smoother pace. Dozens of forgotten
African-American ballers would have made the grade or arrived much
sooner.

Finally, Rens owner Bob Douglas would have thrived if given a fair
chance in the newly established NBA. He could have shared his genius
with the league during its infancy as a fellow owner and general manager alongside greats like Ned Irish, Les Harrison, Leo Ferris, Danny
Biasone, and Eddie Gottlieb. Just maybe, Douglas's wisdom and popularity, as well as his formula for success and knack for spotting talent,
would have helped the league avoid its early struggles to become better
sooner.

Skipping years ahead to the 2016–17 NBA playoffs, the racially
integrated New York Renaissance—with some European, African, or
South American players on their roster—might have met LeBron James

and his Cleveland Cavaliers in the Eastern Conference Championship. The ninety-four-year-old Rens would have been the oldest team in the league, by far. But their rapid-motion unselfish offense and smothering help-defense would still be the cornerstone of the franchise's timeless playing style.

Alas, none of that came to be. Clifton's errant pass sailed into the sideline din, thwarting the path of history, and leaving us with *it might have been*.

Epilogue

After his Rens folded, Robert "Bob" Douglas retired from basketball and promoted the Renaissance Ballroom & Casino in Harlem, an entertainment complex that was the team's former home court. He was enshrined in the Naismith Memorial Basketball Hall of Fame in 1972, the first African American to be so honored.

Once the NBA began signing black players, Abe Saperstein cut his ties with the league and began emphasizing comedy and, brilliantly, taking the Globetrotters on international tours in Mexico, Hawaii, Europe, and Asia. In subsequent years, the tricks and antics of his players stoked the imaginations of countless fans of all races and ethnicities, in rural towns as well as inner cities. He was enshrined in the Naismith Memorial Basketball Hall of Fame in 1971.

Sweetwater Clifton signed with the New York Knicks in 1950, becoming one of the first three African-American players in the NBA. He played eight seasons in the NBA, retiring in 1958. For many years, Clifton supported neighborhood causes in Harlem and in his native Chicago. He was well loved and an accessible idol who inspired people, sometimes with his sheer presence. Today, the New York Knicks' annual Sweetwater Clifton City Spirit Award honors community members who are local heroes through their efforts and contributions that make a significant difference in the lives of others. Nat "Sweetwater" Clifton was enshrined in the Naismith Memorial Basketball Hall of Fame in 2012.

31

What If Game 7 of the 2016 World Series Had Turned Into Every Sports Movie Ever Made?

Josh Levin

"Firm front leg!"

It's funny what pops into your head during Game 7 of the World Series. When Kris Bryant closed his eyes, he found himself swinging a bat in Las Vegas in 2003, on a diamond that was more brown than green.

"Elevate it!"

Bryant's front leg stayed firm, just like his dad had taught him, and the ball elevated and elevated and kept on elevating. He'd never hit one that far. It's possible no eleven-year-old ever had.

With the Cubs up 6–4 and Aroldis Chapman on the hill, Bryant's reverie flew into fast-forward. He fantasized about the dogpile on the mound and the champagne dousing his uniform and the victory parade down Michigan Avenue. Chapman could fling a baseball faster than any man who'd ever lived. Rajai Davis couldn't hit a lick. The ball came in at 97.1 miles per hour. It left Davis's bat at a tick above 101. By the time Bryant turned his head, the game was tied. Seven outs later, the sky opened up, soaking the third baseman's cap with nonalcoholic precipitation. During the rain delay, the Cubs slugger would have some time to slow his breathing and gather his thoughts, to go back to that peaceful, perfect instant when he'd watched a baseball soar deep into the desert night.

Francisco Lindor was six years old, chasing a ball down a hill in Gurabo, Puerto Rico. Addison Russell was playing Little League in Pensacola, Florida, his mom's voice crying out from the back of the metal bleachers. Nobody had asked for these home movies to start rolling. Nobody had invited their moms, dads, *abuelitas*, and *hermanos mayores* to take up residence inside their heads. It just happened, all at once, to everyone decked out in Cubbie blue and Indians red. Every flashback told a story of a lifetime spent running, fielding, throwing, and hitting. Each one of the fifty players who'd suited up for Game 7 was the sum of thousands—tens of thousands—of these small moments, any one of which might float into consciousness as the Cleveland grounds crew covered the brown-and-green infield with a white plastic tarp.

All that hard work was about to pay off. It was gut-check time. It would all come down to this. And also, a dog had wandered into the Cubs clubhouse, and a prepubescent kid had pulled Bryant aside to inform the twenty-four-year-old slugger that he was going to sit the rest of this one out. The pooch was playing third, and he was batting in the three hole, and that was the way it was going to be.

Jason Heyward—a Harley-riding bad boy and air hockey hustler who'd worn out his welcome on his last club on account of hogging all the balls in the outfield—had been the first to notice the golden retriever, and the sad-looking boy tossing pop flies to his pet in the tunnel underneath Progressive Field. That dog was a gamer, a four-legged Willie Mays. The nondog version of Willie Mays—which is to say Willie Mays—had been good enough to lead the New York Giants to a sweep over the Cleveland Indians in the 1954 Series, hadn't he? Heyward went looking for Joe Maddon, to tell him there was nothing in the rulebook that said a dog couldn't earn a spot on the Cubs' postseason roster.

Maddon was a nonconformist, the kind of manager who didn't mind that one of his players insisted on calling him Morris Buttermaker. But Maddon was no longer in charge of the Chicago Cubs. He'd keeled over minutes earlier, just after whispering four final words: "I love you, kid." The skipper's last will and testament spelled out an unusual line of succession. That kid Heyward found wandering in the tunnel—Billy was his name—and his irascible dog Bud were running the ball club now. They'd be the ones to decide if the Cubs won their first World Series in 108 years.

The ghosts of Ernie Banks and Ron Santo would be hitting fourth and fifth, thanks to a disembodied baritone that seemed to have a reasonable grasp of baseball strategy. *Ease their pain,* it said. *Let's play two,* it added. *Are you sure it's a great idea to have a dog hitting third?* the voice continued after a brief pause. *Sure, it can catch a baseball in its mouth. That makes sense. But dogs don't have opposable thumbs. What about that chimp from* Ed? *Which is to say Ed. He can play a little, and I'm sure he could use the work.*

Down the hallway, behind a closed door, the home team had received some disturbing news: A former showgirl named Rachel Phelps had bought the Indians, and she was doing her best to sabotage their season so she could move the franchise to Miami.

"What about Larry Dolan?" asked Lindor, the team's young shortstop. "Isn't he still the principal owner? Also, there's already a team in Miami. The Marlins. They beat the Indians in the World Series back in '97."

"We'll have a chance to fix the plot holes in postproduction!" manager Terry Francona shouted. He'd been a pretty fair player in his day, but he'd washed out of the game because he couldn't dry out. After a stint as the head man of the Rockford Peaches, he'd found his way back to the Show. When the going got tough, he'd let off steam by berating the sensitive Lonnie Chisenhall for his lachrymosity.

"And one more thing," Francona told his squad. "Remember that chimp from *Ed*? He's on the team now. Playing the hot corner. Got a rocket for an arm."

Corey Kluber hit the showers, but there was no hot water. Coco Crisp went to get a quick lift in, but all the barbells were broken.

Goddammit, Rachel Phelps. Mike Napoli prayed that Jobu would take the fear from his bats and got so mad that he turned into a wolf, or maybe that was just the way his beard looked—it had always been really gross and scraggly.

"Did I ask for your excuses?" Francona screamed. "I don't want them to gain another yard. You blitz all night! If they cross the line of scrimmage, I'm gonna take every last one of you out! You make sure they remember, forever, the night they played the Indians!" Lindor tried to tell his manager that he had the wrong sport, but Francona was too busy musing about how Progressive Field had the same measurements as their gym back home in Hickory.

The rain stopped, the tarp came off the field, and Bryan Shaw jogged in from the Indians bullpen wearing a pair of thick black glasses. As the fans sang "Wild Thing," the Cubs' canine third sacker sniffed the Indians chimp, trying to figure out if it was a real-life mammal, a simian-shaped machine, or a primitive animal-robot hybrid with the same agent as Matt LeBlanc.

The Cubs scored a pair of runs in the top of the tenth, thanks to timely hits from Kyle Schwarber and Ben Zobrist, plus a sac fly from the golden retriever that moved pinch runner Albert Almora into scoring position. That voice didn't know what it was talking about. Bud could hit a curveball.

Carl Edwards Jr. got the first two outs in the bottom of the frame, but then Brandon Guyer drew a base on balls, and the light-hitting Davis knocked him home. It was a one-run game with one out to go.

Billy walked to the mound and patted his reliever on the rump. He was going to call on another righty to get the final out. That righty was himself, and he'd changed his name to Henry, because that seemed like a better name for a kid who could whip a fastball due to a botched surgical procedure. Henry's arm had gone limp, though, for reasons that kind of made sense at the time but collapsed under later scrutiny. To get the final out, the noodle-armed child would have to outduel the Indians' wily, sore-kneed catcher Jake Taylor (Tom Berenger), a guy whose actions both on the field and off seemed almost entirely motivated by his obsession with breaking up Rene Russo's impending marriage.

Henry stepped off the mound to gather himself. When the kid's toes came back on the rubber, Taylor pointed to center field. The Indians catcher was calling his shot. Bud barked. Bryant flashed back to that summer night when he'd hit a baseball so far it seemed to fly over the horizon. Ed signaled for a hit and run, then waved it off and began flinging his own poo at the home plate umpire. At least his teammates assumed the poo was Ed's own. The ump, who looked a lot like the guy who'd crooned the National Anthem, indicated via an elaborate series of hand gestures that the feces had just missed the outside corner.

When Taylor pointed to straightaway center for a second time, the Cubs catcher noticed a spot on the hitter's uniform. David Ross had missed the crimson discoloration at first, as he'd been thinking about the Warren Commission and the small of a woman's back. But you don't set the minor-league home run record by missing signs. This was a pool of blood, evidence of an internal injury that had never quite healed.

Ross called for an inside fastball—everyone knows the internally injured can't handle the heat. Henry shook him off. "Meat. Damn Meat," Ross grumbled. He'd seen these types before: million-dollar arm, five-cent head, twelve-year-old's command of situational baseball.

Sixty feet, six inches away, Henry cocked his arm back as far as his ligaments would allow and let the horsehide loose. It was an Eephus pitch, a skyscraping parabola, a toss that took several lifetimes to reach its highest point and another handful of generations to arc down to the batter's box. "Juuuuuust a bit freeze-dried," said Indians announcer Harry Doyle, who'd briefly been distracted by a bag of desiccated-looking apricots.

The lights that hung high above Progressive Field sparked and popped. A hundred tiny balls of fire lit up the Cleveland sky and the Cuyahoga River. Jake Taylor's wool uniform might have burst into flames as he lifted his bat off his shoulder. But the catcher wasn't swinging for the fences. He was squaring around to bunt.

Bud had been playing deep and close to the line. "Shit," the dog muttered. He charged in as the ball dinked off Taylor's bat, grabbed the seams between his teeth, and ran across the infield grass, over the mound, and through the billowing smoke. Taylor was sprinting, too, as fast as his balky knees would carry him. Paw. Foot. Paw. Foot. Paw. Foot.

The mammals' metatarsals touched the bag simultaneously. At least, that was how it looked in real time. The home-plate ump did the moonwalk, went into a split, and twirled his right and left index fingers around his ears. He was calling for a review.

It was the strangest thing anyone had ever seen: a World Series decided by instant replay. Sports talk radio would call it a travesty, an outrage, a farce. For chrissakes, let the adult men and children and the disembodied voice and the various furry creatures and ghosts decide the game on the field, even if that field is in the process of being consumed by the largest conflagration seen in Cleveland since June of 1969.

The ruling came down. The home-plate ump raised his first. Bud's claw had grazed the bag first. Taylor was out. The Cubs had won.

Kris Bryant got his dogpile and a couple of bottles' worth of Dom in his hair and a spot near the front of that parade on Michigan Avenue, just one car behind the dog that had ended Chicago's misery. He'd visualized each moment, and every moving image he'd seen in his head had come to life. Game 7 of the World Series. Chicago Cubs 8, Cleveland Indians 7. First title in more than a century. From beginning to end, the game had gone according to script. He'd just thought Enrico Palazzo was going to stop Reggie Jackson from killing the queen.

Acknowledgments

My thanks and gratitude must start with Katya Rogers who, one day, casually mentioned to Daniel Greenberg, "I think Mike Pesca might be good for that."

And I was. Or it was. Or mostly he was. So the next thanks goes to Daniel for shepherding this whole thing. Twelve was a dream to work with. Many authors think of their publishers or editors like snaggle-toothed teens speak of orthodontists. But I had such a great experience with Sean Desmond and all the pros at Twelve. Truly wonderful.

My mother is a huge sports fan, which makes sense considering her father was an all-NYC second baseman and, legend goes, even better at football. His genes seem to have skipped every generation since, but the passion still persists. My dad raised me to root for the Knicks, Jets, Mets, and St. John's. So that's a combined one championship during my life as a sentient being, but other than that he never guided me wrong. We were even in a fantasy football league when I was ten years old. The next year we drafted rookie Marcus Allen and won it all, as I recall. I also remember going to Jets games at Shea Stadium and rooting hard for Patriots WR Stanley Morgan.

"What are you guys, huge Stanley Morgan fans?" asked the guy in the row in front of us. This was at a time when explaining fantasy football took twenty minutes, so I just said, "He's my uncle."

I need to thank Mary Wilson, Chris Berube, and Andrea Silenzi. I could trust in their skill and effort every day so no one ever suspected that I was totally phoning it in on *The Gist* while I concentrated on this, the much, much more important effort. Thanks to Julia Turner for looking the other way even though she, like, totally knew I was half-assing it.

I want to thank Jon Kaye, Craig Jacobs, Jeremy Gittler, Dave Lichtman, Gideon Berger, Adam Goldstein, Joe Lorge, Mark Ader, Mike Ragonese, and Jason Whitney. Your sports-loving peers as a twelve-to-sixteen-year-old determine the depth of your passion as an adult. I grew up surrounded by such insane sports fans that when I got to college people would remark, "You know more about sports than anyone I ever met." And I'd think, "Sure, I'm about eighteenth on my high school list."

The following friends and colleagues provided insight and sounding boards as I executed this project: Brett Garfinkel, Pete Moore, Matt Levine, Eric Mercer, Eric Cantor, Elliot Liffman, Paul Blutter, David Folkenflik, Zoe Chace, David Golder, and the aforementioned Lichtman and Whitney.

Josh Levin and Stefan Fatsis not only wrote chapters, but offered insights and were great partners for years on the podcast *Hang Up and Listen*—my one regret is that there is no mention of Zelmo Beatty within these pages. Thanks to Andy Bowers for inventing that show as well as the other one I've been completely shirking to write this thing.

The following editors helped shaped my sports voice at NPR: Quinn O'Toole, Steve Drummond, Uri Berliner, and Martha Little. Special thanks to Steve Inskeep, Rachel Martin, Robert Siegel, David Green, and Linda Wertheimer, for always being enthusiastic advocates for my contributions on air. That really matters. And a huge thanks to Jay Kernis, Bob Garfield, and Brooke Gladstone, who belong in the "mentors" category.

To Milo, Emmett, and Michelle. I love you all so much. I wish there were some sort of point system to tell you as much.

Finally, I want to thank everyone I can think of who ever bought me a ticket to a sporting event. Dad, Mom, Michelle, Josh Kamin, Lion, Matthew Hiltzik, Howard Dolch, Jonathan Prince, Seth Podair, Steven Feit, Chris Altieri (wrestling), Lichtman, Whitney, Jason Klarreich, Alan Jacobs, Ed Goldstein, Keith Hernandez, Josh King, Jon Holtz, Craig Rothfeld, Jeff Traugot (rides to jai alai count), Pete, Eric, and Lee Galkin. Apologies to those I forgot; please do remind me of that great game we saw, where Steve Zungul netted two in the final quarter or Mike Augustyniak provided a key block to pull within sixteen.

Stanley Morgan is not actually my uncle.

Notes

Chapter 27: What If Nixon Had Been Good at Football?

1. Stephen E. Ambrose, *Nixon*, vol. 1, *The Education of a Politician 1913–1962* (New York: Simon & Schuster, 1988).
2. Ibid.
3. Evan Thomas, *Being Nixon: A Man Divided* (New York: Random House, 2015).
4. William Flynn, "Life Story of Vice President Nixon: Never Got into Game, but He Was Too Nervous to Eat," *Boston Globe*, 21 October 1955.
5. Thomas, *Being Nixon*.
6. Matt Coker, "11 Richard Nixon College Football Moments," *OC Weekly*, 23 January 2013.
7. Thomas, *Being Nixon*.
8. Flynn, "Life Story."
9. Conrad Black, *Richard M. Nixon: A Life in Full* (New York: PublicAffairs, 2007).
10. Robert M. Collins, "Richard M. Nixon: The Psychic, Political, and Moral Uses of Sport," *Journal of Sport History* 10, no. 2 (Summer 1983): 83–84.
11. Michael Beschloss, "The President Who Never Earned His Varsity Letter," *New York Times*, 14 November 2014.
12. Cited in Melvin Small, ed., *A Companion to Richard M. Nixon* (New York: Wiley, 2007), p. 89.
13. Beschloss, "The President Who Never Earned His Varsity Letter."
14. Douglas Brinkley and Luke Nichter, eds., *The Nixon Tapes, 1971–1972* (New York: Houghton Mifflin Harcourt, 2014).

Chapter 30: What If Nat "Sweetwater" Clifton's Pass Hadn't Gone Awry?

1. *Chicago Stadium Review, Tenth Annual World's Championship Basketball Tournament, Official Program*, 8–11 April 1948.
2. For more details, please see Susan J. Rayl, *The New York Renaissance Professional Black Basketball Team, 1923–1950*, dissertation for Doctor of Philosophy, Pennsylvania State University, Department of Exercise and Sport Sciences, August 1996.

3. See, for example, *Daily Capital Journal (Salem, Oregon)*, 10 April 1948.

4. "Real Estate, For Rent," *New York Age*, 4 December 1948.

5. *People's Voice*, 15 February 1947, p. 28, as referenced by Rayl, *The New York Renaissance Professional Black Basketball Team, 1923–1950*.

6. The ABL had three black players: Bobby Wright with the New York Gothams, Larry Doby with the Paterson Crescents, and Preston Wilcox with the Hartford Hurricanes. For more details please see Rayl, *The New York Renaissance Professional Black Basketball Team, 1923–1950*.

7. *Muncie (Indiana) Evening Press*, 26 December 1947.

8. *Woodstock (Illinois) Daily Sentinel*, 3 January 1947.

9. *New York Age*, 2 November 1946.

10. *Chicago Tribune*, 23 March 1942.

11. George Kroker, "Fan's Fare," *Decatur (Illinois) Herald*, 23 February 1942.

12. *Cincinnati Enquirer*, 15 August 1948.

13. *Pittsburgh Courier*, 8 February 1947.

14. "Rates Clifton Best Young Star," *Pittsburgh Courier*, 14 February 1948.

15. *Richmond (Indiana) Palladium-Item*, 16 December 1947.

16. *Minneapolis Morning Tribune*, 19 February 1948.

17. Author's in-person interview with George Crowe, 24 April 2009.

18. *Chicago Defender*, 17 April 1948.

19. Application for Marriage License, Indiana Marriage Licenses, 1948, vol. 139, p. 130.

20. John A. Kirk, ed., *Race and Ethnicity in Arkansas: New Perspectives* (Fayetteville, AR: University of Arkansas Press, 2014). For more on the viciousness of white Arkansas landowners against black sharecroppers, see David Krugler, "America's Forgotten Mass Lynching: When 237 People Were Murdered in Arkansas," *Daily Beast*, 16 February 2015.

21. *Minneapolis Morning Tribune*, 31 July 1948.

22. *Oakland Tribune*, 8 August 1948.

23. Ron Thomas, *They Cleared the Lane: The NBA's Black Pioneers* (Lincoln, NE: University of Nebraska Press, 2002), p.22. According to Thomas, an authority on the topic, Carl Bennett, then general manager of the Fort Wayne Pistons, confirmed the existence of an unwritten rule barring African Americans from the white pro leagues and eventually the NBA.

24. Eventually, league owners would sour on their arrangement with Saperstein, because he would push them into changing their schedules to suit his Globetrotters enterprise and threaten to quit their arrangement if they did not agree. See *Rochester Democrat and Chronicle*, 29 November 1949: "Originally scheduled to play the Royals, the Trotters were matched with the Celts when Abe Saperstein, manager of the Negro cagers, required a schedule change. In a three-way telephone conversation last night with Maurice Podoloff, president of the NBA, and owner Les Harrison of the Royals, Saperstein declared he wanted a release from the contract, for his Globetrotters are no longer eager to play league teams.

Podoloff and Harrison finally yielded after a heated discussion with Saperstein, Royal officials announced."

25. Thomas, *They Cleared the Lane*, p. 22.

26. *Syracuse (New York) Post-Standard*, 18 December 1948.

27. *Muncie (Indiana) Star Press*, 1 July 1949.

28. Ibid.

29. Ibid.

30. Ibid.

31. *Sheboygan Press*, 1 August 1949.

32. *Hartford Courant*, 2 July 1949. Note that the Butler Fieldhouse was renamed as the Hinkle Fieldhouse in 1965, after Paul D. "Tony" Hinkle, who had been the school's basketball coach since the Fieldhouse opened in 1928. He also coached football and baseball teams during his Butler career.

33. Ironically, two Indianapolis Olympians players, Alex Groza and Ralph Beard, were suspended from the NBA for life following the 1950–51 season after they confessed to point shaving during their college careers at Kentucky. The team folded in 1953.

34. *Canandaigua Daily Messenger*, 28 July 1949.

35. *St. Louis Post-Dispatch*, 4 August 1949. "In the big shuffle four teams, Providence and Indianapolis of the BAA and Hammond and Dayton of the NBL were dropped from the ranks," said one wire services release. "The NBL eliminated Hammond, Ind. and Dayton, O.," it continued. When a new committee was organized within the NBA to handle player disputes, the description of its additional purpose struck a similarly revealing tone. "This committee also will decide what's to be done with the players on the four teams wiped out," it said.

36. "Oshkosh Out by Gosh," *Wilmington Journal News*, 10 September 1949.

37. *Lafayette Journal and Courier*, 14 December 1949.

38. As quoted in Thomas, *They Cleared the Lane*, p. 22.

Index

About the Contributors

Foreword
by Malcolm Gladwell

Malcolm Gladwell has been a staff writer at the *New Yorker* since 1996. He is the author of *The Tipping Point, Blink, Outliers, What the Dog Saw*, and *David and Goliath*. He is the host of the podcast *Revisionist History*.

Introduction
by Mike Pesca (Editor)

Mike Pesca covered sports and news for National Public Radio for ten years. He has contributed to the *Washington Post, Basketball Prospectus, Baseball Prospectus*, and *Inside the NFL*. He is the host of *Slate*'s daily news and opinion podcast *The Gist*.

Chapter 1: What If Muhammad Ali Had Gotten His Draft Deferment?
by Leigh Montville

Leigh Montville is a former columnist at the *Boston Globe* and former senior writer at *Sports Illustrated*. He is the author of several books, including *Evel, The Mysterious Montague, The Big Bam, Ted Williams, At the Altar of Speed, Manute, Why Not Us?*, and *Sting Like A Bee: Muhammad Ali vs. the United States of America, 1966–1971*.

Chapter 2: What If Football Had Been Deemed Too Boring in 1899?
by Jason Gay

Jason Gay is the sports columnist for the *Wall Street Journal* and the author of *Little Victories: Perfect Rules for Imperfect Living*. His work has appeared in *Vogue*, *GQ*, *Rolling Stone*, *Outside*, and the *New York Observer*.

Chapter 3: What If the United States Had Boycotted Hitler's Olympics?
by Shira Springer

Shira Springer covers stories at the intersection of sports and society for NPR and WBUR. She also writes a regular column on women's sports for the *Boston Globe* and features for the *Boston Globe Magazine*.

Chapter 4: What If the 2017 Golden State Warriors Traveled Through Time to Play the Greatest Teams in NBA History?
by Ethan Sherwood Strauss

Ethan Sherwood Strauss worked as a beat reporter covering the Golden State Warriors for ESPN before and during their rise. His article "You Won't Believe How Nike Lost Steph Curry to Under Armour" set ESPN's record for long-form page views.

Chapter 5: What If Horse Racing Was Still the Most Popular Sport in America?
by Peter Thomas Fornatale

Peter Thomas Fornatale is the host of the *Daily Racing Form*'s *Players' Podcast*. He is the coauthor of three *New York Times* best sellers with professional wrestler Chris Jericho. His latest book is *Betting with an Edge*, coauthored with professional horse player Mike Maloney.

Chapter 6: What If I Hadn't Written That Fan Letter to Dan Majerle in April 1993?
by Jesse Eisenberg

Jesse Eisenberg is an Academy Award–nominated actor, a contributor to the *New Yorker*, and the author of *Bream Gives Me Hiccups: And Other Stories*.

Chapter 7: What If Wayne Gretzky Hadn't Been an Oiler?
by Katie Baker

Katie Baker is a staff writer at the *Ringer* specializing in covering hockey and the NHL. She was a staff writer for the duration of Grantland's existence and has written for *Deadspin*, the *New York Times Magazine*, *The Awl*, the *Wall Street Journal*, and *New York*.

Chapter 8: What If Major League Baseball Had Started Testing for Steroids in 1991?
by Ben Lindbergh

Ben Lindbergh is a staff writer for the *Ringer*, where he hosts two podcasts, *Achievement Oriented* and *The Ringer MLB Show*. He also hosts the *Effectively Wild* podcast for FanGraphs. He is a former staff writer for FiveThirtyEight and Grantland, a former editor in chief of *Baseball Prospectus*, and the *New York Times* best-selling coauthor of *The Only Rule Is It Has to Work: Our Wild Experiment Building a New Kind of Baseball Team*.

Chapter 9: What If Bucky Dent Hadn't Homered over the Green Monster in 1978?
by Stefan Fatsis

Stefan Fatsis is the author of *Word Freak*, *A Few Seconds of Panic*, and *Wild and Outside*, and is a cohost of *Slate*'s sports podcast *Hang Up and Listen*. He has written for *Slate*, the *Wall Street Journal*, the *New York Times*, *Sports Illustrated*, and other publications. He listened to the Yankees–Red Sox playoff game on a transistor radio during junior varsity soccer practice in Pelham, New York, and he sprinted around the field in rapturous glee after Dent's homer.

Chapter 10: What If Jerry Tarkanian Had Beaten the NCAA and Liberated College Basketball?
by Jonathan Hock

Jonathan Hock is an eleven-time Emmy Award–winning documentarian. He has directed or produced seven films for ESPN's Peabody Award–winning 30 for 30 series, including "The Best That Never Was" (2010), "Unguarded" (2011), "Survive and Advance" (2013), and "Of Miracles and Men" (2015).

Chapter 11: What If Football Were Reinvented Today?
by Nate Jackson

Nate Jackson is the author of the *New York Times* best seller *Slow Getting Up*. He played six seasons in the National Football League as a wide receiver and a tight end. His writing has appeared in *Deadspin*, *Slate*, the *Daily Beast*, *BuzzFeed*, the *Wall Street Journal*, and the *New York Times*.

Chapter 12: What If There Had Always Been Sports PR Flacks?
by L. Jon Wertheim

L. Jon Wertheim is executive editor of *Sports Illustrated* and a contributing correspondent at *60 Minutes*.

Chapter 13: What If... Title IX Never Was?
by Mary Pilon

Mary Pilon is the author of *The Monopolists* and *The Kevin Show*. Her work has been featured in *The Best American Sports Writing* (2014). Her writing regularly appears in the *New Yorker*, *Esquire*, *Bloomberg Businessweek*, *Vice*, *New York*, and the *New York Times*.

Chapter 14: What If Tom Brady Hadn't Stepped In/Taken Over for an Injured Drew Bledsoe?
by Steve Kornacki

Steve Kornacki is a national political correspondent for NBC News and MSNBC. His book on American politics in the 1990s is due out in 2018.

Chapter 15: What If the 1999 U.S. Women's National Soccer Team Had Lost the Women's World Cup?
by Louisa Thomas

Louisa Thomas is the author of two books, including *Louisa: The Extraordinary Life of Mrs. Adams*. She is a contributor to the *New Yorker*'s website.

Chapter 16: What If the Olympics Had Never Dropped Tug-of-War?
by Nate DiMeo

Nate DiMeo is the creator of the *Memory Palace*, a storytelling podcast about America's past. He's been the artist in residence at the Metropolitan Museum of Art and a finalist for a Peabody Award and the Thurber Prize for American Humor.

Chapter 17: What If Billie Jean King Had Lost to Bobby Riggs?
by Wayne Coffey

Wayne Coffey is the author of more than thirty books, among them five *New York Times* best sellers. He has been writing about tennis for three decades.

Chapter 18: What If Mike Tyson Had Beaten Buster Douglas?
by Jeremy Schaap

Jeremy Schaap is a co-anchor of *E:60* on ESPN and the host of *The Sporting Life* on ESPN Radio. He's been honored with the RFK Journalism Award, two Edward R. Murrow Awards, and eleven Emmy Awards. He is also the author of *Cinderella Man*, a *New York Times* best seller, and *Triumph: The Untold Story of Jesse Owens and Hitler's Olympics*.

Chapter 19: What If? A Tour Through NBA Injury History
by Neil Paine

Neil Paine is a senior sportswriter at FiveThirtyEight. Before joining FiveThirtyEight, Neil was a basketball analytics consultant for the Atlanta Hawks and also worked for Sports Reference LLC.

Chapter 20: What If the Dodgers Had Left Brooklyn?
by Robert Siegel

Robert Siegel has been a host of the National Public Radio program *All Things Considered* since 1987.

Chapter 21: What If a Blimp Full of Money Had Exploded over World Track Headquarters in 1952?
by Paul Snyder

Paul Snyder is a San Antonio–raised, New York–seasoned former Division I track athlete based out of Flagstaff, Arizona. He's written for *Running Times, Mayer Magazine*, and CitiusMag.com.

Chapter 22: What If Baseball Teams Only Played Once a Week?
by Will Leitch

Will Leitch is a senior writer for *Sports on Earth* and a contributing editor for *New York* magazine. Leitch was the founding editor of *Deadspin* and is the author of four books, including *Are We Winning? Fathers and Sons in the New Golden Age of Baseball*. He hosts the daily podcast *The Will Leitch Experience*.

Chapter 23: What If Bobby Fischer Had Received Proper Psychiatric Help?
by Dylan Loeb McClain

Dylan Loeb McClain is a former staff editor and chess columnist for the *New York Times*. He is a FIDE master level player.

Chapter 24: What If Basketball Rims Were Smaller Than Basketballs?
by Jon Bois

Jon Bois is the creative director of SB Nation Labs. He produces two video series, *Pretty Good* and *Chart Party*, and is the author of *17776*.

Chapter 25: What If the AFL–NFL Merger Had Been Complicated by the Jets' Loss in Super Bowl III?
by Michael MacCambridge

Michael MacCambridge is the author of *America's Game: The Epic Story of How Pro Football Captured a Nation, Chuck Noll: His Life's Work*, and other books.

Chapter 26: What If the National League Had the DH?
by Rob Neyer

Rob Neyer started his career working for Bill James and STATS and worked for ESPN.com as a columnist for fifteen years. He has written or cowritten six books about baseball.

Chapter 27: What If Nixon Had Been Good at Football?
by Julian E. Zelizer

Julian E. Zelizer is the Malcolm Stevenson Forbes, Class of 1941 Professor of History and Public Affairs at Princeton University. He is also a CNN political analyst. Zelizer is the author of numerous books about American political history, including *The Fierce Urgency of Now: Lyndon Johnson, Congress, and the Battle for the Great Society*.

Chapter 28: What If Bill Walton Had Healthy Knees?
by Bob Ryan

Bob Ryan is the author of many books, including *Forty-Eight Minutes: A Night in the Life of the NBA*, *Wait Till I Make the Show: Baseball in the Minor Leagues*, and *The Boston Celtics: The History, Legends, and Images of America's Most Celebrated Team*. He appears regularly on various ESPN shows and has contributed to the *Boston Globe* for nearly fifty years.

Chapter 29: What If Roger Bannister Trained Today?
by Liam Boylan-Pett

Liam Boylan-Pett is a writer, working mostly in sports for publications like *SB Nation*, *Bleacher Report*, and *Runner's World*. He studied creative writing at Columbia University before heading to Georgetown University to earn his master's degree in journalism. The Bath, Michigan, native was the 315th American to run a sub-four-minute mile.

Chapter 30: What If Nat "Sweetwater" Clifton's Pass Hadn't Gone Awry?
by Claude Johnson

Author and historian **Claude Johnson** is the author of *Black Fives: The Alpha Physical Culture Club's Pioneering African American Basketball Team*,

1904–1923, as well as the founder and executive director of the Black Fives Foundation, a tax-exempt public charity whose mission is to research, preserve, teach, and honor the pre-NBA history of African Americans in basketball.

Chapter 31: What If Game 7 of the 2016 World Series Had Turned into Every Sports Movie Ever Made?
by Josh Levin

Josh Levin is the editorial director of *Slate* and the host of the podcast *Hang Up and Listen*. His writing has appeared in *Sports Illustrated*, the *Atlantic*, GQ, and *Play: The New York Times Sports Magazine*.

MISSION STATEMENT

Twelve strives to publish singular books by authors who have unique perspectives and compelling authority. Books that explain our culture, that illuminate, inspire, provoke, and entertain. Our mission is to provide a consummate publishing experience for our authors, one truly devoted to thoughtful partnership and cutting-edge promotional sophistication that reaches as many readers as possible. For readers, we aim to spark that rare reading experience—one that opens doors, transports, and possibly changes their outlook on our ever-changing world.

5/18